THE BEATLES ON RECORD

THE BEATLES ON RECORD

J. P. RUSSELL

CHARLES SCRIBNER'S SONS
New York

Copyright © 1982 J. P. Russell

Library of Congress Cataloging in Publication Data

Russell, J. P. (Jeff P.)
 The Beatles on record.

 Previously published as: The Beatles album file and
complete discography.
 Discography: p.
 1. Beatles. 2. Beatles—Discography. I. Title.
II. Title: Beatles album file and complete discography.
ML421.B4R87 1982 016.7899'12454'00922   82-10331
ISBN 0-684-17777-3 (cloth)
ISBN 0-684-17783-8 (pbk.)

1 3 5 7 9 11 13 15 17 19 F/C 20 18 16 14 12 10 8 6 4 2

Printed in the United States of America.

Acknowledgements

I should like to thank Pickwick International/Contour Records for their courteous permission to reproduce the sleeve of The Beatles Featuring Tony Sheridan; A.F.E. (UK) Ltd., for their courteous permission to reproduce the sleeve of The Beatles Historic Sessions, EMI Records Ltd., for their courteous permission to reproduce all EMI Parlophone, Capitol and Apple record sleeves.

Omnibus Press, London and Quick Fox, New York for their courteous permission to reproduce the quotes on pages 14, 50, 61, 62, 75 and 79 which are from The Beatles In Their Own Words compiled by Miles.

I should also like to thank Mike Heatley of EMI Record's International Division for his assistance and information.

Most of all I should like to thank my wife Linda, to whom this book is dedicated.

J.P.R.
Merseyside, 1982

Contents

THE BEATLES ON RECORD

1   The Beatles and their Recorded Music

The Beatles were the biggest phenomenon the world of music has ever known. Their music still brings joy and excitement to millions of people, and never before or since has so much been said or written about any recording artists. They captured the hearts and affection of the world's youth and created a mystique that fascinates fans even now, twelve years after they split up and went their different ways.

In those ten years many books have been published, giving various accounts of their success. Their history is well documented elsewhere, particularly in Hunter Davies's excellently researched *The Beatles: The Authorised Biography*, and Philip Norman's *Shout: The True Story of the Beatles*, but until now there has not been a book dealing *solely* with the group's record releases. I have decided to fill that gap with this collection of information, some of which has never been published before.

I have tried to avoid the trap that some previous discussions of the Beatles' songs have fallen into, namely losing sight of the original music while attempting highly technical explanations and over-analysis of the lyrics. I have returned to the original music — it's there and it will be there for a long time, to listen to and enjoy, not to analyse.

This book encompasses the Beatles' recordings made together and *not* records made individually by John, Paul, George or Ringo, either before or after they split up; the information relating to them would fill another volume. However, you will find information relating to every song the Beatles officially issued on record, the titles of both albums and individual tracks, release dates, author credits, timings and comments on each track with details of who plays and sings what, and the odd bits and pieces included here and there.

The first part of the book has been set out chronologically, in the order of release of albums in the UK and then in the USA. The inevitable exceptions to this are The Beatles First and The Beatles' Historic Sessions.

Although not issued until 1964 and 1981, respectively, these albums were recorded prior to the Beatles' EMI/Parlophone signing, and I have therefore included them before the Please Please Me album. Also, the Magical Mystery Tour and Hey Jude albums although not issued in Britain until 1976 and 1979, respectively, have been placed in their American order of release i.e. as the follow-up albums to Sgt. Pepper's Lonely Hearts Club Band and Abbey Road, because they contain material from that period. I have included the Beatles Box, which although not generally available in the stores, is obtainable through EMI's mail order division, World Records. Also covered for interest and completness is The Songs Lennon and McCartney Gave Away, an album including songs recorded by other artists, written by Lennon and McCartney but never issued by the Beatles.

Following the chapters on British albums are chapters on the records released in the USA by Capitol Records. The albums discussed are those from Meet The Beatles to Revolver and the American Rarities — 13 albums althogether. They are in chronological order and each track is usefully cross-referenced to a British album. These 13 albums are the only American albums listed separately, as all albums between Sgt. Pepper's Lonely Hearts Club Band and Love Songs were issued in basically the same order on both sides of the Atlantic.

After the album reviews, Chapter 43 *Recording Oddities* discusses alternative versions and recording oddities issued by the Beatles. These have been a favourite topic amongst Beatles' fans for years. In Chapter 44 *The Unreleased Tracks* I have listed some 215 songs recorded by the Beatles in one form or another, but never released.

Lastly comes the Discography, giving a complete listing of all Beatles' records released in the UK and the USA up to May 1982.

Included is the first EMI/Parlophone releases of 1982 — Reel Music, an album containing 14 of the songs as featured in the Beatles' five films — along with a single release featuring sections of 8 of those songs edited together in the form of a medley and entitled The Beatles Movie Medley.

Future imminent releases by EMI in 1982 are at least two of the many unreleased tracks, How Do You Do It? and Leave My Kitten Alone, as part of the 20th anniversary celebration of the release of Love Me Do on 5 October 1982. Hopefully, EMI will issue more than two of the unreleased tracks as there are a considerable number of them (see Chapter 44 *The Unreleased Tracks*) and in particular What's The New Mary Jane? This song was forever going to be the next single and is a track that EMI cannot deny possessing as test pressings of the recording are already in circulation.

Interestingly, earlier in 1981, in July, an exciting record came to light — the first record cut by John Lennon, Paul McCartney and possibly George Harrison. The record, of which there is believed to be only one copy in existence, was recorded in a small studio in Liverpool in 1958 when John and Paul were members of the now legendary group, The Quarry Men. The A-side is a version of Buddy Holly's That'll Be The Day with an unmistakeable John Lennon lead vocal. The B-side is a previously unheard of and unknown song In Spite Of All The Danger. Various sources say it is either a Lennon and McCartney song or a Harrison and McCartney song — as yet no-one can quite agree.

Paul McCartney sought, and was granted, a High Court injunction against the record's sale by its original owner, Duff Lowe, one-time pianist with The Quarry Men. Sothebys valued the single at $10,000 but the court ordered that it be handed over to Paul McCartney. Hopefully, for the pleasure of Beatles' fans everywhere, McCartney will allow the record to be copied and put on sale.

Throughout the book, I have sought to identify the actual *known* writer of a song — John Lennon or Paul McCartney — even when the official and registered composing credit is Lennon *and* McCartney.

Like Beatles' fans everywhere my hopes of seeing the Beatles re-form were destroyed by the radio announcement which I heard at 7.00 a.m. GMT on Tuesday 9 December 1980. With the murder of John Lennon in New York, shortly after his return into the music scene after five years of self-imposed exile, a little bit died in all of us.

Ironically, his death led to Paul, George and Ringo getting together to record a George Harrison song, All Those Years Ago, as a tribute to John.

My tribute to John Lennon, and to the memory of the Beatles, is this book — written by a fan for other fans everywhere as a guide to Beatles' records and, for the newer generation, as an introduction to the fabulous sound of the Beatles.

Jeff Russell
Merseyside, 1982

THE BRITISH ALBUMS

Originally issued as
THE BEATLES FIRST
Polydor 236 201
Release Date : 19 March 1964;
re-issued 4 August 1967.
Then re-issued on Contour records as:

THE EARLY YEARS
Contour 287001
Release Date : 18 June 1971
and

THE BEATLES FEATURING TONY
SHERIDAN (Illustrated)
Contour CN 2007
Release Date : 4 June 1976

Producer : Bert Kaempfert
Running Time : 31:34

SIDE ONE : Ain't She Sweet; Cry For A Shadow; (Let's Dance); My Bonnie; Take Out Some Insurance On Me Baby; (What'd I Say).

SIDE TWO : Sweet Georgia Brown; The Saints; (Ruby Baby); Why; Nobody's Child; (Ya-Ya).

The Beatles' first album, recorded in Hamburg in 1961, features eight recordings made by the Beatles in their pre-Parlophone days. It is sketchy with only two tracts that could honestly be called Beatles' recordings. Six tracks feature the Beatles backing Tony Sheridan, and four more another group called The Beat Brothers, who were not, as many thought, the Beatles recording under a pseudonym. These four tracks were included solely to pad out the album — the only connection between the two groups being that both backed Tony Sheridan.

The history behind this album is similar to the story of the meeting between the Beatles and Brian Epstein, only in this case it was Bert Kaempfert. Kaempfert, having heard reports of a group playing around the clubs in Hamburg's red light district who were attracting a great deal of interest, went to investigate. Arriving at the Top Ten Club in the notorious Reeperbahn, he witnessed an impressively enthusiastic group, Tony Sheridan and The Beatles. Kaempfert was aware of the effect they had on the audience. What he was not aware of at the time, however, was that Tony Sheridan and The Beatles were not all members of the same group. He approached them and finally persuaded them to sign a recording contract with him for an initial period of twelve months, during which time they were to record a minimum of four titles.

The first recordings the Beatles made with Bert Kaempfert were My Bonnie, The Saints, Cry For A Shadow and Why (Can't You Love Me Again). The line-up for these recordings was John Lennon, Paul McCartney, George Harrison and Pete Best (Stuart Sutcliffe having left the group to study art). The first release from this session was a single My Bonnie / The Saints, which was released in Germany on Polydor 24 673 in June 1961. The record sold extremely well and the Beatles were soon in the German Top Ten. In September of 1961, after the success of the single, Polydor put together an E.P. containing My Bonnie, Why (Can't You Love Me Again), Cry For A Shadow and The Saints. Although this didn't sell as well as the single, the Beatles had a second recording session with Polydor at which they recorded Ain't She Sweet, Take Out Some Insurance On Me Baby, Sweet Georgia Brown and Nobody's Child. These new titles remained unissued until 1964, with the exception of Sweet Georgia Brown, which was included on an E.P. issued in Germany in October 1962. Then, after the success of the Beatles' first five singles and first two L.P.s on Parlophone, Polydor resurrected all eight tracks. Initially they issued Ain't She Sweet / Take Out Some Insurance On Me Baby (Polydor NH 52 317) on 29 May 1964, but amidst a host of Parlophone No. 1s, this reached only No. 29 in the charts. The remaining six Polydor tracks were issued as singles, but again, none reached the top fifty. Polydor, determined to have some success with their Beatles' recordings, took all eight tracks plus four recorded by Tony Sheridan and The Beat Brothers and subsequently compiled this album, again without much luck. To date this album has been reissued three times but has never sold in sufficient quantities to make any money. Although these recordings hint at what was to come on future well-produced recordings, they are only of interest to Beatles' collectors, mainly for historical rather than musical value.

In addition to these eight recordings there are reputed to be three more made during these sessions. Two feature John Lennon on lead — Some Other Guy and Rock and Roll Music; the third track, Kansas City, features Tony Sheridan. It is doubtful, however, that these exist. One could argue that if they did they would have been included on the album in place of the four tracks by The Beat Brothers.

SIDE ONE

Ain't She Sweet (Yellen−Ager) 2:12

John Lennon : Rhythm Guitar and Solo Vocal
Paul McCartney : Bass Guitar
George Harrison : Lead Guitar
Pete Best : Drums

This opening track features John Lennon's first officially recorded vocal performance. (This is the only recording on the album to feature any of the Beatles on lead vocal.) John gives the song the distinctive Lennon treatment; his raw nasal vocal almost jumps out of the speakers. The instrumental backing accentuates John's vocal without imposing on it. Overall the recording comes across well, although in places it sounds rather shallow. This was no doubt due to Bert Kaempfert's production techniques which, although flawless with his own orchestra, just did not work with a beat group. Although everyone who heard the finished recording thought it was marvellous, the Beatles were disappointed and dismissed it as something of a joke. They sold the rights to Polydor because they simply had not achieved the sound they wanted. Eighteen months later they were to meet George Martin, who was to bring out that distinctive 'Beatles' sound'.

Cry For A Shadow (Lennon−Harrison) 2:22

John Lennon : Rhythm Guitar
Paul McCartney : Bass Guitar
George Harrison : Lead Guitar
Pete Best : Drums

Co-written by John and George, this instrumental is the only published (or unpublished) Lennon-Harrison collaboration. As with Ain't She Sweet the Beatles were disappointed with the recording and sold the rights of it to Polydor Records. The opening and main theme was thought up by George Harrison; John Lennon later added the rhythm sections. It is an interesting, although simple, piece of music consisting of opening and main theme, which is played through three times, with a few other bars added for the ending. George Harrison's lead guitar playing here is by far the best on the album (he is not given the opportunity on other tracks). The music is given more excitement by various screams and shouts from the four Beatles. The title was not chosen until after the recordings were finished. The toss of a coin decided that Cry For A Shadow and not Beatle Bop would be used. The Beatles had, in any case, felt that the latter was rather coy so it was dismissed and Cry For A Shadow was agreed.

Let's Dance (Lee) 2:34
Tony Sheridan and The Beat Brothers

My Bonnie (Pratt) 2:06
Tony Sheridan and The Beatles

John Lennon : Rhythm Guitar and Backing Vocal
Paul McCartney : Bass Guitar and Backing Vocal
George Harrison : Lead Guitar and Backing Vocal
Pete Best : Drums
Tony Sheridan : Lead Vocal

This is the most famous track on the album, the A-side of the single issued in Germany in 1961, and the cause of the meeting between Brian Epstein and the Beatles. Tony Sheridan's lead vocal is given a rousing musical and vocal backing by the Beatles who also supply some enthusiastic hand clapping. The Beatles had included hand clapping in their backing during live performances, and it was a sound that they would use many times on future recordings.

Take Out Some Insurance On Me Baby
(Singleton—Hall) 2:52
Tony Sheridan and The Beatles

John Lennon : Rhythm Guitar
Paul McCartney : Bass Guitar
George Harrison : Lead Guitar
Pete Best : Drums
Tony Sheridan : Solo Vocal

Unfortunately, from here on the album gets steadily worse. On this track Tony Sheridan sounds rather like a poor man's Elvis Presley, singing an uninteresting song in an equally uninteresting manner. The Beatles do a far better job of the backing than Tony Sheridan does with the lyrics.

What'd I Say (Charles) 2.37
Tony Sheridan and The Beat Brothers

SIDE TWO

Sweet Georgia Brown (Bernie—Pinkard—Casey) 2:03
Tony Sheridan and the Beatles

John Lennon : Rhythm Guitar and Backing Vocal
Paul McCartney : Bass Guitar and Backing Vocal
George Harrison : Lead Guitar and Backing Vocal
Pete Best : Drums
Tony Sheridan : Lead Vocal

Tony Sheridan's lead vocal again leaves much to be desired, but, with the Beatles very enthusiastic backing he manages to get away with it. Incidentally, in 1963 Sheridan re-recorded the vocals with specially adapted lyrics referring to the length of the Beatles' hair and the then recently formed Beatles' Fan Club. This is the version here. The original appears only on the 1962 German. E.P. (Polydor 21485).

The Saints (Trad. Arr. Sheridan) 3:19
Tony Sheridan and The Beatles

John Lennon : Rhythm Guitar
Paul McCartney : Bass Guitar
George Harrison : Lead Guitar
Pete Best : Drums
Tony Sheridan : Solo Vocal

The B-side of that now famous single, though not as good as the A-side, still features some exciting music from the Beatles. Tony Sheridan's vocals are once again not as good as the backing he is given.

Ruby Baby (Leiber—Stoller) 2:49
Tony Sheridan and The Beat Brothers

Why (Can't You Love Me Again) (Crompton—Sheridan) 2:55
Tony Sheridan and The Beatles

John Lennon : Rhythm Guitar and Backing Vocal
Paul McCartney : Bass Guitar and Backing Vocal
George Harrison : Lead Guitar and Backing Vocal
Pete Best : Drums
Tony Sheridan : Lead Vocal

Partly written by Tony Sheridan, this pleading song suits his voice perfectly, and at last we have his real singing voice without an Elvis Presley impersonation. The Beatles provide an adequate musical backing, again with hand clapping.

Nobody's Child (Foree—Coben) 2:58
Tony Sheridan and The Beatles

John Lennon : Rhythm Guitar
Paul McCartney : Bass Guitar
George Harrison : Lead Guitar
Pete Best : Drums
Tony Sheridan : Solo Vocal

Unfortunately Tony Sheridan's impersonation of Elvis is back on this track and his inclusion of a wolf howl totally destroys the already poor rendition. One can understand, when listening to this track, why the Beatles preferred to dismiss the album.

Ya-Ya (Robinson—Dorsey—Lewis) 2:47
Tony Sheridan and The Beat Brothers

When the Beatles returned to Liverpool in October 1961 they brought a few copies of My Bonnie with them for their friends. One person to receive a copy was Bob Wooller, the DJ at the Cavern Club, who gave the record a considerable amount of play. Soon, several members of the club were asking for the record at the nearby music shop, NEMS (North End Music Stores).

The manager, Brian Epstein, knew that the record was not in stock but wanted to know who the artists were so that he could obtain it. Brian was told that the record was by a German group called The Beatles. He made enquiries around Liverpool and found that the Beatles were not German but English and above all, a local group who were currently playing at the Cavern Club just around the corner from his music shop. Intrigued, he went along to the Cavern Club to find out more about them and their record. He watched their performance and recognised the four scruffy lads who came into his shop on Saturday afternoons to listen to records, but never bought anything. He also could not fail to notice the enormous amount of excitement they generated within the audience. It seemed as though the moment they appeared on stage the atmosphere became electrically charged. Brian was fascinated. How could these four scruffs have so much effect on an audience? No wonder he was having so many requests for their record.

After their performance, Brian met the Beatles and found out that the record was on the Polydor label. He then began extensive enquiries amongst record importers, but drew a blank. Being the businessman that he was, he then contacted Polydor Records in Germany and imported 200 copies himself. Brian also made enquiries about how to go about managing a group. Receiving what he considered to be sufficient information, he invited the Beatles along to his office to discuss the possibility of becoming their manager.

The Beatles informed Brian that they were under a management contract to Allan Williams. Brian also learned that their recording contract with Polydor Records still had two years to run. He went along to see Allan Williams. Allan, glad to get rid of the Beatles, readily agreed that Brian could have them, adding that the Beatles had caused him nothing but trouble. It was a decision that he was soon to regret.

Brian then contacted Polydor Records who informed him that they were only interested in the Beatles as a backing group for Tony Sheridan, and that they had no plans whatsoever to record the Beatles on their own. After some discussion Polydor Records released the Beatles totally and unconditionally from their contract. Both situations now resolved, the Beatles, witnessed by Alistair Taylor (Brian's personal assistant), signed the contract which made Brian Epstein their new manager. (Brian himself never signed that contract, but never revealed why.)

The first thing Brian did was to take over from Pete Best the responsibility for making bookings for the group. Next, he talked them into wearing suits on stage and told them to work out a regular stage performance in which they were to play only their best numbers. He also banned them from smoking, eating, drinking alcohol or chewing during their performances, and before every booking would issue each of the Beatles with typewritten instructions as to where the booking was and what time they were to be there (usually at least half an hour prior to the start of the performance).

Having organised the Beatles and given them a new appearance, the next task, Brian decided, was to get his newly signed Beatles a recording contract.

The Decca Tapes
Circuit LK 4438-1 (Bootleg)
Producer : Mike Smith
Release Date : Unreleased
Running Time : 33:14

The Decca Tapes is a bootleg album consisting of fifteen of the recordings made by the Beatles at a London audition for Decca Records Ltd on 1 January 1962. The record as 'illegally' available has no connection whatsoever with the Decca Record Company Ltd. Both the author and publishers of this book deplore the actions and practices of bootleggers. This 'album' has been included in this book solely for its historical and informative value.

SIDE ONE: Like Dreamers Do; Till There Was You; The Sheik of Araby; To know Her Is To Love Her; Take Good Care of My Baby; Memphis; Sure To Fall.

SIDE TWO: Hello Little Girl; Three Cool Cats; Crying, Waiting, Hoping; Love Of The Love; September In The Rain; Besame Mucho; Searchin'.

Brian Epstein, determined to get the Beatles a recording contract, managed to convince Mike Smith, an A & R man from Decca Records, to give them an audition, on 1 January 1962. The Beatles ran through their stage act in the relatively calm and controlled environment of the recording studio. Mike Smith, impressed with their recordings, gave the Beatles a second audition on 9 January 1962. Although Decca turned the Beatles down, and the recordings on this album which come from those audition sessions were never intended for release, they are good. In recent years they have slipped into the hands of bootleggers who have somehow managed to obtain a copy of the original master tapes and produced an excellent album, comparable in sound quality to any officially released album. Its musical content and enthusiasm can be compared with the officially available Please Please Me album, even though there are a few duff notes here and there.

The 15 tracks on this album include early versions of Money and Till There Was You which the Beatles eventually re-recorded and included on the album With The Beatles in 1963. The remaining 13 tracks include Beatles' versions of Hello Little Girl, Like Dreamers Do and Love Of The Loved, which they later gave away to other recording artists. As yet these have never been officially issued by the Beatles.

This album looks and sounds like any other, until, on closer examination (especially of the sleeve), certain inconsistencies are revealed. First, the sleeve quotes a Decca Records catalogue number, LK 4438-1, implying it is an official release, but then also included is the EMI record care warning 'Important, this record is intended for use only on special stereophonic reproducers.....' These two conflicting statements indicate that the album is obviously a bootleg.

The sleeve includes a most official looking track listing, complete with writer credits and lead vocal information. It gives the usual producer, engineer and photographer credits, and across the bottom of the sleeve is the address (fictitious) of Circuit Records in Finchley, London. The sleeve notes, entitled 'The Untold Story of the Decca Tapes', are wildly fictitious. They tell us that an album, supposedly titled The Original Beatles, was released in 1962, including 14 of these 15 tracks and that ten were also released as singles in the same year. The writer, Grid Leek, in his attempts to convince the reader that the story is true even quotes Decca catalogue numbers for the fictitious singles and album. Three of the five numbers quoted for these singles do date from the period described, but two date from mid-1961. Oviously the writer did a great deal of research to trace catalogue numbers from 1962, but his research was not thorough enough. Below is a list of the records, complete with fictitious catalogue numbers and release dates which were supposed to have been issued by Decca Records.

Singles

F11339	Three Cool Cats/Hello Little Girl	19 January 1962
F11364	Sheik of Araby/September In The Rain	23 February 1962
F11405	Memphis/Love Of The Loved	20 April 1962
F11487	Searchin'/Like Dreamers Do	15 June 1962
F11533	Sure To Fall/Money	17 August 1962

Album

| LK4437 | The Original Beatles | 28 September 1962 |

These notes do include real catalogue numbers and release dates of official records such as My Bonnie and Love Me Do. They also document the meeting between Brian Epstein and Mike Smith of Decca, but then tell a fictitious (although highly enjoyable) tale of the Beatles' attempts to secure a recording contract with Decca. The notes even state that when the Beatles signed their recording contract with EMI, Decca decided to put together the 14-track album The Original Beatles and issue it on 28 September 1962, exactly one week before EMI issued Love Me Do. A final comment relating to these highly enjoyable sleeve notes; right at the bottom there is the line 'NOTE: The untold story of the Decca Tapes is a work of historical fiction.' Back to reality, and the track listing of this album.

SIDE ONE

Like Dreamers Do (Lennon–McCartney)   2:29

John Lennon : Rhythm Guitar
Paul McCartney : Bass Guitar and Solo Vocal
George Harrison : Lead Guitar
Pete Best : Drums

This song was eventually recorded in 1964 by the Applejacks (Decca F11916) and produced by Mike Smith who also produced this version. Paul sings lead vocal in a slightly toned down Little Richard voice. The recording generates as much excitement as any official release, although because this was an audition tape a certain amount of fear can be heard in Paul's voice. The backing sounds more enthusiastic than on the Polydor sessions, and Pete Best's performance is much improved from the monotonous drumming on those recordings.

Money (Gordy–Bradford)   2:18

John Lennon : Rhythm Guitar and Lead Vocal
Paul McCartney : Bass Guitar and Backing Vocal
George Harrison : Lead Guitar and Backing Vocal
Pete Best : Drums

This is the first of two tracks the Beatles re-recorded and officially issued on the album With The Beatles. Unlike the official version, this is much faster and instead of piano it starts with John Lennon's rhythm guitar. The lead vocal also comes from John. He sounds like he would during a live performance, and the echo given to his voice emphasises this effect. The backing vocals from Paul and George are sung in a similar way to the released version, but musically it doesn't compare — the song on With The Beatles is far superior.

Till There Was You (Willson)   2:53

John Lennon : Rhythm Guitar
Paul McCartney : Bass Guitar and Solo Vocal
George Harrison : Lead Guitar
Pete Best : Drums

This was also re-recorded and officially released by the Beatles on the With

The Beatles album. Paul's lead vocal is backed by his own bass guitar, George's lead guitar and Pete Best's drumming. The song is given a similar treatment to that of the released version, although the lead guitar and drums don't seem at ease.

The Sheik of Araby (Snyder—Wheeler—Smith)   1:38

John Lennon : Rhythm Guitar
Paul McCartney : Bass Guitar
George Harrison : Lead Guitar and Solo Vocal
Pete Best : Drums

Although one of the best, this is unfortunately one of the shortest tracks on the album. George gives a rousing rendition of the ancient song and is given an equally rousing backing. John inserts some ad-lib comments, which give the song a lighter feel than other recordings on the album and turn it into a send-up. This is a good recording, although the ending is sloppy.

To Know Her Is To Love Her (Spector)   2:30

John Lennon : Rhythm Guitar and Lead Vocal
Paul McCartney : Bass Guitar and Backing Vocal
George Harrison : Lead Guitar and Backing Vocal
Pete Best : Drums

This was originally recorded by the Teddy Bears in 1958 and produced by the now legendary Phil Spector. The Beatles stick closely to Phil Spector's original arrangement, but change the title and lyrics from a female to male point of view. John again sings lead vocal, with Paul and George supplying the da, da, da, backing.

Take Good Care Of My Baby (Goffin—King)   2:22

John Lennon : Rhythm Guitar and Harmony Vocal
Paul McCartney : Bass Guitar and Harmony Vocal
George Harrison : Lead Guitar and Lead Vocal
Pete Best : Drums

Lead vocals are from George with harmonies in places from John and Paul. The Beatles stick closely to the original Bobby Vee recording.

Memphis (Berry)   2:15

John Lennon : Rhythm Guitar and Solo Vocal
Paul McCartney : Bass Guitar
George Harrison : Lead Guitar
Pete Best : Drums

John's lead vocal on this late fifties Chuck Berry standard is by far one of his best performances on the album. It puts Chuck Berry's original version to shame although the Beatles do not stray far from his original arrangement.

Sure To Fall (Perkins — Cantrell — Claunch)   1:59

John Lennon : Rhythm Guitar and Harmony Vocal
Paul McCartney : Bass Guitar and Lead Vocal
George Harrison : Lead Guitar and Harmony Vocal
Pete Best : Drums

The old Carl Perkins number is given the Beatles' treatment, with lead vocal
from Paul and harmonies from John and George here and there. This is
either a very straight-faced send-up or Paul has stage fright. Nevertheless it
is still an enjoyable track.

SIDE TWO

Hello Little Girl (Lennon — McCartney)   1:35

John Lennon : Rhythm Guitar and Lead Vocal
Paul McCartney : Bass Guitar and Lead Vocal
George Harrison : Lead Guitar
Pete Best : Drums

Although the shortest track on the album, it is most definitely the best. It was
written by John, who once said of the song, 'This was one of the first songs I
ever finished. I was then about 18 and we gave it to the Fourmost. I think it
was the first song of my own that I ever attempted to do with the group.'
The Fourmost did record this song in 1963 with the Beatles' future producer,
George Martin. In comparison to the Fourmost's recording, this leaves much
to be desired. The lead vocal is a duet between John and Paul, with John
singing solo in places. For the chorus they are joined by George. Later, after
the Beatles had signed with Parlophone, they re-recorded Hello Little Girl
and made a version better than both this and the Fourmost's recording.

Three Cool Cats (Leiber — Stoller)   2:20

John Lennon : Rhythm Guitar and Backing Vocal
Paul McCartney : Bass Guitar and Backing Vocal
George Harrison : Lead Guitar and Lead Vocal
Pete Best : Drums

George is in excellent form on lead vocal in this complete send-up of the
1959 Coasters hit. John and Paul aid and abet with the various humorous
interjections of 'I want that little chick' and 'Hey man, save one chick for me'.
This comes across as a less than serious attempt to record the song.

Crying, Waiting, Hoping (Holly)   1:58

John Lennon : Rhythm Guitar and Backing Vocal
Paul McCartney : Bass Guitar and Backing Vocal
George Harrison : Lead Guitar and Lead Vocal
Pete Best : Drums

The Beatles recorded quite a few Buddy Holly songs. Unfortunately they released only Words of Love on the Beatles for Sale album. The lead vocal on this song comes from George, with backing vocals from John and Paul.

Love Of The Loved (Lennon–McCartney)   1:47

John Lennon : Rhythm Guitar
Paul McCartney : Bass Guitar and Solo Vocal
George Harrison : Lead Guitar
Pete Best : Drums

Eventually given away to Cilla Black who recorded it in 1963, this is a McCartney song. Here he sings lead vocal backed by the incessant riff that appears throughout the recording. Again, like Hello Little Girl and Like Dreamers Do, the Beatles re-recorded this in 1963, and again like the two previous titles, the newer recording is yet to be released.

September In The Rain (Warren)   1:50

John Lennon : Rhythm Guitar
Paul McCartney : Bass Guitar and Solo Vocal
George Harrison : Lead Guitar
Pete Best : Drums

Originally a hit for Dinah Washington in 1961, this must definitely be one of the strongest tracks on the Decca Tapes. Paul gives the song a true Beatles' feel in the mold of I Saw Her Standing There. This is probably the only track that sounds as though the Beatles are thoroughly enjoying themselves.

Besame Mucho (Velazquez–Shaftel)   2:33

John Lennon : Rhythm Guitar and Backing Vocal
Paul McCartney : Bass Guitar and Lead Vocal
George Harrison : Lead Guitar and Backing Vocal
Pete Best : Drums

This must be one of the Beatles all-time favourite songs. Although they never officially released it, various versions by the Beatles crop up now and again on bootleg records. During the early sixties the Beatles recorded this song for a number of radio broadcasts. It also cropped up a few years later during the sessions for Let It Be as a much better, although never released version. Paul always sings the lead vocal, with backing from John and George. They do an excellent job on this old 1930s song that was revived in 1959 by the Coasters. This track, like others on the album, does not stray very far from the original arrangement, although in my opinion the result is better.

Searchin' (Leiber–Stoller)   2:57

John Lennon : Rhythm Guitar and Backing Vocal
Paul McCartney : Bass Guitar and Lead Vocal
George Harrison : Lead Guitar and Backing Vocal
Pete Best : Drums

The closing track of the album is another song originally recorded by the Coasters; this one dates back to 1957. The Beatles featured it now and again in their stage act. Paul sings lead vocal, with John and George adding harmonies for the chorus. The two sections of falsetto that can be heard come from John Lennon, who nervously tries to inject some humour into the situation.

Having completed their recording session the Beatles returned to Liverpool and awaited Decca's decision. Three months later, in March 1962, Brian Epstein received a reply from Decca — they had turned the Beatles down. Disappointed, but still hopeful, Brian took the audition tapes to every record label he could find, and in quick succession was turned down by Pye, Philips, Columbia, and just about every other record label in London. A rather despondant Brian, determined that somebody was going to like the Beatles, decided to have one final try before giving up.

Deciding that the best way to present the Beatles was by having records made from the tapes, he ended up in the HMV shop in London's Oxford Street. Here, for approximately £1.50 you could get an album made from tapes; Brian subsequently did just that. The cutting engineer, impressed with what he was hearing, recommended that Brian take his records upstairs to the offices of Ardmore and Beechwood, whose offices were located above the HMV shop. There, Brian met Syd Coleman, who, after hearing the records, recommended that he go to see a friend of his called George Martin at Parlophone. The following day Brian went along to see George Martin and played him the tapes. George was not very impressed after hearing the tapes, but decided to take a chance and agreed to give the Beatles a recording test on Wednesday 6 June 1962.

On that date, the Beatles gave their first performance for their future producer, George Martin. Although again not too impressed, he had a feeling that there was something there — a certain something that he knew needed to be brought out. After the audition, George told Brian and the Beatles that he would give them a decision within a month. Having been disappointed by Decca's decision, the Beatles didn't pay much attention to George Martin' comment and, rather dejected, returned to Liverpool and subsequently to Hamburg to play an engagement at the Star Club. Meanwhile, George Martin was listening to the audition tapes over and over again. He could hear the Beatles' potential, but there was something not quite right with the drumming which was not regular enough, and, in his opinion did not give the right sort of sound. George informed Brian Epstein that he was prepared to sign the Beatles to a recording contract, but they would have to find a new drummer — he was not prepared to sign Pete Best.

The Beatles, still in Hamburg, received the following telegram from Brian, CONGRATULATIONS BOYS, EMI REQUEST RECORDING SESSION, PLEASE REHEARSE NEW MATERIAL. This was what they had waited months for. Upon their return from Hamburg, Brian found out that John, Paul and George had decided independently that they wanted Pete Best out and Ringo Starr in. He was now faced with the unenviable task of sacking Pete Best.

With Ringo Starr as the new drummer, George Martin offered them a recording contract in which he agreed to record two singles in the first year. The date set for the first recording session, when they were to record two tracks for release as a single, was Tuesday 4 September 1962. The two tracks selected for that first single were Love Me Do/P.S. I Love You and the single was issued on 5 October 1962. Within a few weeks it had reached number 17 in the charts (the lowest position that any Beatles record issued on Parlophone was to reach during their entire recording career).

The Beatles were delighted, and so was George Martin — so delighted that he set up a second session for the follow-up. That second session was set for Monday 26 November 1962 and produced Please Please Me/Ask Me Why, although George Martin wanted the Beatles to record How Do You Do It? (later a hit for another Liverpudlian group, Gerry and The Pacemakers). The Beatles although not enthusiastic about How Do You Do It? made a recording of it to please George Martin. After the second session the Beatles set off for Hamburg again to fulfil a two-week Christmas residency at the Star Club, which was to last from 18 to 31 December 1962. During that two-week period, Ted 'Kingsize' Taylor made some recordings on a domestic tape recorder with a single microphone, amongst which were recordings of the Beatles.

**THE BEATLES HISTORIC
SESSIONS** (2 L.P's)
AFE   AFELD 1018
Producer : None
Release Date : 25 September
1981
Running Time : 75:20

The Beatles Historic Sessions

JOHN LENNON
PAUL McCARTNEY
GEORGE HARRISON
RINGO STARR
STUART SUTCLIFFE

SIDE ONE: I'm Gonna Sit Right Down And Cry Over You; I Saw Her Standing There; Roll Over Beethoven; Hippy Hippy Shake; Sweet Little Sixteen; Lend Me Your Comb; Your Feets Too Big.
SIDE TWO: Twist and Shout; Mr. Moonlight; A Taste Of Honey; Besame Mucho; Reminiscing; Kansas City/Hey Hey Hey Hey; Where Have You Been All My Life.

SIDE THREE: Till There Was You; Ain't Nothin' Shakin'; To Know Her Is To Love Her; Little Queenie; Falling In Love Again; Ask Me Why; Be Bop A Lula; Hallelujah, I Love Her So.
SIDE FOUR: Sheila; Red Sails In The Sunset; Everybody's Trying To Be Baby; Matchbox; Talkin' 'bout You; Shimmy Shimmy; Long Tall Sally; I Remember You.

Previously issued in part, and in various forms, as

The Beatles Live! At the Star Club in Hamburg; Germany, 1962
Lingasong LNL1
The Beatles/Early Years 1   Phoenix Records PHX 1004
The Beatles/Early Years 2   Phoenix Records PHX 1005
Rare Beatles Phoenix Records PHX 1011

When originally issued on 25 May 1977 by Lingasong Records as The Beatles Live! At the Star Club in Hamburg, Germany; 1962. (LNL 1), the album contained only 26 songs. However, in the present form it contains all 30 numbers that are available for release. In fact, there were 32 tracks recorded at the time, but the two unreleased tracks are merely alternate versions of Roll Over Beethoven and To Know Her Is To Love Her.

The recordings as available on the double L.P. were originally made in the Star Club in Hamburg, Germany sometime between the 18 and 31 December 1962. Ted 'Kingsize' Taylor of Kingsize Taylor and the Dominoes set up a domestic tape recorder and a single microphone and over the two-week period made some 20 hours of recordings of a number of Liverpool groups including the Beatles. The recordings were then virtually forgotten about until the Beatles became famous. Taylor then offered the recordings to the Beatles' manager Brian Epstein who, after listening to them, turned Taylor down. Epstein nevertheless offered him £20 for the recordings, which Taylor refused. The tapes were then put aside and lost somewhere in Liverpool, by which time they had achieved legendary status. In the early 1970's whilst cleaning out an office that he had once occupied, Allan Williams, the Beatles' first manager, came across the tapes. Williams then attempted to sell the tapes around various record companies, trying unsuccessfully to have them released. The lack of interest caused Williams, in conjunction with a brand new record label, to have them issued as Lingasong Records.

It is reputed that Lingasong took the tapes and spent £40,000 transfering the original 3¾ inches per second mono recordings on to professional 16-track tape. With the aid of various filters, equalisers and compressers they set about trying to clean up the recordings. Unfortunately, someone was rather heavy-handed with the filters; in a number of cases, parts of the original recording have been filtered out. However, when AFE Audio Fidelity Enterprises obtained the tapes, they re-mixed them to sound as close as possible to the original mono sound. Whilst they cannot be regarded as high quality — the original mono recording was scarcely that anyway — the overall sound is superior to that on the Lingasong released versions. This is borne out by a comparison of the L.P.s if played one after the other, the Historic Sessions having a sound and mixing quality far superior to The Beatles Live! at the Star Club in Hamburg, Germany; 1962.

In many ways the sleeve of this album is also far better than the original Lingasong release. It now looks like a Beatle album as well as sounding more or less like a Beatle album. Unfortunately, there are three mistakes on the printed sleeve information. Firstly, underneath the proclamation The Beatles Historic Sessions are the listed names of the Beatles: John Lennon, Paul McCartney, George Harrison, Ringo Starr and Stuart Sutcliffe. Tragically Stuart Sutcliffe does **not** appear on this album; he died of a cerebral haemmorage on 10 April 1962, eight months before the recordings were made.

The second and third 'mistakes' are in the song listing. AFE list a song entitled Can't Help It/Blue Angel which on listening turns out to be Buddy Holly's Reminiscing. Also, Hallellujah, I Love Her So and Be Bop A Lula feature vocals by Horst Obber, one of the Star Club waiters (not Horst Fascher, as Chris White's sleeve notes state); the musical backing though is still by the Beatles.

Despite its inaccurate sleeve information this album does contain some interesting music, including pre-Parlophone recordings of I Saw Her Standing There and Ask Me Why. The musical arrangements used by the Beatles on these two Lennon and McCartney classics are very similar to those used on their first Parlophone album Please Please Me some two months later. Also John's rendition of the Isley Brothers Twist and Shout is comparable to the version included on Please Please Me. Another eight songs on this album can also be compared with their later studio versions, and it is interesting to note how George Martin seems to have used the Beatles' own arrangements on the various rock and roll standards they recorded. Excluding EMI and BBC recordings, the only two titles with no known studio recordings are Falling In Love Again and I Remember You.

Besides this double album, these recordings have also been issued by Phoenix Records (an AFE subsidiary) as three separate albums entitled The Beatles/Early Years 1 (PHX 1004), The Beatles/Early Years 2 (PHX 1005) and Rare Beatles (PHX 1011) 22 January 1982. Each of these albums contains ten of the 30 tracks as included on this album. The first two albums feature the Dezo Hoffman portrait photographs which date from 1962. The third sleeve features the same photograph used on the back of the sleeve of the Historic Sessions. An additional rarity aspect of The Beatles/Early Years 1 is that just before I Saw Her Standing There begins, John Lennon can be heard reciting the first line of the song.

SIDE ONE

I'm Gonna Sit Right Down and Cry Over You
(Thomas—Biggs)   2:30

John Lennon : Rhythm Guitar and Lead Vocal
Paul McCartney : Bass Guitar and Backing Vocal
George Harrison : Lead Guitar and Backing Vocal
Ringo Starr : Drums

I Saw Her Standing There (Lennon—McCartney)   2:25

John Lennon : Rhythm Guitar and Harmony Vocal
Paul McCartney : Bass Guitar and Lead Vocal
George Harrison : Lead Guitar
Ringo Starr : Drums

Roll Over Beethoven (Berry)   2:17

John Lennon : Rhythm Guitar
Paul McCartney : Bass Guitar
George Harrison : Lead Guitar and Solo Vocal
Ringo Starr : Drums

Hippy Hippy Shake (Romero)   1:42

John Lennon : Rhythm Guitar
Paul McCartney : Bass Guitar and Solo Vocal
George Harrison : Lead Guitar
Ringo Starr : Drums

Sweet Little Sixteen (Berry)   2:50

John Lennon : Rhythm Guitar and Solo Vocal
Paul McCartney : Bass Guitar
George Harrison : Lead Guitar
Ringo Starr : Drums

Lend Me Your Comb (Wise – Weisman – Twomey)   1:45

John Lennon : Rhythm Guitar and Lead Vocal
Paul McCartney : Bass Guitar and Lead Vocal
George Harrison : Lead Guitar
Ringo Starr : Drums

Your Feets Too Big (Benson – Fisher)   2:21

John Lennon : Rhythm Guitar and Harmony Vocal
Paul McCartney : Bass Guitar and Lead Vocal
George Harrison : Lead Guitar
Ringo Starr : Drums

SIDE TWO

Twist and Shout (Medley – Russell)   2:12

John Lennon : Rhythm Guitar and Lead Vocal
Paul McCartney : Bass Guitar and Backing Vocal
George Harrison : Lead Guitar and Backing Vocal
Ringo Starr : Drums

Mr Moonlight (Johnson)   2:10

John Lennon : Rhythm Guitar and Lead Vocal
Paul McCartney : Bass Guitar and Harmony Vocal
George Harrison : Lead Guitar
Ringo Starr : Drums

A Taste Of Honey (Marlow – Scott)   1:55

John Lennon : Rhythm Guitar and Backing Vocal
Paul McCartney : Bass Guitar and Lead Vocal
George Harrison : Lead Guitar and Backing Vocal
Ringo Starr : Drums

Besame Mucho (Velazque–Shaftel)   2:40

John Lennon : Rhythm Guitar and Backing Vocal
Paul McCartney : Bass Guitar and Lead Vocal
George Harrison : Lead Guitar and Backing Vocal
Ringo Starr : Drums

Reminiscing (Curtis)   1:41

John Lennon : Rhythm Guitar
Paul McCartney : Bass Guitar
George Harrison : Lead Guitar and Solo Vocal
Ringo Starr : Drums

Kansas City (Leiber–Stoller)/Hey Hey Hey Hey
(Penniman)   2:10

John Lennon : Rhythm Guitar and Backing Vocal
Paul McCartney : Bass Guitar and Lead Vocal
George Harrison : Lead Guitar and Backing Vocal
Ringo Starr : Drums

Where Have You Been All My Life (Mann–Weil)   1:45

John Lennon : Rhythm Guitar and Lead Vocal
Paul McCartney : Bass Guitar and Backing Vocal
George Harrison : Lead Guitar and Backing Vocal
Ringo Starr : Drums

SIDE THREE

Till There Was You (Willson)   1:55

John Lennon : Rhythm Guitar
Paul McCartney : Bass Guitar and Solo Vocal
George Harrison : Lead Guitar
Ringo Starr : Drums

Ain't Nothin' Shakin'
Colacrai–Fontaine–Lampert–Cleveland)   1:15

John Lennon : Rhythm Guitar
Paul McCartney : Bass Guitar
George Harrison : Lead Guitar and Solo Vocal
Ringo Starr : Drums

To Know Her Is To Love Her (Spector)   3:05

John Lennon : Rhythm Guitar and Harmony Vocal

Paul McCartney : Bass Guitar and Harmony Vocal
George Harrison : Lead Guitar and Lead Vocal
Ringo Starr : Drums

Little Queenie (Berry)   3:57

John Lennon : Rhythm Guitar
Paul McCartney : Bass Guitar and Solo Vocal
George Harrison : Lead Guitar
Ringo Starr : Drums

Falling In Love Again (Hollander-Connelly)   1:58

John Lennon : Rhythm Guitar
Paul McCartney : Bass Guitar and Solo Vocal
George Harrison : Lead Guitar
Ringo Starr : Drums

Ask Me Why (Lennon—McCartney)   2:30

John Lennon : Rhythm Guitar and Lead Vocal
Paul McCartney : Bass Guitar and Backing Vocal
George Harrison : Lead Guitar and Backing Vocal
Ringo Starr : Drums

Be Bop A Lula (Vincent—Davis)   2:28

John Lennon : Rhythm Guitar
Paul McCartney : Bass Guitar
George Harrison : Lead Guitar
Ringo Starr : Drums
Horst Obber : Solo Vocal

Hallelujah, I Love Her So (Charles)   2:07

John Lennon : Rhythm Guitar
Paul McCartney : Bass Guitar
George Harrison : Lead Guitar
Ringo Starr : Drums
Horst Obber : Solo Vocal

SIDE FOUR

Sheila (Roe)   1:55

John Lennon : Rhythm Guitar
Paul McCartney : Bass Guitar
George Harrison : Lead Guitar and Solo Vocal
Ringo Starr : Drums

Red Sails In The Sunset (Kennedy—Williams)   2:00

John Lennon : Rhythm Guitar
Paul McCartney : Bass Guitar and Solo Vocal
George Harrison : Lead Guitar
Ringo Starr : Drums

Everybody's Trying To Be My Baby (Perkins)   2:25

John Lennon : Rhythm Guitar
Paul McCartney : Bass Guitar
George Harrison : Lead Guitar and Solo Vocal
Ringo Starr : Drums

Matchbox (Perkins)   2:35

John Lennon : Rhythm Guitar and Solo Vocal
Paul McCartney : Bass Guitar
George Harrison : Lead Guitar
Ringo Starr : Drums

Talkin' 'Bout You (Berry)   1:50

John Lennon : Rhythm Guitar and Solo Vocal
Paul McCartney : Bass Guitar
George Harrison : Lead Guitar
Ringo Starr : Drums

Shimmy Shimmy (Massey—Sheubert)   2:18

John Lennon : Rhythm Guitar and Lead Vocal
Paul McCartney : Bass Guitar and Lead Vocal
George Harrison : Lead Guitar
Ringo Starr : Drums

Long Tall Sally (Johnson—Penniman—Blackwell)   1:50

John Lennon : Rhythm Guitar
Paul McCartney : Bass Guitar and Solo Vocal
George Harrison : Lead Guitar
Ringo Starr : Drums

I Remember You (Mercer—Schertzinger)   1:51

John Lennon : Harmonica
Paul McCartney : Bass Guitar and Solo Vocal
George Harrison : Lead Guitar
Ringo Starr : Drums

PLEASE PLEASE ME
Parlophone PMC 1202;
                PCS 3042
Producer : George Martin
Release Date : 22 March 1963
Running Time : 31:48

SIDE ONE: I Saw Her Standing There; Misery; Anna (Go To Him); Chains; Boys; Ask Me Why; Please Please Me.

SIDE TWO: Love Me Do; P.S. I Love You; Baby It's You; Do You Want To Know A Secret; A Taste Of Honey; There's A Place; Twist And Shout.

The Beatles' first album for Parlophone combines their two previously issued singles Love Me Do/P.S. I Love You and Please Please Me/Ask Me Why with ten newly recorded songs. Four of the new songs are Lennon—McCartney originals, while the remaining six are Beatles' versions of some of their favourite songs, which they had been including in their live performances at the Cavern Club in Liverpool and the Star Club in Hamburg for quite some time prior to gaining a recording contract with EMI.

Despite the success of the two singles—Please Please Me had just reached No. 1—EMI were still not convinced that the Beatles were going to last. However, wanting to cater to the overwhelming demand for their records EMI requested that the Beatles make an album as soon as possible, and preferably call it Please Please Me so that it would be instantly recognizable to the buyers of the single.

George Martin initially planned to record a live album capturing all the excitement of a Beatles performance at the Cavern Club in Liverpool, but the idea proved to be impractical and was quickly dismissed. He then decided that the Beatles should make the album in a recording studio although it would still consist of songs that they would have performed on a live album.

On 11 February 1963 the Beatles, with George Martin, entered EMI's Abbey Road studios to record the remaining tracks on this album in one long exhaustive recording session, from 10 a.m. to 11 p.m. As he had not decided upon the content of this album, George Martin asked the Beatles to run quickly through some of their favourite songs. From these he selected nine of the final ten album titles. The tenth was Twist and Shout. With the contents now decided, and with the knowledge that the Beatles had been playing these songs for years, Martin started the recording session.

Thirteen hours, ten songs and £400 later the album was finished. To record an album, mix it and have it ready to go into production in one day is no mean feat but they managed it. Incidentally it is interesting to note that at the time of recording Lennon and McCartney had written nearly 100 songs, and were heavily criticised for not including more of their own songs on this album. However, EMI were delighted with the recordings. A decision was made that upon release of the album, two tracks from it should also be issued as a single.

To combat EMI's plan, and with the knowledge that four of the tracks had already been issued as singles, the Beatles had a further recording session on 4 March 1963, which produced From Me To You and Thank You Girl. These were released as a single, on 12 April 1963, two weeks after the release of the album. Like its predecessor, Please Please Me, this single went to No. 1.

The release of the album changed the British music scene. Previously the British album chart had been filled with film sound-track albums, recordings of London and Broadway musicals and, with the exception of Elvis Presley and two or three other American artists, very little else. The only British pop music artists before the Beatles who had had any sort of success in the British album charts were Cliff Richard and the Shadows.

SIDE ONE

I Saw Her Standing There (Lennon–McCartney) 2:50

John Lennon : Rhythm Guitar and Harmony Vocal
Paul McCartney : Bass Guitar and Lead Vocal
George Harrison : Lead Guitar
Ringo Starr : Drums

A great opener to the album, this was initial proof that Lennon and McCartney could and would write good old rock and roll. It is hard to imagine a better start to the Beatles' first album than Paul counting in 'one—two—three—four.' Paul's lead vocal with harmonies from John is backed by some excellent 'Shadows'-style lead guitar from George. The recording features some of the Beatles' early 'trademarks'—handclapping, used to add more excitement to an already exciting recording, and 'oooo' which was to be put to good use on future recordings. Overall, this is a good chunk of pounding rock and roll that featured in Beatles' live performances and was a huge favourite amongst members at both the Cavern and the Star clubs.
 On 28 November 1974 John Lennon recorded this song with Elton John. After a concert given by Elton John at Madison Square Garden, Lennon joined him on stage and announced this song 'we thought we'd do a number of an old estranged fiancé of mine, called Paul.'

Misery (Lennon–McCartney) 1:43

John Lennon : Rhythm Guitar and Lead Vocal
Paul McCartney : Bass Guitar and Lead Vocal
George Harrison : Lead Guitar
Ringo Starr : Drums

The lead vocal on this up-tempo ballad sounds double-tracked; it is, in fact, a close-harmony duet between John and Paul, and is a fine example of how they blended their two voices to sound like one. It is fine proof that not only could Lennon and McCartney write songs, but they could also sing.

Anna (Go To Him) (Alexander) 2:56

John Lennon : Rhythm Guitar and Lead Vocal
Paul McCartney : Bass Guitar and Backing Vocal
George Harrison : Lead Guitar and Backing Vocal
Ringo Starr : Drums

John's powerful pleading lead vocals do justice to this Arthur Alexander song, which Arthur had recorded a year earlier for the Dot label. Arthur Alexander, as John Lennon later revealed, was a big influence on his early writing. This song and the equally mournful You Better Move On, recorded by the Rolling Stones, are two of Arthur's songs made internationally famous for him.

Chains (Goffin—King) 2:21

John Lennon : Rhythm Guitar, Harmonica and Harmony Vocal
Paul McCartney : Bass Guitar and Harmony Vocal
George Harrison : Lead Guitar and Lead Vocal
Ringo Starr : Drums

The musical introduction to this Goffin—King song, originally recorded by the American girl group The Cookies, heralds the first appearance on the album of John's harmonica. The vocals are a three-part harmony between John, Paul and George, with George singing solo between the chanting chorus line that dominates the song.

Boys (Dixon—Farrell) 2:24

John Lennon : Rhythm Guitar and Backing Vocal
Paul McCartney : Bass Guitar and Backing Vocal
George Harrison : Lead Guitar and Backing Vocal
Ringo Starr : Drums and Lead Vocal

This song, originally recorded by the Shirelles, gives Ringo his first appearance on the album as vocalist. He belts out the lyrics in fine form, sounding like any good rock and roller should. John, Paul and George supply the 'bop-shoo-wop' backing as Ringo hurtles his way through his beloved Shirelles song. Luther Dixon and Wes Farrell must have found this to be a good rendition of their song.

Ask Me Why (Lennon—McCartney) 2:24

John Lennon : Rhythm Guitar and Lead Vocal
Paul McCartney : Bass Guitar and Harmony Vocal
George Harrison : Lead Guitar and Harmony Vocal
Ringo Starr : Drums

Released as the B-side to the Beatles' second single for Parlophone, Please Please Me, this is the first song on the album not to have been recorded at the 11 February session. One of John's early attempts at ballad writing, it features him on lead vocal with some very pleasant harmonies from Paul and George. Another of the Beatles' early trademarks, falsetto, can be heard on this song.

Please Please Me (Lennon—McCartney) 2:00

John Lennon : Rhythm Guitar, Harmonica and Lead Vocal
Paul McCartney : Bass Guitar and Harmony Vocal
George Harrison : Lead Guitar and Harmony Vocal
Ringo Starr : Drums

Two minutes of sheer excellence. This highly commercial recording, was the title track of the album and also the title of the Beatles' second single for Parlophone, which shot to No. 1 within weeks of being released. John's lead vocal is given some fine close harmony backing from Paul and George. The track is interspersed with some interesting harmonica from John. This recording has always fascinated me because so much is condensed into such a short space of time. Paul has since given George Martin credit for improving the tempo of this track, which was the main reason for its success.

SIDE TWO

Love Me Do (Lennon–McCartney) 2:19

John Lennon : Harmonica and Lead Vocal
Paul McCartney : Bass Guitar and Lead Vocal
George Harrison : Acoustic Guitar and Harmony Vocal
Ringo Starr : Tambourine
Andy White : Drums

This recording was the A-side of the Beatles' first single for Parlophone. (The next track, P.S. I Love You was the B-side.) Released on 5 October 1962, it hovered around the lower half of the Top Twenty at No. 17. It was on the chart for six weeks—which by later standards was short. The recording is dominated by John's harmonica. The main lead vocals are a duet from John and Paul, with John singing solo at various times. The lyrics are sparse but with the dominant harmonica and John's asthmatic Liverpudlian 'scouse' vocals it was definitely an 'ear catcher' in 1962.

There are two recordings of Love Me Do; one features Ringo on drums and the other features a session musician, Andy White. This version is the 'Andy White' version (with Ringo on tambourine). The single featured Ringo on drums.

The reason for the two recordings, was that after Ringo replaced Pete Best, George Martin had not heard him play and had brought in Andy White just in case Ringo's drumming didn't match up to expectations. Martin insisted that the Beatles use Andy White as the drummer, but the Beatles wanted Ringo. As a compromise two recordings were made. None of the Beatles was particularly pleased either about a session musician being used on their records, or about the fact that Ringo had been given a tambourine, and they all insisted that the version featuring Ringo on drums be released as the single. The version featuring Ringo is included on Record 1 of the Beatles Box.

P.S. I Love You (Lennon–McCartney) 2:02

John Lennon : Acoustic Guitar and Lead Vocal
Paul McCartney : Bass Guitar and Lead Vocal
George Harrison : Lead Guitar
Ringo Starr : Maraccas
Andy White : Drums

Previously released as the B-side to Love Me Do, this sounds rather like a Paul McCartney re-write of John Lennon's Ask Me Why, although it is still a very pleasant song.

Baby It's You (David—Williams—Bacharach)   2:36

John Lennon : Rhythm Guitar and Lead Vocal
Paul McCartney : Bass Guitar and Backing Vocal
George Harrison : Lead Guitar and Backing Vocal
Ringo Starr : Drums
George Martin : Piano

This easygoing ballad was previously recorded by one of the Beatles' favourite groups, The Shirelles. John's lead vocals are backed by Paul and George who supply the 'sha, la, la, la, la' backing. John Lennon's ability to change the tone, pitch and feeling in his voice is finely displayed on this recording.

Do You Want To Know A Secret (Lennon—McCartney)   1:55

John Lennon : Rhythm Guitar and Backing Vocal
Paul McCartney : Bass Guitar and Backing Vocal
George Harrison : Lead Guitar and Lead Vocal
Ringo Starr : Drums

George Harrison's first appearance on the album as a vocalist is on this song, of which John Lennon was once quoted as saying 'I wrote this one for George.' Unfortunately for George the whole recording is badly mixed, with George's lead guitar mixed into oblivion somewhere down the right channel, and John and Paul's backing vocals given far too much echo, producing an out-of-keeping, almost ethereal atmosphere. The song was later recorded by Billy J. Kramer and The Dakotas and reached No. 1 in the British charts.

A Taste Of Honey (Marlow Scott)   2:02

John Lennon : Rhythm Guitar and Harmony Vocal
Paul McCartney : Bass Guitar and Lead Vocal
George Harrison : Lead Guitar and Harmony Vocal
Ringo Starr : Drums

Taken from the theme music of the film of the same name, A Taste Of Honey has been recorded by many musicians, from blues singers to classical orchestras. This song featured in the Beatles' early stage performances, was very popular in the early sixties, and was a good vehicle for Paul McCartney's voice. John and George supply harmonies.

There's A Place (Lennon—McCartney)   1:44

John Lennon : Rhythm Guitar, Harmonica and Lead Vocal
Paul McCartney : Bass Guitar and Harmony Vocal
George Harrison : Lead Guitar
Ringo Starr : Drums

The tight harmony of John and Paul, with John singing solo at times, combine perfectly with the wailing soulful harmonica on this fine example of John's early ballad writing. This is an extremely pleasant, well recorded song.

Twist And Shout (Medley—Russell) 2:32

John Lennon : Rhythm Guitar and Lead Vocal
Paul McCartney : Bass Guitar and Backing Vocal
George Harrison : Lead Guitar and Backing Vocal
Ringo Starr : Drums

This is the strongest track on the album, and one of the few songs that I imagine Lennon and McCartney must have wished they had written themselves. Originally recorded by the Isley Brothers in 1962, this Phil Medley and Bert Russell song was a Beatles' show-stopper at early concerts, the song that most people would remember after the show was over. John's rasping, leathery vocals turn the invitation to twist and shout into a demand. The chunky combination of the lead and rhythm guitar, coupled with Paul's chugging bass guitar and Ringo's tight drum beat makes this a truly magnificent recording. According to legend, when the Beatles had finished the recordings for the Please Please Me album they still had some studio time left. So, in one take, they recorded Twist and Shout. Every time I listen to the track I wonder how long it took John Lennon to recover from the sore throat he must have suffered after the recording.

WITH THE BEATLES
Parlophone PMC 1206; PCS 3045
Producer : George Martin
Release Date : 22 November 1963
Running Time : 32:44

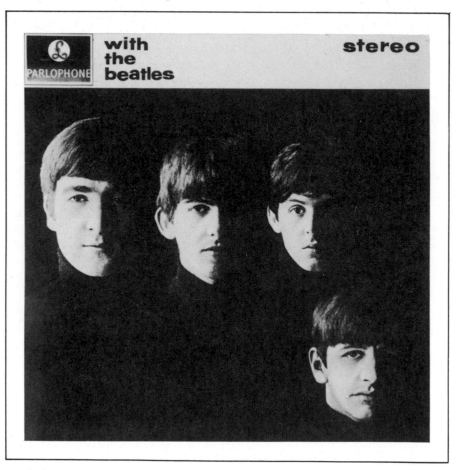

SIDE ONE: It Won't Be Long; All I've Got To Do; All My Loving; Don't Bother Me; Little Child; Till There Was You; Please Mister Postman.

SIDE TWO: Roll Over Beethoven; Hold Me Tight; You Really Got A Hold On Me; I Wanna Be Your Man; Devil In Her Heart; Not A Second Time; Money.

The Beatles' second album for Parlophone features 14 newly recorded songs. Seven of them were written by Lennon—McCartney, one by George Harrison and the remaining six are a further selection of the Beatles' personal favourites.

After the huge success of the Please Please Me album it was important to follow it with another equally good, if not better, album. This the Beatles managed to do. Recorded on 15 July 1963, this album feels more self-confident, with the Beatles sounding more relaxed in their singing and playing. On three of the tracks the Beatles are joined by their producer, George Martin, on Piano — You Really Got A Hold On Me (the old Miracles number), Lennon and McCartney's Not A Second Time and finally John's powerful rendition of the Janie Bradford and Berry Gordy song, Money.

Unlike Please Please Me, this album is not dependent on earlier single releases. To ensure that none of the tracks was extracted for release as a single, the Beatles recorded, on 19 October 1963, I Want To Hold Your Hand and This Boy. These were issued as a single on 29 November 1963, exactly one week after the release of the album.

SIDE ONE

It Won't Be Long (Lennon—McCartney)   2:11

John Lennon : Rhythm Guitar and Lead Vocal
Paul McCartney : Bass Guitar and Backing Vocal
George Harrison : Lead Guitar and Backing Vocal
Ringo Starr : Drums

John's double-tracked lead vocal on this song is given some neat close-harmony backing from Paul and George. The song is structured in a similar way to Money, the album's closing track, inasmuch as John sings the statement-style lyrics and Paul and George reply with 'yeah-yeah'. The recording also makes use of a repetitive, although not over-obvious or annoying, riff.

All I've Got To Do (Lennon—McCartney)   2:05

John Lennon : Rhythm Guitar and Lead Vocal
Paul McCartney : Bass Guitar and Harmony Vocal
George Harrison : Lead Guitar
Ringo Starr : Drums

This recording starts with an unusual semi-blues/country beat. It then moves at a much faster pace before reverting to the earlier beat. John handles the lyrics perfectly, with Paul supplying harmonies. The combination works extremely well.

All My Loving (Lennon—McCartney)   2:04

John Lennon : Rhythm Guitar and Harmony Vocal
Paul McCartney : Bass Guitar and Lead Vocal
George Harrison : Lead Guitar and Harmony Vocal
Ringo Starr : Drums

Paul's first lead vocal performance on the album on All My Loving has become one of the Beatles' standards, recorded by many artists in many styles. Paul's voice is double-tracked on this powerful song which tears along at a furious pace. The song starts and stops, but unobtrusively, and makes effective use of a second or so of silence - an effect to be used often on future recordings. Listen to George's country and western guitar playing during the instrumental break; it fits in with the rest of the track perfectly to make this one of Paul McCartney's most likeable songs.

Don't Bother Me (Harrison)   2:28

John Lennon : Rhythm Guitar and Tambourine
Paul McCartney : Bass Guitar and Claves
George Harrison : Lead Guitar and Solo Vocal
Ringo Starr : Drums, Bongos and Loose-Skinned Arabian Bongo

This was the first George Harrison song to appear on a Beatles' album, although not his first composition as he had written, with John, the instrumental Cry For A Shadow which was included on the Polydor album The Beatles First.

This song would probably never have been written had it not been for Bill Harry, editor/owner in the early sixties of the Merseyside newspaper *Merseybeat*. He repeatedly teased George, asking him when he was going to start writing songs like John and Paul. Giving in finally, George came up with Don't Bother Me in reply to Bill Harry's persistent questioning. It was a good first song from George. It is structured like All My Loving, starting and stopping in a similar manner. In addition to the normal instrumentation, George's double-tracked lead vocals are backed with Paul beating out the rhythm on claves, John joining in on tambourine, and Ringo on loose-skinned Arabian bongo.

Little Child (Lennon–McCartney)   1:46

John Lennon : Rhythm Guitar, Harmonica and Lead Vocal
Paul McCartney : Bass Guitar, Piano and Lead Vocal
George Harrison : Lead Guitar
Ringo Starr : Drums

John's harmonica leads into this rhythm and blues song, one of few such to be recorded by the Beatles. The lead vocal is a duet between John and Paul, although John predominates. His superb blues harmonica contribution is very derivative of Cyril Davies, the exponent of some fine harmonica playing on many British rhythm and blues records during the late fifties and early sixties when he worked with Alexis Korner's Blues Incorporated.

Because of the influence of Cyril Davies on John, and that of Nicky Hopkins (another early British exponent of rhythm and blues) on Paul, who plays piano on the track, the call and answer of the vocals versus the harmonica and piano gives the song a Rolling Stones feel.

Till There Was You (Willson) 2:12

John Lennon : Acoustic Guitar
Paul McCartney : Bass Guitar and Solo Vocal
George Harrison : Acoustic Guitar
Ringo Starr : Bongos

Taken from the stage show/film *The Music Man,* this song had been used for a long time by the Beatles in their stage performances. It always went down extremely well with members of both the Cavern and Star clubs and was used as a slow melodic 'breather' in between the up-tempo dance beat songs. With almost magical control the Beatles would always bring an audience to near silence whenever they performed this number. For proof of this listen to the album The Beatles' Historic Sessions. The lead vocal is a solo from Paul with John and George playing acoustic guitars and Ringo tapping out a gentle beat on a set of bongos. The only electrically operated instrument on this track is Paul's bass guitar.

Please Mister Postman (Holland) 2:34

John Lennon : Rhythm Guitar and Lead Vocal
Paul McCartney : Bass Guitar and Harmony Vocal
George Harrison : Lead Guitar and Harmony Vocal
Ringo Starr : Drums

Another early favourite of the Beatles, this one-time American chart-topper for the American girl group the Marvelettes, features John Lennon on lead vocals with Paul and George adding harmonies and some interesting backing vocals. What sounds like a duet between John and Paul is actually John's voice double-tracked. This is another song that I imagine the Beatles wished they had written themselves.

SIDE TWO

Roll Over Beethoven (Berry) 2:44

John Lennon : Rhythm Guitar
Paul McCartney : Bass Guitar
George Harrison : Lead Guitar and Solo Vocal
Ringo Starr : Drums

With John's rhythm guitar chugging away, George double-tracks the lead vocals for this rendition of the Chuck Berry classic. The Beatles performed this song quite often during their early days at the Cavern and Star clubs, and it was a popular request number. An early live recording of the song can be heard on the album The Beatles' Historic Sessions.

Hold Me Tight (Lennon—McCartney) 2:30

John Lennon : Rhythm Guitar and Backing Vocal
Paul McCartney : Bass Guitar and Lead Vocal
George Harrison : Lead Guitar and Backing Vocal
Ringo Starr : Drums

Paul is on lead vocal for this one with John and George adding energetic backing vocals and joining on chorus. Paul sings with a slightly Little Richard sound similar to I Saw Her Standing There on the first album. Both songs show Paul's increasing interest in writing his own rock and roll songs.

You Really Got A Hold On Me (Robinson) 2:58

John Lennon : Rhythm Guitar and Lead Vocal
Paul McCartney : Bass Guitar and Backing Vocal
George Harrison : Lead Guitar and Lead Vocal
Ringo Starr : Drums
George Martin : Piano

The lead vocal for this song, originally recorded by the American group the Miracles, is brilliantly handled by John. It is not the easiest of songs to sing, but he does it well. George duets with John and alternates with him on the main line of the song. Paul joins them both for the chorus, while George Martin adds a dramatic piano.

In the late fifties and early sixties, American soul was virtually unknown in Britain, and almost nobody had heard of the Miracles or Smokey Robinson. It was not until the Beatles and other Liverpudlian groups started to put out their versions of American records such as You Really Got a Hold On Me that interest in the originals began to grow. Smokey Robinson later went on to write such classics as The Tracks Of My Tears and The Tears Of A Clown.

I Wanna Be Your Man (Lennon—McCartney) 1:59

John Lennon : Rhythm Guitar, Hammond Organ and Harmony Vocal
Paul McCartney : Bass Guitar and Harmony Vocal
George Harrison : Lead Guitar
Ringo Starr : Drums, Maraccas and Lead Vocal

After the public response to Ringo's performance of the Shirelles' number Boys on Please Please Me, John and Paul came up with I Wanna Be Your Man for him. Ringo handles the lyrics professionally, with a helping hand from John and Paul on chorus. The instrumentation for this track is supplemented by a Hammond organ played by John and maraccas added by Ringo.

After failing to reach the Top Twenty with their first single Come On, the Rolling Stones recorded I Wanna Be Your Man as their follow-up and the song took them to Number 12 in the British charts.

Devil In Her Heart (Drapkin)   2:23

John Lennon : Rhythm Guitar and Harmony Vocal
Paul McCartney : Bass Guitar and Harmony Vocal
George Harrison : Lead Guitar and Lead Vocal
Ringo Starr : Drums and Maraccas

When the Beatles got hold of this song (originally recorded by the American girl group the Donays) they changed the lyrics slightly for George to sing. He handles the song skillfully, and John and Paul add harmonies and backing vocals. During their career the Beatles were to record in many styles; on this track they play a samba beat, and the final chord could almost have been replaced with a vocal 'cha, cha, cha'.

Not A Second Time (Lennon – McCartney)   2.03

John Lennon : Acoustic Guitar and Solo Vocal
Paul McCartney : Not Present
George Harrison : Not Present
Ringo Starr : Drums
George Martin : Piano

The last Lennon and McCartney song on the album features a double-tracked vocal from John with George Martin on piano. This is one of their few early songs without backing vocals. The trade is backed by Martin, John on acoustic guitar and Ringo on drums.

This is the song that William Mann of *The Times* described so graphically in 1963. After writing about Lennon and McCartney at great length as '... the outstanding English composers of 1963...' Mann then gave a review of This Boy and continued with the following '... but harmonic interest is typical of their quicker songs too, and one gets the impression that they think simultaneously of harmony and melody, so firmly are the major tonic sevenths and ninths build into their tunes, and the flat submediant key switches, so natural in the Aerolian cadence at the end of Not A Second Time (The chord progression that ends Mahler's Song of the Earth)...' to which John Lennon replied 'Really it was chords just like any other chords'.

Money (Bradford – Gordy)   2.47

John Lennon : Rhythm Guitar and Lead Vocal
Paul McCartney : Bass Guitar and Backing Vocal
George Harrison : Lead Guitar and Backing Vocal
Ringo Starr : Drums
George Martin : Piano

John shouts out his demands for 'money' with the full force of his raw leathery voice. Paul and George add the backing answers to his demands, and Ringo adds an almost hypnotic 'jungle' beat on drums. George Martin is again featured on piano, which is one of the predominant instruments on this powerful rendition. The song was partly written by the boss of Motown Records, Berry Gordy, and originally recorded by the American artist Barratt Strong for the American Anna record label in 1959; it was then re-issued on the Motown label in 1960.

A HARD DAY'S NIGHT
Parlophone PMC 1230; PCS 3058
Producer : George Martin
Release Date : 10 July 1964
Running Time : 29:53

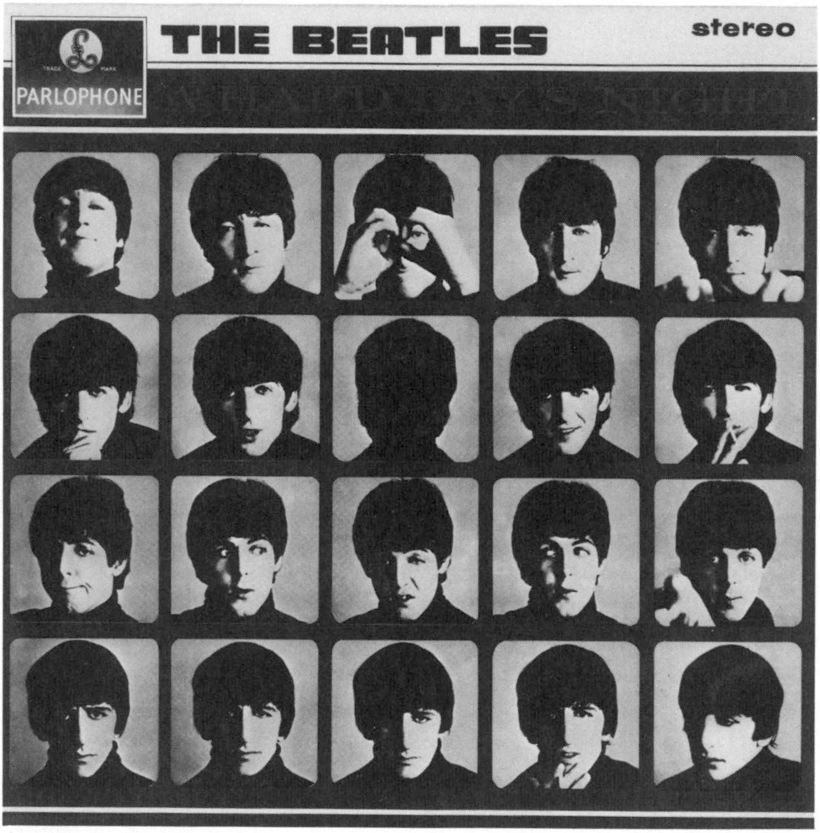

SIDE ONE: A Hard Day's Night; I Should Have Known Better; If I Fell; I'm Happy Just To Dance With You; And I Love Her; Tell Me Why; Can't Buy Me Love

SIDE TWO: Any Time At All; I'll Cry Instead; Things We Said Today; When I Get Home; You Can't Do That; I'll Be Back.

The soundtrack album from the Beatles' first film features 13 new Lennon and McCartney songs; this was to be the only Beatles' album to consist entirely of Lennon and McCartney compositions. Future albums always contained at least one track written by George Harrison and in two cases tracks written by Ringo Starr.

The first side features seven new songs used in the film, from the powerful opening title track to the slow melodic And I Love Her. The soundtrack also used some of the Beatles' older songs such as I Wanna Be Your Man, Don't Bother Me, All My Loving and She Loves You but these are not included on the album. The second side has a further selection of Lennon and McCartney originals including I'll Cry Instead, which, although written for the film, was not considered strong enough for inclusion by the film's director, Dick Lester. Amongst the remaining five tracks is You Can't Do That, issued with Can't Buy Me Love as a single some three months prior to the release of this album. Upon release of the album the title track along with Things We Said Today was also issued as a single.

The film, which also stars Wilfred Brambell (as Paul's mythical grandfather), depicts two days in the lives of the Beatles from boarding a train in Liverpool (shot at Paddington Station, London) on their way to give the concert which is shown at the end of the film. It has some hilarious moments and is highly enjoyable.

SIDE ONE

A Hard Day's Night (Lennon–McCartney)   2:32

John Lennon : Rhythm Guitar and Lead Vocal
Paul McCartney : Bass Guitar and Harmony Vocal
George Harrison : Lead Guitar
Ringo Starr : Drums
George Martin : Piano

The opening chord of this strong opening track shows typical Beatles' originality and sounds more like the end of a record than the beginning. As the chord fades, John double-tracks the lead vocals with Paul harmonising in part and sometimes also singing lead vocals. In the excellent instrumental break in the middle George's guitar sounds like a harpsichord and Ringo's backing beat rounds the whole thing off. A good strong solid opening track which in the film is played over the opening titles.

I Should Have Known Better (Lennon–McCartney)   2:42

John Lennon : Acoustic Guitar, Harmonica and Solo Vocal
Paul McCartney : Bass Guitar
George Harrison : Lead Guitar
Ringo Starr : Drums

John's wailing harmonica introduces this song which also features him on lead vocals in a double-tracked solo with an extremely energetic backing. The song makes an early appearance in the film, where the Beatles are seen playing cards in the train.

If I Fell (Lennon–McCartney) 2:16

John Lennon : Acoustic Guitar and Lead Vocal
Paul McCartney : Bass Guitar and Lead Vocal
George Harrison : Lead Guitar
Ringo Starr : Drums

This pleasant up-tempo ballad opens with a solo vocal from John on the first verse before he is joined by Paul in a duet for the rest of the song. In the film the Beatles are seen performing this during rehearsals for a television show.

I'm Happy Just To Dance With You
(Lennon–McCartney) 1:59

John Lennon : Rhythm Guitar and Backing Vocal
Paul McCartney : Bass Guitar and Backing Vocal
George Harrison : Lead Guitar and Lead Vocal
Ringo Starr : Drums and Loose-Skinned Arabian Bongo

George is on lead vocals for this song, written for him by John. The 'Oh-oh' backing comes from John and Paul, and Ringo's loose-skinned Arabian bongo producing a hollow thumping sound makes its second appearance on a Beatles' record (its first was on Don't Bother Me on With The Beatles).

And I Love Her (Lennon–McCartney) 2:27

John Lennon : Acoustic Guitar
Paul McCartney : Acoustic Guitar and Solo Vocal
George Harrison : Claves and Acoustic Guitar Solo
Ringo Starr : Bongos

Paul McCartney's earliest ballad has become an international standard recorded by scores of artists each with a different treatment. George Martin's orchestral version is included on the American album; there, the song features Paul on lead vocals, first double-tracked then triple-tracked to add his own harmonies. It also features a striking and memorable acoustic guitar riff accompanied by claves, two further acoustic guitars and bongos.

Tell Me Why (Lennon–McCartney) 2:04

John Lennon : Rhythm Guitar and Lead Vocal
Paul McCartney : Bass Guitar and Harmony Vocal
George Harrison : Lead Guitar
Ringo Starr : Drums

The vocals on this track are an interesting and unusual three-part harmony between John and Paul, with John's vocals double-tracked and Paul harmonising. The recording also features an effective use of falsetto, by John and Paul, who manage to sound like a crowd of children.

Can't Buy Me Love (Lennon—McCartney)   2:15

John Lennon : Rhythm Guitar
Paul McCartney : Bass Guitar and Solo Vocal
George Harrison : Lead Guitar
Ringo Starr : Drums

Previously issued as a single, three months before this album, the song features a double-tracked vocal from Paul and sounds rather like a re-write of A Hard Day's Night, minus the opening chord. The recording also features an interesting double-tracked guitar during the instrumental break. The Beatles first recorded Can't Buy Me Love in a theatre dressing room. The recording started with the verses instead of the chorus as it does here. Only three of the Beatles were on that recording, John and Paul singing and playing guitar and Ringo adding the backing beat, courtesy of a suitcase. George had gone to the toilet, and at the end of the song there is the sound of the toilet being flushed. The Beatles wanted to issue that version as a single but George Martin was not amused so this recording was made instead.

SIDE TWO

Any Time At All (Lennon—McCartney)   2:10

John Lennon : Acoustic Guitar and Solo Vocal
Paul McCartney : Bass Guitar and Piano
George Harrison : Lead Guitar
Ringo Starr : Drums

A lively song featuring a solo vocal from John and enthusiastic backing that includes a guitar/piano duet between George and Paul during the instrumental break. Neither this nor the remaining five tracks on this side of the album are featured in the film *A Hard Day's Night*.

I'll Cry Instead (Lennon—McCartney)   1:44

John Lennon : Acoustic Guitar, Tambourine and Lead Vocal
Paul McCartney : Bass Guitar and Lead Vocal
George Harrison : Lead Guitar
Ringo Starr : Drums

This country and western influenced song written by John for inclusion in the film features a lead vocal duet between John and Paul with George playing some neat country and western/rockabilly guitar.

Things We Said Today (Lennon—McCartney)   2:35

John Lennon : Acoustic Guitar, Tambourine and Harmony Vocal
Paul McCartney : Bass Guitar and Lead Vocal
George Harrison : Lead Guitar
Ringo Starr : Drums

The opening riff is reminiscent of the Shadows' Guitar Tango, although it was

42

uncharacteristic for the Beatles to borrow from other artists' material. Paul double-tracks the lead vocals with John harmonising in places. The song is a pleasant up-beat ballad written by Paul.

When I Get Home (Lennon – McCartney)   2:14

John Lennon : Rhythm Guitar and Lead Vocal
Paul McCartney : Bass Guitar and Harmony Vocal
George Harrison : Lead Guitar
Ringo Starr : Drums

Lead vocals are from John on this one with Paul harmonising in parts. Unfortunately the overemphatic use of the line 'whoa-ho' overshadows the rest of the song.

You Can't Do That (Lennon – McCartney)   2:33

John Lennon : Rhythm Guitar and Lead Vocal
Paul McCartney : Bass Guitar and Harmony Vocal
George Harrison : 12 String Lead Guitar and Harmony Vocal
Ringo Starr : Drums, cowbell and Bongos

This was previously issued as the B-side to Can't Buy Me Love. John's gravelly lead vocal shouts out the lyrics in an attempt at being Wilson Pickett (as he admitted later) and Paul and George harmonise on the chorus. Ringo bangs out a metallic beat on a cowbell and for good measure bongos are added.

I'll Be Back (Lennon – McCartney)   2:22

John Lennon : Acoustic Guitar and Lead Vocal
Paul McCartney : Bass Guitar, Acoustic Guitar and Harmony Vocal
George Harrison : Acoustic Guitar
Ringo Starr : Drums

The closing track is a pleasant up-tempo ballad featuring a double-tracked lead vocal from John, with Paul harmonising in places. The sentiment of the title was a nice way to finish the album.

BEATLES FOR SALE
Parlophone PMC 1240; PCS 3062
Producer : George Martin
Release Date : 4 December 1964
Running Time : 36:58

SIDE ONE: No Reply; I'm A Loser; Baby's In Black; Rock And Roll Music; I'll Follow The Sun; Mr. Moonlight; Kansas City/Hey Hey Hey Hey.

SIDE TWO: Eight Days A Week; Words Of Love; Honey Don't; Every Little Thing; I Don't Want To Spoil The Party; What You're Doing; Everybody's Trying To Be My Baby.

For this album Lennon and McCartney wrote eight new songs, and added a further six from the vast repertoire of other material which they had been performing for some time. Three of the new songs, Eight Days A Week, No Reply and I'm A Loser, were all considered as possible singles; the Beatles once again did not want to issue a single from the album. Instead, John came up with I Feel Fine and Paul with She's A Woman, which were issued as a single on 27 November 1964, one week prior to the release of this album.

The Beatles had just completed their second major tour of the USA when they began work on this album during mid to late September 1964 and their obvious exhaustion can be heard in some of the tracks. On Every Little Thing and I Don't Want To Spoil The Party, for example, the vocals sound rather weary and slightly strained. But, as they had issued an album in time for the Christmas market of 1963 they had planned to do the same for Christmas 1964 and so recording continued. (Each year they were to repeat this, and issued Christmas albums until 1969.)

In spite of the strain which shows through on a couple of tracks, this album contains some of the Beatles' classic early recordings, such as John's powerful rendition of the old Chuck Berry standard Rock and Roll Music, and the Roy Lee Johnson classic Mr Moonlight, along with Paul's new song I'll Follow The Sun.

As with the previous three albums, both George and Ringo feature on one track each. Ringo sings the old Carl Perkins standard Honey Don't and George takes lead vocal on another Carl Perkins track, Everybody's Trying To Be My Baby.

The sleeve photographs for this album also reveal the strain in the form of four unsmiling Beatles. The inner photograph shows the Beatles standing against a background of photographs of various music hall and film stars, pieced together to form a collage. This is an obvious forerunner to the sleeve of the 1967 Sgt. Pepper album.

SIDE ONE

No Reply (Lennon—McCartney)   2:15

John Lennon : Acoustic Guitar and Lead Vocal
Paul McCartney : Bass Guitar and Harmony Vocal
George Harrison : Lead Guitar and Harmony Vocal
Ringo Starr : Drums
George Martin : Piano

This strong opening track features a double-tracked lead vocal from John, with Paul helping here and there and George joining them for the chorus. They go straight into the lyrics without musical introduction or opening chorus. This was a style of writing used by John and Paul for quite some time. It was often George Martin who would add a chorus as an introduction before the main lyrics.

I'm A Loser (Lennon—McCartney)   2:31

John Lennon : Acoustic Guitar, Harmonica and Lead Vocal
Paul McCartney : Bass Guitar and Harmony Vocal
George Harrison : Lead Guitar
Ringo Starr : Drums and Tambourine

Lead vocals again are from John with Paul harmonising in parts and joining John for the chorus. At the time of writing, John had become influenced by Bob Dylan. Here he uses many of Dylan's expressions and nuances.

Baby's In Black (Lennon−McCartney) 2:02

John Lennon : Acoustic Guitar and Lead Vocal
Paul McCartney : Bass Guitar and Lead Vocal
George Harrison : Lead Guitar
Ringo Starr : Drums and Tambourine

Lead vocals on this track are a duet between John and Paul. Some 18 months after this recording, the Rolling Stones and a group called Los Bravos had hit records with Paint It Black and Black is Black, respectively, both of which were probably inspired by this song. All three tracks convey the black feeling of lost love.

Rock And Roll Music (Berry) 2:02

John Lennon : Rhythm Guitar, Piano and Solo Vocal
Paul McCartney : Bass Guitar and Piano
George Harrison : Acoustic Guitar
Ringo Starr : Drums
George Martin : Piano (with John and Paul)

John's leathery vocals make a far better job of this Chuck Berry classic than Berry ever did, and do the song justice. It tears along at neck-breaking speed. John, as well as singing, joins George Martin *and* Paul McCartney to add the piano for the backing. Yes, they are all on the same piano, and all at the same time.

I'll Follow The Sun (Lennon−McCartney) 1:46

John Lennon : Acoustic Guitar and Harmony Vocal
Paul McCartney : Acoustic Guitar and Lead Vocal
George Harrison : Lead Guitar
Ringo Starr : Bongos

Paul's lead vocal on this song is mostly double-tracked with John harmonising in places. Ringo adds some gentle taps on a set of bongos and George's lead guitar puts in a brief appearance during the instrumental break of this very pleasant, relaxing song.

Mr. Moonlight (Johnson) 2:35

John Lennon : Acoustic Guitar and Lead Vocal
Paul McCartney : Bass Guitar, Hammond Organ and Harmony Vocal
George Harrison : Lead Guitar and African Drum
Ringo Starr : Bongos

John screams out the opening of Mr. Moonlight with all the power and expression that the Lennon larynx can supply. As can be guessed, he is the lead vocalist on this track with Paul harmonising in parts. Paul also plays a dramatic Hammond organ sounding like a cross between the phantom of the opera and Reginald Dixon. Ringo adds the backing beat on a set of bongos, while George supplies that hollow 'thump' on an ancient African drum.

Kansas City (Leiber – Stoller)/**Hey Hey Hey Hey**
(Penniman)   2:30

John Lennon : Rhythm Guitar and Backing Vocal
Paul McCartney : Bass Guitar and Lead Vocal
George Harrison : Lead Guitar and Backing Vocal
Ringo Starr : Drums
George Martin : Piano

Originally, it was Paul McCartney's idea to join Kansas City together with Little Richard's hit Hey Hey Hey Hey, and the Beatles had used this medley during their early stage performances. It was recorded here exactly as they always performed it, with Paul on lead vocal using his Little Richard voice and John, George and Ringo supplying the 'hey hey hey hey' backing for the second song. There was an error on the album cover, listing this track as Kansas City. This was corrected on the actual record label, by adding the Hey Hey Hey Hey credit, and on later covers of albums which included the track.

SIDE TWO

Eight Days A Week (Lennon – McCartney)   2:43

John Lennon : Rhythm Guitar, Acoustic Guitar and Lead Vocal
Paul McCartney : Bass Guitar and Harmony Vocal
George Harrison : Lead Guitar
Ringo Starr : Drums

The fade-in, build-up of guitars at the beginning of this track, thought to be innovative at the time, has since been copied many times. John's lead vocal is double-tracked, and he also supplies his own harmonies for this song. Many people considered this to be dedicated to Brian Epstein, because of his problems at that time — trying to divide his management attentions between too many groups and solo artists, and literally trying to live 'eight days a week'.

However, the song was written by John when the Beatles were approached to make a second film, tentatively called *Eight Arms to Hold You*. John set about writing a song with the same title, but it turned out as Eight Days A Week; then John came up with Help!, after which the title of the film was changed.

Words Of Love (Holly)   2:10

John Lennon : Rhythm Guitar and Lead Vocal
Paul McCartney : Bass Guitar and Lead Vocal
George Harrison : Lead Guitar
Ringo Starr : Drums and Packing Case

John and Paul's close harmony on this, the only Buddy Holly song that the Beatles released on record, is the best example of how John and Paul blended their voices. Buddy Holly was one of Paul McCartney's favourite American artists, so much so that he has since bought all publishing rights to every Buddy Holly song.

That hand clapping sound on the backing is Ringo playing a packing case!

Honey Don't (Perkins) 2:56

John Lennon : Acoustic Guitar and Tambourine
Paul McCartney : Bass Guitar
George Harrison : Lead Guitar
Ringo Starr : Drums and Solo Vocal

On Ringo's usual one track per album opportunity, he eases his way through the words of this old Carl Perkins song, producing his own sing-a-long style that suited his voice so well, and that he was to use on many future recordings.

Carl Perkins was present at the session when this and some of his other songs were recorded by the Beatles. He was reported to have thoroughly enjoyed watching the session, although he did not take part. (In 1982, Perkins joined Paul McCartney for a song on McCartney's album Tug of War.)

Every Little Thing (Lennon–McCartney) 2:01

John Lennon : Acoustic Guitar and Lead Vocal
Paul McCartney : Bass Guitar, Piano and Lead Vocal
George Harrison : Lead Guitar
Ringo Starr : Drums and Timpani

More close harmonies from John and Paul on this track, which has the interesting inclusion of a timpani drum, played by Ringo, to accentuate sections of the song; George adds some very pleasant country and western style guitar.

I Don't Want To Spoil The Party (Lennon–McCartney) 2:33

John Lennon : Acoustic Guitar and Lead Vocal
Paul McCartney : Bass Guitar and Lead Vocal
George Harrison : Lead Guitar
Ringo Starr : Drums and Tambourine

John and Paul again harmonise on lead vocals, sounding very much as they do on Words of Love. This interesting track has a 'square-dance' style backing, although John and Paul's vocals sound rather tired.

What You're Doing (Lennon—McCartney)   2:30

John Lennon : Acoustic Guitar and Backing Vocal
Paul McCartney : Bass Guitar and Lead Vocal
George Harrison : Lead Guitar
Ringo Starr : Drums
George Martin : Piano

On many Beatles' early recordings, they paid homage to various artists.
Here, they pay tribute to Phil Spector.
The drum intro is a straight lift from the Spector-produced Be My Baby by
the Ronettes. It is even used again at the end, exactly as it is on the Ronettes'
record. The vocals on this track come from Paul.

Everybody's Trying To Be My Baby (Perkins)   2.24

John Lennon : Acoustic Guitar and Tambourine
Paul McCartney : Bass Guitar
George Harrison : Lead Guitar and Solo Vocal
Ringo Starr : Drums

The second Carl Perkins song to be included on this album, recorded at the
same session as Honey Don't, features George on lead vocals (although he is
swamped somewhat by echo) and country and western guitar.

HELP!
Parlophone PMC 1255; PCS 3071
Producer : George Martin
Release Date : 6 August 1965
Running Time : 33:06

SIDE ONE: Help!; The Night Before; You've Got To Hide Your Love Away; I Need You; Another Girl; You're Going To Lose That Girl; Ticket To Ride.

SIDE TWO: Act Naturally; It's Only Love; You Like Me Too Much; Tell Me What You See; I've Just Seen A Face; Yesterday; Dizzy Miss Lizzy.

The Beatles' fifth album for Parlophone was also the sound track from their second film. The first side contains seven of the eight Beatles' songs featured in the film (the eighth, She's A Woman is not included on this album). Amongst the seven tracks, Another Girl and Ticket To Ride feature Paul McCartney playing lead guitar for the first time on record. The second side has four Lennon and McCartney originals; It's Only Love, with an unusual quavering guitar sound, Tell Me What You See, I've Just Seen A Face and the brilliant Yesterday.

Of the other three tracks featured on the second side, You Like Me Too Much is written by George Harrison and Act Naturally and Dizzy Miss Lizzy are two of the last non-Beatle written songs that they recorded. Bad Boy, although recorded at the same time, was unavailable in Britain for 18 months, when it was included on the compilation album A Collection of Beatles Oldies. Previously the track was available on the American album Beatles VI (Capitol ST 2358).

With Help! the Beatles began to progress away from the simple 'three guitar and drums' towards a more complex sound, particularly on tracks such as You've Got To Hide Your Love Away, It's Only Love and Yesterday. The latter features Paul and a string quartet. (The progression was particularly noticeable four months later when the Rubber Soul album was issued.)

The sleeves of the British and American albums differ greatly. The American sleeve is basically an advertisement for the film, being a gatefold with stills from the film and information about it.

Also, on the front cover of the American sleeve, someone has made the amusing mistake of rearranging the four photographs of the Beatles so that the semaphore which is supposed to spell out H-E-L-P! on the British sleeve actually spells out H-P-E-L!

SIDE ONE

Help! (Lennon – McCartney)   2:16

John Lennon : Acoustic Guitar and Lead Vocal
Paul McCartney : Bass Guitar and Backing Vocal
George Harrison : Lead Guitar and Backing Vocal
Ringo Starr : Drums and Tambourine

John's nasal lead vocals are supported by Paul and George on chorus and backing. This is one of the first Beatles' lyrics not to have a boy meets girl/boy loses girl situation. It is a real plea from John for help, comparing the situation he found himself in at the time to earlier, less complicated days. He said later 'I meant it – it's real. The lyric is as good now as it was then. It is no different, and it makes me feel secure to know that I was aware of myself then. I was just singing "help" and I meant it.'

The Night Before (Lennon – McCartney)   2:33

John Lennon : Electric Piano and Backing Vocal
Paul McCartney : Bass Guitar and Lead Vocal
George Harrison : Lead Guitar and Backing Vocal
Ringo Starr : Drums

Double-tracked lead vocals are from Paul with backing vocals from John and George effectively mixed into the song like fragments of a half-remembered dream. The electric piano is played by John.

You've Got To Hide Your Love Away
(Lennon—McCartney)   2:08

John Lennon : Acoustic Guitar and Solo Vocal
Paul McCartney : Acoustic Guitar
George Harrison : Acoustic Guitar
Ringo Starr : Tambourine
Session Musicians : Flutes

John Lennon's most intriguing lyrics show the influence of Dylan. The vocal is a solo from John; just near the end he is joined by flutes.

I Need You (Harrison) 2:28

John Lennon : Acoustic Guitar and Backing Vocal
Paul McCartney : Bass Guitar and Backing Vocal
George Harrison : Lead Guitar and Lead Vocal
Ringo Starr : Drums

A double-tracked lead vocal from George on this, his own song, proves that he could write songs as good as John and Paul's.
　　The backing vocals and pleasant harmony are added by John and Paul. The eerie guitar sound played by George is achieved with the volume/tone control pedal which he was to use on a number of other tracks during 1965. At the end of the song it sounds as if he will play a guitar solo, but not having mastered the pedal he decided against it.

Another Girl (Lennon—McCartney)   2:02

John Lennon : Acoustic Guitar and Backing Vocal
Paul McCartney : Bass Guitar, Lead Guitar and Lead Vocal
George Harrison : Lead Guitar and Backing Vocal
Ringo Starr : Drums

Lead vocals are from Paul on this track, with John and George harmonising on the main line and chorus. The song has the same syncopated beat used in She's A Woman. The lead guitar is played by Paul for the first time on a Beatles' album and his solo at the end is really worth listening to.

You're Going To Lose That Girl (Lennon—McCartney)   2:18

John Lennon : Acoustic Guitar and Lead Vocal
Paul McCartney : Bass Guitar, Piano and Backing Vocal
George Harrison : Lead Guitar and Backing Vocal
Ringo Starr : Drums and Bongos

John's nasal lead vocal again works perfectly on this song, with Paul and George adding the backing vocals, plus some vocal support on chorus. Lead guitar comes from George, and Ringo adds bongos.

Ticket To Ride (Lennon–McCartney)   3:03

John Lennon : Rhythm Guitar, Tambourine and Lead Vocal
Paul McCartney : Bass Guitar, Lead Guitar and Harmony Vocal
George Harrison : Lead Guitar
Ringo Starr : Drums

Previously issued as a single, this song features John mainly on lead vocal with Paul harmonising in parts and making his second appearance on lead guitar.

SIDE TWO

Act Naturally (Morrison–Russell)   2:27

John Lennon : Acoustic Guitar
Paul McCartney : Bass Guitar and Harmony Vocal
George Harrison : Lead Guitar
Ringo Starr : Drums and Lead Vocal

Lead vocals are from Ringo, his only appearance as a vocalist on the album. Paul helps out with some harmony vocals, while John and George play the country and western/rockabilly guitars in the backing.

It's Only Love (Lennon–McCartney)   1:53

John Lennon : Acoustic Guitar, Tambourine and Solo Vocal
Paul McCartney : Bass Guitar
George Harrison : Lead Guitar
Ringo Starr : Drums

This started life with the intriguing title of That's A Nice Hat, before John wrote the lyrics. George Martin recorded an orchestral interpretation of the original instrumental, and included it on his orchestral version of the Help! album. This must be John's first inoffensive wandering into expanded consciousness lyrics as the song starts with the words 'I get high'. The quavering lead guitar is more experiments by George on the volume/tone control pedal, use of which he did not perfect until Yet It Is.

You Like Me Too Much (Harrison)   2:34

John Lennon : Acoustic Guitar and Electric Piano
Paul McCartney : Steinway Piano and Harmony Vocal
George Harrison : Lead Guitar and Lead Vocal
Ringo Starr : Drums and Tambourine
George Martin : Steinway Piano (with Paul)

George provides lead vocals, with harmonies from Paul on the chorus. The piano introduction features Paul and George Martin on the same Steinway. John plays electric piano in the backing and on the call and answer style instrumental break, which also features lead guitar from George. George's talent as a song writer is seen in this song as well as in I Need You featured on the first side of this album.

Tell Me What You See (Lennon–McCartney)   2:35

John Lennon : Washboard and Lead Vocal
Paul McCartney : Bass Guitar, Electric Piano and Lead Vocal
George Harrison : Lead Guitar and Tambourine
Ringo Starr : Drums and Claves

The vocal structure for this song is unusual with John and Paul duetting on the statement style lyrics and Paul singing solo on the 'answers'. Paul also plays the electric piano in the backing.

I've Just Seen A Face (Lennon–McCartney)   2:04

John Lennon : Acoustic Guitar
Paul McCartney : Acoustic Guitar and Solo Vocal
George Harrison : Acoustic Guitar
Ringo Starr : Drums and Maraccas

This track started life as an instrumental entitled Aunty Gin's Theme; it was also recorded by George Martin under that title. Paul's lyrics show slight Dylan influence although the song is more like an up-tempo Rocky Racoon.

Yesterday (Lennon–McCartney)   2:04

John Lennon : Not Present
Paul McCartney : Acoustic Guitar and Solo Vocal
George Harrison : Not Present
Ringo Starr : Not Present
Session Musicians : String Quartet

Paul McCartney's most famous song to date started life as an instrumental entitled Scrambled Eggs and has the same history as both It's Only Love and I've Just Seen A Face. For the first time, none of the other Beatles appear on this recording, and it can be classified as a Paul McCartney solo song. It features a solo vocal from Paul, who also plays an acoustic guitar backed by a string quartet.

Dizzy Miss Lizzy (Williams) 2:51

John Lennon : Hammond Organ and Solo Vocal
Paul McCartney : Bass Guitar
George Harrison : Lead Guitar
Ringo Starr : Drums

John Lennon's leathery lead vocals are once again put to effective use on this Larry Williams song which was another of the Beatles' Cavern Club standards. They stick closely to the original arrangement of the song, but include some 'oooo's and 'ows' to give it more of a live sound.

RUBBER SOUL
Parlophone PMC 1267; PCS 3075
Producer : George Martin
Release Date : 3 December 1965
Running Time : 34:50

SIDE ONE: Drive My Car; Norwegian Wood (This Bird Has Flown); You Won't See Me; Nowhere Man; Think For Yourself; The Word; Michelle.

SIDE TWO: What Goes On; Girl; I'm Looking Through You; In My Life; Wait; If I Needed Someone; Run For Your Life.

This sixth album from the Beatles showed a new musical direction. Here they move even further away from the instant pop product of their first five albums towards the second stage of their recording career. The album contains some of the Beatles most classic mid-sixties songs, like Norwegian Wood and Girl, which sound as fresh now as they did in 1965. It was after the release of this album, and the realisation that its contents could not be reproduced live, that the Beatles decided to give up live performances and concentrate solely on making records.

On this album John gives a foretaste of the events of 1967 with the mysterious lyrics of The Word and a glimpse into his past with In My Life. Paul dabbles with the French language for the lyrics of Michelle. George, as on Help!, has two songs included, Think For Yourself and If I Needed Someone, and Ringo joins forces with John and Paul to come up with the country and western flavoured What Goes On. On two of these tracks, the Beatles try out new instruments. George tries out the sitar on John's Norwegian Wood and Paul tries out the newly invented fuzz bass guitar on George's Think For Yourself.

The sleeve of this album shows, like the Beatles For Sale, four unsmiling faces. Beatles' fans complained at the time that the photograph made the Beatles look rather anaemic. However, the music is far from being anaemic.

SIDE ONE

Drive My Car (Lennon — McCartney)   2:25

John Lennon : Tambourine and Lead Vocal
Paul McCartney : Bass Guitar, Piano and Lead Vocal
George Harrison : Lead Guitar and Backing Vocal
Ringo Starr : Drums

Paul uses his Little Richard voice once again for a duet with John on lead vocals, and George joins them here and there throughout the song for the chorus. George also plays some nice blues sounding guitar on the intro and during the instrumental break. Paul plays piano during this blues/Motown influenced song.

Norwegian Wood (This Bird Has Flown)
(Lennon — McCartney)   2:00

John Lennon : Acoustic Guitar and Lead Vocal
Paul McCartney : Bass Guitar and Harmony Vocal
George Harrison : Sitar
Ringo Starr : Tambourine

The first classic track on the album reveals, in the introduction, George playing a sitar for the first time. The sitar was featured in the incidental music for the Beatles' second film *Help!* George was fascinated by its sound and acquired one. He achieved his effect by tuning his new 'weird' instrument to western notes. As usual this led the way for other artists to copy the Beatles' innovation and many records featuring the sitar, some good and some bad, were soon on the market. The song, which is really an account of a love affair set to music, has John on lead with additional vocals in places from Paul.

You Won't See Me (Lennon–McCartney)   3:19

John Lennon : Tambourine and Backing Vocal
Paul McCartney : Bass Guitar, Piano and Lead Vocal
George Harrison : Lead Guitar and Backing Vocal
Ringo Starr : Drums
Mal Evans : Hammond Organ

Here, Paul is on lead vocals with John and George supplying harmony for chorus and backing. Mal Evans, one of the Beatles' roadies, is heard for the first time playing the Hammond organ. The piano is played by Paul.

Nowhere Man (Lennon–McCartney)   2:40

John Lennon : Acoustic Guitar and Lead Vocal
Paul McCartney : Bass Guitar and Lead Vocal
George Harrison : Lead Guitar and Lead Vocal
Ringo Starr : Drums

John initially brought this surrealistic character to life as a self description. Later, after his admission of drug taking, the character became one of the focal points for analysts who decided that the 'Nowhere Man' was anything from a drug pusher to the captain of the Yellow Submarine.
    John, Paul and George harmonise for the a capella intro, then John sings lead vocals, with Paul and George adding backing harmonies and joining John for the chorus.

Think For Yourself (Harrison)   2:16

John Lennon : Tambourine and Backing Vocal
Paul McCartney : Fuzz Bass Guitar and Backing Vocal
George Harrison : Lead Guitar and Lead Vocal
Ringo Starr : Drums and Maraccas

The first of two tracks on the album written by George features him on lead vocal with John and Paul harmonising in places. Paul can also be heard trying out the then newly invented fuzz bass guitar. Obviously he cannot have been impressed by it because it was four years before he was to use it again on a Beatles' record.

The Word (Lennon–McCartney)   2:42

John Lennon : Rhythm Guitar and Lead Vocal
Paul McCartney : Bass Guitar, Piano and Lead Vocal
George Harrison : Lead Guitar and Lead Vocal
Ringo Starr : Drums and Maraccas
George Martin : Harmonium

A foretaste of what was to come later with All You Need Is Love. The phrase 'the word is love' and the 'love one another' theme were both to be adopted by the hippy movement.
    John, Paul and George harmonise with John mainly singing lead. George

Martin plays harmonium and Paul joins in on piano. The recording seems to fade out rather early, giving the impression of an incomplete ending.

Michelle (Lennon – McCartney)   2:42

John Lennon : Acoustic Guitar and Backing Vocal
Paul McCartney : Bass Guitar and Lead Vocal
George Harrison : Acoustic Guitar and Backing Vocal
Ringo Starr : Drums

Written by Paul for the daughter of an American millionaire, Michelle features Paul on lead vocals with John and George adding the close harmony backing. This was another of the Beatles' songs to become an all-time standard. The song lapses into French now and again as with the phrase 'Ma belle' ('My beautiful') and 'Sont les mots qui vonts trés bien ensemble' ('These are words that go together very well'). When Michelle was issued in France as the title track of an E.P. (the French did not then release singles, all 45 rpm records were E.P.s), it shot to the number one spot.

SIDE TWO

What Goes On (Lennon – McCartney – Starkey)   2:44

John Lennon : Rhythm Guitar and Backing Vocal
Paul McCartney : Bass Guitar and Backing Vocal
George Harrison : Lead Guitar
Ringo Starr : Drums and Lead Vocal

Co-written by John, Paul and Ringo, this song provided Ringo with another of the sing-a-long, rockabilly numbers that always seemed to suit his voice. John and Paul provide the harmony vocals for the chorus and George adds some nice country and western style guitar.

Girl (Lennon – McCartney)   2:26

John Lennon : Acoustic Guitar and Lead Vocal
Paul McCartney : Bass Guitar and Backing Vocal
George Harrison : Sitar and Backing Vocal
Ringo Starr : Drums

Lead vocals are from John with Paul and George adding a wordless and the 'tit tit' backing vocal and also joining John for the chorus. There is an interesting section when the backing vocals build up and dissolve along with John's voice into the chorus.

I'm Looking Through You (Lennon – McCartney)   2:20

John Lennon : Acoustic Guitar and Harmony Vocal
Paul McCartney : Bass Guitar and Lead Vocal
George Harrison : Lead Guitar and Tambourine
Ringo Starr : Drums and Hammond Organ

Paul on lead vocals on this semi-rock and roll song reveals the influences of both Little Richard and Buddy Holly. It sounds rather like a re-written version of Buddy Holly's Every Day sung with a Little Richard voice but curiously enough it works. The recording also features Ringo on a Hammond organ mixed so far into the backing it might just as well not be there.

The American stereo version of this track includes two false starts but is then identical to this version.

In My Life (Lennon–McCartney) 2:23

John Lennon : Lead Vocal
Paul McCartney : Bass Guitar and Harmony Vocal
George Harrison : Lead Guitar
Ringo Starr : Drums
George Martin : Piano

Nostalgically John recalls people and places who played an important part in his younger days. The song is beautifully set to unobtrusive music, and is reminiscent of Penny Lane or Strawberry Fields Forever.

Wait (Lennon–McCartney) 2:13

John Lennon : Tambourine and Lead Vocal
Paul McCartney : Bass Guitar and Lead Vocal
George Harrison : Lead Guitar
Ringo Starr : Drums and Maraccas

A lively track, featuring a lead vocal duet between John and Paul that for some reason does not seem to fit in with the previous tracks. It sounds almost as if it was left over from either Beatles For Sale or Help!

If I Needed Someone (Harrison) 2:19

John Lennon : Tambourine and Backing Vocal
Paul McCartney : Bass Guitar and Backing Vocal
George Harrison : Lead Guitar and Lead Vocal
Ringo Starr : Drums
George Martin : Harmonium

A George Harrison composition which shows how he improved with each new song he wrote. This can be compared with a few Lennon and McCartney songs of the same period.

The Beatles make use of an extremely pleasant guitar riff that crops up every now and then and accentuates both the lyrics and style of George Harrison's singing.

Run For Your Life (Lennon–McCartney)   2:21

John Lennon : Acoustic Guitar and Lead Vocal
Paul McCartney : Bass Guitar and Backing Vocal
George Harrison : Lead Guitar and Backing Vocal
Ringo Starr : Drums
George Martin : Tambourine

This is not one of John and Paul's best compositions. It sounds rather like a mixture of their previous Little Child from the album With The Beatles, and the Larry Williams song Bad Boy. Even John Lennon, who wrote it, went on record as not liking it.

REVOLVER
Parlophone PMC 7009: PCS 7009
Producer : George Martin
Release Date : 5 August 1966
Running Time : 35:01

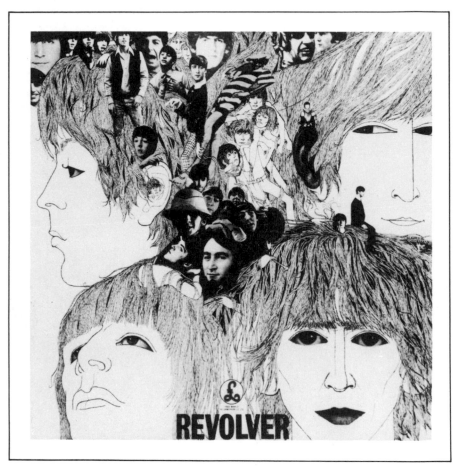

SIDE ONE: Taxman; Eleanor Rigby; I'm Only Sleeping; Love You To; Here, There And Everywhere; Yellow Submarine. She Said, She Said.

SIDE TWO: Good Day Sunshine; And Your Bird Can Sing; For No One; Dr. Robert; I Want To Tell You; Got To Get You Into My Life; Tomorrow Never Knows.

The musical direction the Beatles appeared to be taking with 'Rubber Soul' changed quickly with Revolver. Released eight months after Rubber Soul, this album contains brilliant, diverse music and moves further into the realms of fantasy. Revolver contains some rather interesting social statements from the Beatles in the form of George Harrison's sarcastic comments on Taxman and Paul McCartney's sad tale of loneliness on Eleanor Rigby. Various flights of fantasy and strange lyrics feature on a range of titles from the sing-along Yellow Submarine to the weird and frightening Tomorrow Never Knows.

The sleeve shows a collage of drawings (by Klaus Voormann) and photographs of the Beatles (including two of the photographs previously used on the back of Rubber Soul). A collection of faces, as on the inner photograph of the Beatles For Sale album, is again used just as it would be used again even more effectively on the sleeve of the Sgt. Pepper's Lonely Hearts Club Band album.

Although fans did not realise at the time, the Beatles were to give their last full concert three weeks after the release of this album. Their music had progressed to such a point that with Rubber Soul and Revolver it had become almost impossible to reproduce live.

SIDE ONE

Taxman (Harrison)   2:36

John Lennon : Tambourine and Backing Vocal
Paul McCartney : Bass Guitar and Backing Vocal
George Harrison : Lead Guitar and Lead Vocal
Ringo Starr : Drums

George's first song to make a social comment takes a swipe at the taxman. Lead vocal is from George with backing and harmony vocals from John and Paul. The musical accompaniment is as harsh as the lyrics, with a very strong attacking lead guitar riff.

Eleanor Rigby (Lennon—McCartney)   2:11

John Lennon : Not Present
Paul McCartney : Solo Vocal
George Harrison : Not Present
Ringo Starr : Not Present
Session Musicians : Four Violins, two Violas, and two Cellos

This classic McCartney composition has become another of his 'standards'. Here it features a lead vocal from Paul who double-tracks in part to produce his own harmonies. Like Yesterday on the Help! album, this features only Paul McCartney—John, George and Ringo do not sing or play any instrument on this recording. All of the backing music is played by string octet.

The lyrics make a valid social statement about the loneliness of Eleanor Rigby and Father McKenzie's empty church. It is generally thought that Paul wrote this song after John made his now famous comment 'Christianity will go. It will vanish and shrink. I needn't argue about that. I'm right and I will be proved right. We're more popular than Jesus now. I don't know which will go first, rock and roll or Christianity.....'

I'm Only Sleeping (Lennon—McCartney)   2:58

John Lennon : Acoustic Guitar and Lead Vocal
Paul McCartney : Bass Guitar and Backing Vocal
George Harrison : Lead Guitar and Backing Vocal
Ringo Starr : Drums

The song idles along at tick-over speed and with John's lethargic vocal interpretation creates a lazy, stay-in-bed atmosphere mirroring the lyrics about him lying in bed watching the world go by. The strange guitar sound is George's overdubbed, backwards lead guitar.

Love You To (Harrison)   3:00

John Lennon : Not Present
Paul McCartney : Not Present
George Harrison : Solo Vocal
Ringo Starr : Not Present
Anil Bhagwat : Tabla
Session Musicians : All Other Instruments

After George Harrison had become interested in the sitar and played it on Norwegian Wood he enlisted the help of Anil Bhagwat to play the tabla on this recording, the second of three on the album written by George Harrison, and also the first full scale use of Indian instruments by George for a Beatles' recording. None of the other Beatles appeared on this track.

Here, There And Everywhere (Lennon—McCartney)   2:29

John Lennon : Backing Vocal
Paul McCartney : Acoustic Guitar and Lead Vocal
George Harrison : Lead Guitar and Backing Vocal
Ringo Starr : Drums

This is a gentle but slightly up-tempo ballad from Paul, featuring his lead vocal multi-tracked and spread across the stereo. The wordless backing vocals from John, Paul and George are mixed onto the left-hand channel and blend in with the lead vocal creating the pleasing impression of a single voice.

Yellow Submarine (Lennon—McCartney)   2:40

John Lennon : Acoustic Guitar and Backing Vocal
Paul McCartney : Acoustic Guitar and Backing Vocal
George Harrison : Tambourine and Backing Vocal
Ringo Starr : Drums and Lead Vocal
Chorus : Includes George Martin, Patti Harrison, Mal Evans, Neil Aspinall and Geoff Emerick
Session Musicians : Brass Band

Issued as a single with Eleanor Rigby, on the same day as the album, this is one of the Beatles' most famous sing-along records, with an extremely catchy chorus. The lead vocal comes from Ringo (the only track to feature him as vocalist) with John, Paul and George joining in on chorus. Some of the many sound effects included were John blowing bubbles through a straw into a bucket of water, George swirling water round in another bucket, 'cocktail party' sounds, a brass band, various engine room noises and shouted orders. The final chorus makes use of all the people at the recording – the four Beatles, George Martin, Patti Harrison, roadies Mal Evans and Neil Aspinall, Geoff Emerick and presumably several more. The song was to inspire the cartoon film of the same name, which was released three years after this recording. (See Yellow the Submarine album.)

She Said She Said (Lennon – McCartney)   2:39

John Lennon : Acoustic Guitar and Solo Vocal
Paul McCartney : Bass Guitar
George Harrison : Lead Guitar
Ringo Starr : Drums

This is apparently John Lennon's account of a conversation with Peter Fonda during an LSD trip. If the backing to this track is anything to go by, the trip must have been a chaotic one.

SIDE TWO

Good Day Sunshine (Lennon – McCartney)   2:08

John Lennon : Harmony Vocal
Paul McCartney : Lead Vocal
George Harrison : Harmony Vocal
Ringo Starr : Drums
George Martin : Piano

The lead vocal on this track comes from Paul with harmonies from John, reflecting influences from the thirties with a honky-tonk New Orleans style piano break. This interesting and inventive recording features two separate drum beats, one on each channel of the stereo. With this track the Beatles began successfully experimenting with stereo. On the fade the title/chorus line comes out of each of the speakers alternately.

And Your Bird Can Sing (Lennon – McCartney)   2:02

John Lennon : Rhythm Guitar and Lead Vocal
Paul McCartney : Bass Guitar and Harmony Vocal
George Harrison : Lead Guitar and Harmony Vocal
Ringo Starr : Drums and Tambourine

Lead vocal is from John, with Paul harmonising here and there. The recording features a very prominent lead guitar riff mixed so far forward it becomes part of the main recording rather than part of the backing.

For No One (Lennon–McCartney) 2:03

John Lennon : Not Present
Paul McCartney : Bass Guitar, Piano and Solo Vocal
George Harrison : Not Present
Ringo Starr : Drums and Tambourine
Alan Civil : Horn

This is a very pleasant track featuring a solo vocal from Paul, who also plays a bouncy piano. An unobtrusive horn is played by Alan Civil.

Dr. Robert (Lennon–McCartney) 2:14

John Lennon : Maraccas, Harmonium and Lead Vocal
Paul McCartney : Bass Guitar and Harmony Vocal
George Harrison : Lead Guitar
Ringo Starr : Drums

The lyrics of this song were apparently based on a real character in New York who supplied anyone and everyone with drugs of various kinds. The lead vocals are from John with harmonies in part from Paul.

I Want To Tell You (Harrison) 2:30

John Lennon : Tambourine and Harmony Vocal
Paul McCartney : Bass Guitar, Piano and Harmony Vocal
George Harrison : Lead Guitar and Lead Vocal
Ringo Starr : Drums

Lead vocals are from George, with John and Paul harmonising in places. This is not one of George Harrison's better compositions as it sounds slightly off-key with a rather erratic backing beat.

Got To Get You Into My Life (Lennon–McCartney) 2:31

John Lennon : Tambourine
Paul McCartney : Bass Guitar and Solo Vocal
George Harrison : Lead Guitar
Ringo Starr : Drums
George Martin : Organ
Eddy Thornton : Trumpet
Ian Hamer : Trumpet
Les Conlon : Trumpet
Alan Branscombe : Tenor Sax
Pete Coe : Tenor Sax

This track, heavily influenced by the Motown sound, features a solo vocal from Paul, with brass backing played by Eddy Thornton, Ian Hamer and Les Conlon on trumpets and Alan Branscombe and Peter Coe on tenor sax. A good strong solid track. Later to be recorded by Cliff Bennett and the Rebel Rousers, who had a British Top Ten hit with it.

Tomorrow Never Knows (Lennon–McCartney)   3:00

John Lennon : Tambourine and Solo Vocal
Paul McCartney : Bass Guitar
George Harrison : Sitar and Lead Guitar
Ringo Starr : Drums
George Martin : Piano
Sound effects devised by John and Ringo and arranged by Paul.

Some of the lyrics of this song, originally entitled The Void, come straight from *The Tibetan Book of the Dead*. They are set to hypnotic drum beat with a collage of sound effects made up of backward-running tapes and tape loops, which sound at times rather like a herd of rampaging elephants. John's solo vocal, partly sung through a megaphone, filters through like a nightmare set to music. This is the Beatles' most experimental recording. Lyrics like 'listen to the colour of your dreams' herald the appearance of psychedelia. Curiously, nowhere in the lyrics do the words 'tomorrow never knows' appear. The reason for the title, thought up by John, has never been revealed.

A COLLECTION OF BEATLES OLDIES

Parlophone PMC 7016: PCS 7016
Producer : George Martin
Release Date : 10 December 1966
Running Time : 38:06

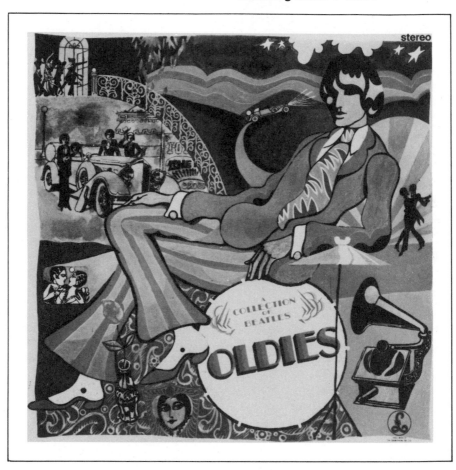

SIDE ONE: She Loves You; From Me To You; We Can Work It Out; Help!; Michelle; Yesterday; I Feel Fine. Yellow Submarine.

SIDE TWO: Can't Buy Me Love; Bad Boy; Day Tripper; A Hard Day's Night; Ticket To Ride; Paperback Writer; Eleanor Rigby; I Want To Hold Your Hand.

Released just in time for the Christmas market of 1966, this collection of previously released album and single tracks was put together because the Beatles did not have an album prepared. After they had finished recording Revolver in June 1966 they were in the first stages of preparing the Sgt. Pepper's Lonely Hearts Club Band album, but its release was six months away. Parlophone felt that the Beatles should have an album issued to corner part of the Christmas market, so this album was quickly compiled and issued just in time.

It included one 'new' track Bad Boy, which, at the time of release of this album, had not been issued in Britain, although it had been available for 18 months as part of the American Beatles VI album (Capitol ST 2358). Amongst the other 15 tracks are seven tracks previously included on Beatles' albums in Britain and six only previously available on singles. Five of these six tracks were available for the first time in Britain in stereo; only She Loves You was a mono recording.

As a 'greatest hits' album this seemed to fit the bill at the time, but more recently all of the tracks have been more sensibly re-packaged — 15 on The Beatles 1962-1966 album and the remaining track, Bad Boy, on the Rarities album. Surprisingly, at the time of release of A Collection of Beatles Oldies there were 19 tracks available that had not been included on any British album, but only seven were used for this album.

SIDE ONE

She Loves You (Lennon–McCartney) 2:18

John Lennon : Rhythm Guitar and Lead Vocal
Paul McCartney : Bass Guitar and Lead Vocal
George Harrison : Lead Guitar
Ringo Starr : Drums

The A-side of the Beatles' fourth single, issued on Parlophone in Britain, features the usual lead vocal duet from John and Paul. The song included the now famous catchy chorus line of 'yeah, yeah, yeah' and the equally famous 'oooo', all which was previously used in I Saw Her Standing There on Please Please Me. If Love Me Do, Please Please Me and From Me To You had not convinced people that the Beatles had staying power the catchy chorus line and excitement generated by She Loves You must surely have done so.

From Me To You (Lennon–McCartney) 1:55

John Lennon : Rhythm Guitar, Harmonica and Lead Vocal
Paul McCartney : Bass Guitar and Lead Vocal
George Harrison : Lead Guitar and Harmony Vocal
Ringo Starr : Drums

With this, the follow-up single to Please Please Me and the Beatles' second number one, they began to prove that they had both musical and song-writing ability. According to some charts Please Please Me only reached number two, and From Me To You was their first number one single. If it was, it began a string of 11 consecutive number one singles — a record that to date has never been equalled. Like so many of the Beatles' early recordings the lead vocal is shared by John and Paul with George joining in here and there and on chorus. The recording also makes very effective use of John's harmonica.

During the early sixties the Beatles had their own BBC radio show, some episodes of which were entitled *From Us To You* which featured a re-worded recording of From Me To You. Although in existence this recording has yet to be issued. Besides this recording there are two different versions of From Me To You available.

We Can Work It Out (Lennon—McCartney) 2:10

John Lennon : Harmonium, Acoustic Guitar and Harmony Vocal
Paul McCartney : Bass Guitar and Lead Vocal
George Harrison : Tambourine
Ringo Starr : Drums

This could be classified as the Beatles' first ever peace song. It pre-dates All You Need Is Love by two years and Give Peace A Chance by four years. Released as a follow up to Help! in 1965 this is the Beatles' eleventh Parlophone single and their ninth number one. By 1965 the Beatles had progressed from the 'beat group' sound of some of their early 1963-64 singles to a more technically and musically proficient group of musicians. Lead vocal on this is by Paul, with John joining in for the chorus and also playing harmonium. At various times the recording lapses into a slow waltz but then picks up again for the verses. John later used the same style for the instrumental break in the middle of Being For The Benefit of Mr. Kite on Sgt. Pepper's Lonely Hearts Club Band.

Help! (Lennon—McCartney) 2:16

John Lennon : Acoustic Guitar and Lead Vocal
Paul McCartney : Bass Guitar and Backing Vocal
George Harrison : Lead Guitar and Backing Vocal
Ringo Starr : Drums and Tambourine

Previously reviewed on the Help! album.

Michelle (Lennon—McCartney) 2:42

John Lennon : Acoustic Guitar and Backing Vocal
Paul McCartney : Bass Guitar and Lead Vocal
George Harrison : Acoustic Guitar and Backing Vocal
Ringo Starr : Drums

Previously reviewed on the Rubber Soul album.

Yesterday (Lennon—McCartney) 2:04

John Lennon : Not Present
Paul McCartney : Acoustic Guitar and Solo Vocal

George Harrison : Not Present
Ringo Starr : Not Present
Session Musicians : String Quartet

Previously reviewed on the Help! album.

I Feel Fine (Lennon – McCartney) 2:17

John Lennon : Rhythm Guitar, Lead Guitar and Lead Vocal
Paul McCartney : Bass Guitar and Backing Vocal
George Harrison : Lead Guitar and Backing Vocal
Ringo Starr : Drums

Previously issued as a single in November 1964 as the follow up to A Hard Day's Night, this is the Beatles' eighth single and sixth consecutive number one. The recording opens with a single note of feedback, then goes into the riff around which the song is constructed. This was the first time that feedback had been used on a record; and it gave ideas to many musicians like Jimi Hendrix who used feedback as a musical note and not just as a noise. Theories at the time about the sound at the beginning of the record included the idea of an amplified humming bee. Infact the Beatles did not use pre-recorded sound effects until 1966, two years later. The lead vocal is from John, with Paul and George joining him on chorus. Paul and George also sing a wordless vocal backing. At the end of the recording there is what sounds like barking dogs but this was Paul playing around. After the Beatles heard the playback they decided to leave it in. As with many of the Beatles' early recordings, there are two different versions of this (see Chapter 43 *Recording Oddities*).

Yellow Submarine (Lennon – McCartney) 2:40

John Lennon : Acoustic Guitar and Backing Vocal
Paul McCartney : Acoustic Guitar and Backing Vocal
George Harrison : Tambourine and Backing Vocal
Ringo Starr : Drums and Lead Vocal
Chorus : Includes George Martin, Patti Harrison, Mal Evans, Neil Aspinall and Geoff Emerick
Session Musicians : Brass Band

Previously reviewed on the Revolver album.

SIDE TWO

Can't Buy Me Love (Lennon – McCartney) 2:15

John Lennon : Rhythm Guitar
Paul McCartney : Bass Guitar and Solo Vocal
George Harrison : Lead Guitar
Ringo Starr : Drums

Previously reviewed on the A Hard Day's Night album.

Bad Boy (Williams) 2:17

John Lennon : Rhythm Guitar, Hammond Organ and Solo Vocal
Paul McCartney : Bass Guitar
George Harrison : Lead Guitar
Ringo Starr : Drums and Tambourine

Previously only available on the American Beatles VI album (Capitol ST 2358). It took 18 months and the release of this album before this track was available in Britain. The lead vocal is a solo from John with some enthusiastic backing from the Beatles. This and another Larry Williams song, Dizzy Miss Lizzy, were the last two songs issued by the Beatles that they did not write.

Day Tripper (Lennon–McCartney) 2:37

John Lennon : Rhythm Guitar, Tambourine and Lead Vocal
Paul McCartney : Bass Guitar and Lead Vocal
George Harrison : Lead Guitar
Ringo Starr : Drums

This was issued as one side of a double A-sided single, the other track being We Can Work It Out. The lead vocal, a duet from John and Paul, sounds rather tired, probably due to the exhaustive concert tour that they had just returned from at the time. The lyrics are reminiscent of Ticket To Ride, but were analysed and misinterpreted shortly after the release of Sgt. Pepper.

A Hard Day's Night (Lennon–McCartney) 2:32

John Lennon : Rhythm Guitar and Lead Vocal
Paul McCartney : Bass Guitar and Harmony Vocal
George Harrison : Lead Guitar
Ringo Starr : Drums
George Martin : Piano

Previously reviewed on the A Hard Day's Night album.

Ticket To Ride (Lennon–McCartney) 3:03

John Lennon : Rhythm Guitar, Tambourine and Lead Vocal
Paul McCartney : Bass Guitar and Harmony Vocal
George Harrison : Lead Guitar
Ringo Starr : Drums

Previously reviewed on the Help! album.

Paperback Writer (Lennon–McCartney) 2:25

John Lennon : Rhythm Guitar and Backing Vocal
Paul McCartney : Bass Guitar and Lead Vocal
George Harrison : Lead Guitar and Backing Vocal
Ringo Starr : Drums

As this is also included on the Hey Jude album, along with its B-side, Rain, it will be discussed with that album.

Eleanor Rigby (Lennon–McCartney) 2:11

John Lennon : Not Present
Paul McCartney : Solo Vocal
George Harrison : Not Present
Ringo Starr : Not Present
Session Musicians : Four Violins, two Violas and two Cellos

Previously reviewed on the Revolver album.

I Want To Hold Your Hand (Lennon–McCartney) 2:24

John Lennon : Rhythm Guitar and Lead Vocal
Paul McCartney : Bass Guitar and Lead Vocal
George Harrison : Lead Guitar and Harmony Vocal
Ringo Starr : Drums

This record, as a single, sold over 5 million copies worldwide. To help sales the Beatles (under pressure) also recorded the song in German. The recording opens with John's rhythm guitar, a sound which builds up to an intense pitch and then explodes as John and Paul begin their lead vocal duet. For the chorus line John and Paul are joined by George and all three add excited hand clapping to make this one of their most powerful early recordings.

**SGT. PEPPER'S LONELY
HEARTS CLUB BAND**
Parlophone PMC 7027 : PCS
7027
Producer : George Martin
Release Date : 1 June 1967
Running Time : 39:02

SIDE ONE: Sgt. Pepper's Lonely Hearts Club
Band; With A Little Help From My Friends;
Lucy In The Sky With Diamonds; Getting
Better; Fixing A Hole; She's Leaving Home;
Being For the Benefit Of Mr. Kite.

SIDE TWO: Within You, Without You; When
I'm Sixty-Four; Lovely Rita; Good Morning,
Good Morning; Sgt. Pepper's Lonely Hearts
Club Band (Reprise); A Day In The Life.

Regarded by many as the Beatles' finest album, Sgt. Pepper has been copied, emulated and drawn from, but never equalled. The title has slipped into everyday language in the music world to describe any artists' new album as being their finest achievement — 'their Sgt. Pepper'.

This album took four months and £50,000 to make — staggering when compared with the Beatles' first Parlophone album, Please Please Me, which was recorded in one 13-hour session and cost £400.

The album's concept began to take shape during the late summer/early autumn of 1966 when Paul came up with the title song. Ideas were then exchanged and it was decided that Sgt. Pepper should be the theme for the album with the track opening the album and appearing again near the end. So the title was recorded twice and the second recording slotted in just before A Day In The Life, the album's final track. The album, in the words of the Beatles themselves, after this point 'generated its own togetherness' and as each new recording was made it seemed to fall into place.

The recording began in December 1966 with Strawberry Fields Forever, When I'm Sixty-Four and Penny Lane, but it was decided to issue Penny Lane/Strawberry Fields Forever as a single, and these tracks were extracted from the recordings already made. After a Christmas break recording recommenced on 19 January 1967 when the Beatles began work on the album's closing track A Day In The Life. Recording continued through to 2 April 1967, when, with the exception of a few final overdubs of strings, the album was completed.

The first rock music album to be issued with a continual theme running through it, Sgt. Pepper was dubbed the first 'concept album'. As a result concept albums of varying degrees of quality by other artists soon began to appear.

Like its contents, the sleeve of this album is highly original. Designed by Peter Blake, from ideas by the Beatles, it shows a collection of faces of people they admired or who had influenced them in various ways. Amongst the fifty-odd faces are W.C. Fields, Aldous Huxley, Fred Astaire, Bob Dylan, Tony Curtis, Laurel and Hardy, Max Miller and a host of others. The only person missing from the collapse of faces was Adolph Hitler (reputed to have been picked by John). His photograph had been selected and blown up to fit in with the rest, but at the last minute it was decided that the inclusion of Adolph Hitler would be in bad taste. The collage also includes wax models of the Beatles themselves, Sonny Liston and Diana Dors, all of which were loaned from Madame Tussaud's in Baker Street, London. Other features of the cover photograph include the Beatles dressed in bright satin uniforms as Sgt. Pepper's band, with their name painted on the brass drum of the kit. The foreground is set out as a garden with the word 'Beatles' spelt out in flowers and also a guitar shaped out of flowers. Across the top of the garden and foreground right are marijuana plants, included as a protest about the non-legalisation of the drug. Statues and ornaments included in the foreground were from various Beatles' homes. The Beatles are holding instruments they did not normally play — John has a French horn, Ringo a trumpet, Paul a Cor anglais and George a flute. A line printed on the back of the sleeve sums up the intention of the album: 'a splended time is guaranteed for all'.

SIDE ONE

Sgt. Pepper's Lonely Hearts Club Band
(Lennon—McCartney)   1:59

John Lennon : Lead Guitar and Backing Vocal
Paul McCartney : Bass Guitar and Lead Vocal
George Harrison : Lead Guitar and Backing Vocal
Ringo Starr : Drums
George Martin : Organ
Session Musicians : Four Horns

The album opens with the sound of an orchestra tuning up and an expectant audience. The 'Sgt. Pepper band' then strike up the first few chords on their guitars, and the album begins. The Beatles had introduced heavy guitar sounds on Rain issued as the B-side to Paperback Writer some 12 months earlier, but here is their first full use of guitars as a sound, as opposed to just backing instruments. The Beatles' instrumentation on this track is supplemented by George Martin on organ (just near the end) and a group of four studio musicians who add the horns, to make the 'Sgt. Pepper band' a semi-rock/brass outfit. Lead vocals are from Paul, who also joins John and George for the backing and the chorus.
    With this album the Beatles started experimenting with stereo and discovered that it actually moved. On this track the chorus starts on the left-hand channel then begins to drift across to the centre of the stereo. When Paul sings again he starts on the right-hand channel.

With A Little Help From My Friends
(Lennon—McCartney)   2:46

John Lennon : Backing Vocal
Paul McCartney : Bass Guitar, Piano and Backing Vocal
George Harrison : Tambourine
Ringo Starr : Drums and Lead Vocal

Ringo is in the vocal spotlight with vocal support from John and Paul on both the backing and the chorus. His vocal performance on this song is rated by many to be one of his best. This is another Lennon and McCartney song that had a working title bearing no relation to the finished song. It started out as Bad Finger Boogie, and is said to have influenced one of the groups signed to the Apple label in their choice of name. They started out as The Ivies and then became Bad Finger.

Lucy In The Sky With Diamonds (Lennon—McCartney)   3:25

John Lennon : Lead Guitar and Lead Vocal
Paul McCartney : Bass Guitar, Hammond Organ and Harmony Vocal
George Harrison : Sitar and Harmony Vocal
Ringo Starr : Drums

John Lennon went on record as saying that his most surrealistic lyrics were inspired, not by an LSD trip as many thought (and some still maintain) but by a painting that his son Julian had brought home from school. When John enquired as to what it was, Julian replied 'It's Lucy in the sky with diamonds'. Lucy, Julian's best friend at school, had inspired Julian to paint a girl on a black background surrounded by stars, which he insisted were not stars but diamonds.

Lead vocals are by John with Paul and George joining in on chorus and also supplying backing vocals. The track opens with what sounds like a string instrument, but this is a Hammond organ. Its in-built special effects were used to produce a harpsichord/celeste sound.

Getting Better (Lennon–McCartney) 2:47

John Lennon : Lead Guitar and Backing Vocal
Paul McCartney : Bass Guitar and Lead/Backing Vocal
George Harrison : Lead Guitar, Tampura and Backing Vocal
Ringo Starr : Drums and Bongos
George Martin : Piano

It certainly is. Paul's lyrics are set to the same syncopated beat that he had used a few years earlier on tracks such as She's A Woman. Lead vocals are from Paul, who also joins John for the backing. George had experimented with the sitar on earlier Beatles' albums and here tries a new Indian instrument, a tampura. This looks like an oversized sitar, but doesn't produce musical notes in terms of western music. Instead, it produces a droning resonant tone that in Indian music is used as it is here — more as a backing tone than as part of the instrumentation. Near the end of the track, George Martin joins in with a piano; interestingly he doesn't actually play the keyboard but strikes the strings instead.

Fixing A Hole (Lennon–McCartney) 2:33

John Lennon : Maraccas and Backing Vocal
Paul McCartney : Harpsichord, Bass Guitar, Lead Guitar and Lead Vocal
George Harrison : Lead Guitar and Backing Vocal
Ringo Starr : Drums

Lead vocal on this one again comes from Paul, who also plays the harpsichord. The guitar solo in the middle is played by George. This is a good up-tempo song from Paul but its lyrics have been misconstrued in my opinion. Paul McCartney commented on this track. 'This song is just about the hole in the road where the rain gets in; a good old analogy — the hole in your make-up which lets the rain in and stops your mind from going where it will. It's you interfering with things ... If you're a junkie sitting in a room *fixing* a hole then that's what it will mean to you, but when I wrote it I meant if there's a crack or the room is uncolourful, then I'll paint it.'

She's Leaving Home (Lennon–McCartney)   3:24

John Lennon : Lead/Backing Vocal
Paul McCartney : Lead/Backing Vocal
George Harrison : Not Present
Ringo Starr : Not Present
Session Musicians : Harp and Strings

This is another classic McCartney ballad, and a sad social statement about a girl running away from home and 'everything that money could buy', because love and attention were missing from her life. Paul had said he was inspired to write the song by a newspaper article which reminded him of the same loneliness he had conveyed in Eleonor Rigby. The vocals are interestingly interwoven. Paul sings a double-tracked lead vocal with John singing here and there. This is the only track on the album where the Beatles do not play any of the backing; they are accompanied by a harp and some sweet sounding violins which were scored by Mike Leander.

Being For The Benefit Of Mr. Kite (Lennon–McCartney)   2:36

John Lennon : Hammond Organ and Solo Vocal
Paul McCartney : Bass Guitar and Lead Guitar
George Harrison : Harmonica
Ringo Starr : Harmonica
George Martin : Wurlitzer Organ and Piano
Mal Evans : Harmonica
Neil Aspinall : Harmonica

John was inspired to write this song by a Victorian circus poster announcing 'being for the benefit of Mr. Kite, a grand circus, The Hendersons, Pablo Fanques Fair ....'. Amongst the acts appearing in the circus was 'Henry The Horse'. John's vivid imagination helped him to collect these characters together and create the lyrics for the track. After reading them and those for Lucy In The Sky With Diamonds, George Martin described John as 'an oral Salvador Dali'. John sings the solo lead vocal on the track and plays Hammond organ. Paul plays a guitar solo and Ringo, George, Neil Aspinall and Mal Evans (the Beatles' roadies) each play a different type of harmonica. George Martin adds a few touches with a Wurlitzer organ, and the whole thing is rounded off with recorded snippets of a Victorian steam organ. To achieve the required random effect with the recording of the fairground organ, it was cut into 12-inch long strips, hurled into the air, then edited back together again, parts being played backwards and parts forward.

SIDE TWO

Within You, Without You (Harrison)   5:03

John Lennon : Not Present
Paul McCartney : Not Present
George Harrison : Tamboura and Solo Vocal
Ringo Starr : Not Present
Neil Aspinall : Tamboura
Session Musicians : Dilruba, Tamboura, Tabla and Sword Mandel
Session Musicians : Eight Violins and three Cellos

Having previously tried his hand at recording Indian music with Love You Too on Revolver George Harrison's dabblings go one further on this track. He merges an assortment of Indian instruments including a dilruba, tabla, a sword mandel and three tambouras, (of which two are played by George and Neil Aspinall) with eight violins and three cellos. This is more of an event than a recording and at five minutes and three seconds it either sends you into a trance or to sleep; depending on your point of view, you either love it or hate it. George is the only member of the Beatles featured and in addition to playing one of the three tambouras he has a solo vocal. The sound of raucous laughter breaks the atmosphere and closes the track.

When I'm Sixty-Four (Lennon−McCartney)   2:38

John Lennon : Lead Guitar and Backing Vocal
Paul Mccartney : Bass Guitar, Piano and Lead/Backing Vocal
George Harrison : Backing Vocal
Ringo Starr : Drums
Session Musicians : Two Clarinets and one Bass Clarinet

The track opens with the sound of two clarinets plus a bass clarinet (played by session musicians). Paul wrote the song for his father who had at the time recently turned 64. Its inoffensive lyrics and its equally inoffensive accompaniment jog along at a pleasant pace and divert us from the Indian temple and the raga-rock of George's extravaganza on the previous track. Lead vocal is from Paul with a three-part harmony backing from John, Paul and George. The piano is played by Paul.

Lovely Rita (Lennon−McCartney)   2:43

John Lennon : Acoustic Guitar, Comb and Paper and Backing Vocal
Paul McCartney : Bass Guitar, Piano, Comb and Paper and Lead/Backing Vocal
George Harrison : Acoustic Guitar, Comb and Paper and Backing Vocal
Ringo Starr : Drums
George Martin : Piano

Lead vocal comes from Paul who also plays piano, although the honky-tonk piano in the middle is George Martin. John, Paul and George sing backing vocals and also use comb and paper to produce the 'sha, sha, sha' sound. The last 60 seconds include a fine blues/jazz piano from Paul and various grunting and groaning noises. The Beatles were to use a similar ending for Magical Mystery Tour later in 1967.

Good Morning, Good Morning (Lennon – McCartney) 2:35

John Lennon : Lead/Backing Vocal
Paul McCartney ; Bass Guitar, Lead Guitar and Backing Vocal
George Harrison : Lead Guitar
Ringo Starr : Drums
Sounds Incorporated : Three Saxophones, two Trombones and one French Horn

This lively track opens with the sound of a cock crowing and then some very solid brass (three saxophones, two trumpets and a French horn) played by Sounds Incorporated, a Liverpudlian group who were great friends of the Beatles. The lead vocal is by John, joined by Paul for the chorus. The guitar solo is by Paul. The ending can only be described as recorded chaos. Amongst the sound effects used are: a fox-hunt (which gallops away across the stereo), bleating sheep, a mooing cow, and a clucking chicken which George Martin had noticed sounded like the opening guitar note of the next track. He carefully edited this so that the clucking sound blended into the guitar note, so we are transported from the farmyard back into the theatre.

Sgt. Pepper's Lonely Hearts Club Band (Reprise)
(Lennon – McCartney) 1:20

John Lennon : Maraccas, Lead Guitar and Lead Vocal
Paul McCartney : Bass Guitar and Lead Vocal
George Harrison : Lead Guitar and Lead Vocal
Ringo Starr : Drums

Paul counts in 'one-two-three-four' to introduce the reprise of the opening track. (If you listen to the counting over headphones you will hear John say 'bye' between the 'two' and 'three' of the count-in.) There is no lead vocalist on this second version — everybody sings the amended lyrics. Unlike on the opening track there are no horns here. The recording does not finish; as it fades out to the sound of an applauding audience, the acoustic guitar and piano of A Day In The Life fade in.

A Day In The Life (Lennon – McCartney) 5:03

John Lennon : Acoustic Guitar, Piano* and Lead Vocal
Paul McCartney : Bass Guitar, Piano, Piano* and Lead Vocal
George Harrison : Bongos and Piano*
Ringo Starr : Drums, Maraccas and Piano*
George Martin : Harmonium*
Mal Evans : Voice Counting, Alarm Clock and Piano*
Session Musicians : 41 Piece Orchestra
*Finale Only

This must be one of the most controversial Beatle recordings. The song, originally began by recounting the news from the daily papers, with a report of a car crash and subsequent death. The second news item was a report of 4,000 potholes in the roads of Blackburn that had been personally counted by a local councillor. John, having written the two segments could not join them together, and asked Paul to fill in the middle section. Paul has been quoted as saying, 'The next bit was another song altogether but it just happened to fit. It was just me remembering what it was like to run up the road to catch a bus to school, having a smoke and going into class. We decided: "bugger this, we're going to write a turn-on song". It was a reflection of my school days — I would have a Woodbine then, and somebody would speak and I would go into a dream. This was the only one in the album written as a deliberate provocation. A stick-that-in-your-pipe .... but what we want is to turn you on to the truth rather than pot'.

When the song begins it fades in from the applause of the previous track. John plays the guitar intro, with Paul joining in on piano. John's cold harsh vocal then begins. When he reaches 'I'd love to turn you on' a 41 piece orchestra begins to play, climbing higher and higher up the musical scale, until suddenly, the noise stops and we hear the sound of an alarm clock. The lyrics continue, and for a second time repeat 'I'd love to turn you on'; the 41 piece orchestra repeats its cacophonos destruction of the musical scale, reaches a climax and suddenly stops. There is then the most unearthly crash on three pianos and a harmonium. The resultant chord is drawn out for a staggering 45 seconds. A few further details might be of interest. The voice that can be heard counting during the 24-bar cacophonous build-up of the orchestra belongs to Mal Evans. The alarm clock was not originally intended for inclusion in the track, but it couldn't be removed, so had to be left in. Paul made use of it to include the line 'woke up, fell out of bed'. The orchestra build-up was recorded four times and then dubbed one on top of the other, slightly out of synchronisation, to give a fuller sound. The three pianos and a harmonium at the end are played or struck by members of the Beatles plus George Martin. This was also recorded four times then sychronised to give an unearthly sound.

The 20,000 Hz Tone   0:08

This tone was added as a gesture from the Beatles to all the dogs in Britain so that there would be something on the L.P. for them too! This is included only on British copies of the album.

The Inner Groove   0:02

This two seconds of nonsense was a snippet of conversation which sounded good when edited from a recording of the party given by the Beatles after they had finished the piano parts at the end of A Day In The Life. They decided they would like to fill the inner groove with something and this is what they chose.

MAGICAL MYSTERY TOUR
Parlophone PCTC 255
Producer : George Martin
Release Date : 19 November 1976
Running Time : 36:32

SIDE ONE: Magical Mystery Tour; The Fool On The Hill; Flying; Blue Jay Way; Your Mother Should Know; I Am The Walrus.

SIDE TWO: Hello Goodbye; Strawberry Fields Forever; Penny Lane; Baby You're A Rich Man; All You Need Is Love.

The idea for the film, of which the first side of this album is the sound track, was originally conceived by Paul McCartney as early as March 1967, although filming didn't begin until Monday 11 September 1967. The invitation to the Beatles to appear as the British contribution to the worldwide television broadcast *Our World* in which they performed All You Need Is Love (which is also included on this album) caused the delay between conception and realisation of the idea.

The Beatles invited various friends and fan club secretaries to be included in the film. Amongst these was their old mate, Victor Spinetti, who appears in the film as a recruiting sergeant. (He had also appeared in the Beatles' two previous films, *A Hard Day's Night* and *Help!*) The Beatles decided that the coach used in the film should have a special logo along the side. This logo can be found on the front cover of the album. The tour, on film, begins in a side street just off Baker Street by the London Planetarium and then continues through the West of England. In the main the film was ad-libbed; the result was interesting though somewhat crazy. Weird characters emerge from the imaginations of the Beatles to feature in the various songs in the film—characters such as 'The Fool On The Hill', 'The Walrus', 'The Man Of A Thousand Voices' and 'The Egg Men'.

The album, although not made available in Britain until 1976, was available in the USA from 1967. It consists of the contents of the two E.P. set issued in Britain on 8 December 1967 along with the A- and B-sides of the three singles the Beatles issued in 1967. When the album was issued in Britain, EMI did a straight pressing from the American album. This left much to be desired as three of the tracks, Penny Lane, Baby You're A Rich Man and All You Need Is Love are in fake stereo.

In 1973, EMI decided to issue a cassette version of the Magical Mystery Tour album. This cassette contained stereo versions of all the tracks included on the album, including a stereo version of Baby You're A Rich Man, which had previously been unavailable in Britain, although it was included on European pressings of the album. The cassette also includes the re-recorded version of All You Need Is Love (see the Yellow Submarine album), although the album contains the original single version of the song. The album has the catalogue number PCTS 255, but the cassette in addition to the usual cassette prefix of TC, has the confusing number PCS 3077 which places it in between the Rubber Soul (PCS 3075) and Revolver (PCS 7009) albums.

It is interesting that the Beatles' entire 1967 record releases are contained on the Sgt. Pepper's Lonely Hearts Club Band and Magical Mystery Tour albums.

SIDE ONE

Magical Mystery Tour (Lennon—McCartney)   2:48

John Lennon : Acoustic Guitar and Backing Vocal
Paul McCartney : Bass Guitar, Piano and Lead Vocal
George Harrison : Lead Guitar and Backing Vocal
Ringo Starr : Drums and Tambourine
Session Musicians : Three Trumpets

The strong opening track features Paul on lead vocal and he joins John and

George to sing the answer-style backing.

The influences of Penny Lane and Lovely Rita show through on this track, with three trumpets and jazz/blues piano. The Beatles expanded their use of stereo on this track, placing sounds and voices to create the effect of the movement of the Magical Mystery Tour coach.

The Fool On The Hill (Lennon—McCartney)   3:00

John Lennon : Harmonica and Maraccas
Paul McCartney : Piano, Recorder, Flute and Solo Vocal
George Harrison : Lead Guitar and Harmonica
Ringo Starr : Finger Cymbals

Paul is the solo vocalist accompanying himself on piano, double-tracked recorder and flute. John and George add harmonicas and Ringo joins in with finger cymbals. George can be heard on lead guitar in the backing. The song is in the classic McCartney ballad style and has become a standard, rating nearly as well as his classics Yesterday and Michelle.

Flying (Lennon—McCartney—Harrison—Starkey)   2:16

John Lennon : Mellotron and Chanting
Paul McCartney : Assorted Guitars and Chanting
George Harrison : Assorted Guitars and Chanting
Ringo Starr : Drums, Maraccas and Chanting

The only track to have been issued and composed by all four Beatles, this is the second of only two instrumentals ever released by them. The other was the Lennon-Harrison 1961 composition Cry For A Shadow. John plays the main theme of this instrumental on a Mellotron. Paul and George add an assortment of guitars and all four Beatles produce the chanting heard later. The ending fades into an assortment of sound effects and backward-running tapes and tape loops put together by John and Ringo for this recording.

Blue Jay Way (Harrison)   3:50

John Lennon : Tambourine
Paul McCartney : Bass Guitar and Backing Vocal
George Harrison : Hammond Organ, Lead and Backing Vocal
Ringo Starr : Drums
Session Musician : Cello

George leaves Indian music for a while to record the story of Derek Taylor (the Beatles' publicist) being lost in fog in Los Angeles whilst trying to find Blue Jay Way, where George was staying at the time. The recording fades in immediately after the previous track as if the two are joined together. This is the only track to feature phasing (an electronic effect produced by playing the recording on two tape machines, slightly out of synchronisation, to produce a swirling, swishing effect). George's double-tracked lead vocals, backed mainly by himself on Hammond organ and Ringo on drums, are all phased throughout — quite an achievement, as phasing tends to slip after a while. The engineering expertise of George Martin kept the whole recording phased. The backing also includes a cello, various electronic sounds and backing vocals played forwards and backwards.

Your Mother Should Know (Lennon – McCartney)   2:33

John Lennon : Organ and Backing Vocal
Paul McCartney : Bass Guitar, Piano and Lead/Backing Vocal
George Harrison : Tambourine, Tabla and Backing Vocal
Ringo Starr : Drums

Paul's fascination with the twenties and thirties began to show on When I'm Sixty-Four on Sgt. Pepper, when he did a very good Noel Coward impression. His fascination continues with this similar song. Paul sings lead vocal and joins John and George for the backing vocals. The backing also includes Paul on piano, John on organ and at the end, George on an Indian tabla. The vocals start off on the left-hand channel for the first verse and switch to the right hand-channel for the second verse, then back to the left-hand channel for the third and final verse.

I Am The Walrus (Lennon – McCartney)   4:35

John Lennon : Mellotron and Lead Vocal
Paul McCartney : Bass Guitar and Backing Vocal
George Harrison : Tambourine and Backing Vocal
Ringo Starr : Drums
Session Musicians : Eight Violins, four Cellos and three Horns
Choir : Six Boys and Six Girls (Children of Michael Sammes Singers)

Definitely the most intriguing track the Beatles recorded. There are four separate edits of this recording; this one features the opening riff played by John on the Mellotron repeated four times (although the British single and E.P. has the opening riff repeated six times (see Chapter 43 *Recording Oddities*). He is then joined by eight violins, four cellos and Ringo on drums. The nonsensical flow of John's lyrics brings to mind his two books *In His Own Write* and *Spaniard In The Works*. Strange phrases like 'sitting on a cornflake', 'yellow matter custard', 'crabalocker fishwife', 'expert texpert choking smokers', 'semolina pilchard' and 'elementary penguin' seem to fit into the interwoven collage of sound that he wanted to create.

On the line 'yellow matter custard' John is joined by three horns, various voices, oscillations and discordant sounds from a radio plugged into the recording console. When the recording stops we hear a snatch of noise and oscillations from the radio, then the music starts again, this time in fake stereo. The sound is mixed into mono on the right-hand channel with the 'highs' from the mix on the left-hand channel.

The radio, as legend goes, was coming through live onto the tape and two lines spoken by two separate voices fit perfectly with the lyrics, for after John sings 'I am the egg man' the first voice says 'are you sir?'. John then continues with 'they are the egg men' and the second voice says 'A man may take you for what you are'. It was apparently John's idea to plug the radio into the recording console, and it was him playing around with the dial, which caused the noises and voices to be added to the recording.

In addition to the music and the radio in the backing are six boys and girls, the children of the Michael Sammes Singers. The boys can be heard singing 'Oompah, oompah, stick it up your jumpah', and the girls are singing 'everybody's got one'. John then tunes the radio into a Shakespeare play and at the end of the recording we hear 'sit ye down father, rest you'.

SIDE TWO

Hello Goodbye (Lennon–McCartney) 3:24

John Lennon : Lead Guitar, Organ and Backing Vocal
Paul McCartney : Bass Guitar, Piano, Bongos, Conga Drum and
    Lead/Backing Vocal
George Harrison : Lead Guitar, Tambourine and Backing Vocal
Ringo Starr : Drums and Maraccas
Session Musicians : Two Violas

This was released as a single three weeks prior to the Magical Mystery Tour double E.P. set, with I Am The Walrus, a 'taster' from the E.P. set, on the B-side. This is the only song, except for the six Magical Mystery Tour recordings, that features in the film. Paul sings lead and joins John and George for the backing vocals. The guitars are played by John and George, and Paul plays piano and the bongos and conga drum on the Maori finale. John also plays the organ that can be heard near the end of the song before the Maori finale begins; session men added the violas that crop up now and again throughout the recording.

Strawberry Fields Forever (Lennon–McCartney)   4:05

John Lennon : Lead Guitar, Harpsichord and Solo Vocal
Paul McCartney : Bass Guitar, Piano, Bongos and Flute
George Harrison : Lead Guitar and Timpani
Ringo Starr : Drums
Mal Evans : Tambourine
Philip Jones : Alto Trumpet
Session Musicians : Two Cellos and two Horns

With this song John immortalised forever Strawberry Fields, a Salvation Army orphanage in Liverpool, not far from Penny Lane. He traces a slightly surrealistic trip to Strawberry Fields and reveals the confused state of an orphan's mind—'nothing is real'. The Beatles made two recordings of Strawberry Fields Forever, and after listening to the playback John decided that he liked the first half of one recording and the second half of the other. There was one problem—they were in different keys. John entrusted the necessary editing to George Martin. To edit the two together, George Martin had to speed up the first section and slow down the second so that they were approximately in the same key.
   There are two oddities on this recording of which only one has been publicised. The first is a Morse code message, tapped out just after John sings 'Let me take you down...'. The Morse message consists of two letters, J and L. It is surprising that this has not received more attention. The second oddity included on this recording sparked off rumours of Paul McCartney's

death. At the end of the recording, John can be heard to say 'cranberry sauce'. Many people, however, decided that John was saying 'I buried Paul'.

Penny Lane (Lennon–McCartney)   3:00

John Lennon : Piano and Harmony Vocal
Paul McCartney : Bass Guitar, Arco String Bass, Flute and Lead Vocal
George Harrison : Conga Drum and Firebell
Ringo Starr : Drums
George Martin : Piano
David Mason : Piccolo Trumpet
Phillip Jones : Trumpet

Penny Lane has been known to Liverpool's residents for years as the name of a bus terminus. There is nothing particularly special about Penny Lane—it looks the same as any other road in the area—but like the Stawberry Fields Salvation Army Home, the Beatles have immortalised Penny Lane in the words of their song. Paul's reminiscence of Liverpool is finely displayed in his lyrics, although with a slight surrealism.

Paul's lead vocal is backed up by John who, with George Martin, also adds piano. Paul besides singing lead also adds string bass and a flute. The piccolo trumpet which crops up here and there, was added by David Mason of the London Symphony Orchestra. Phillip Jones, who was also with the LSO plays the trumpet on this track and also on Strawberry Fields Forever.

When the record was circulated in late January 1967 to radio stations in the USA and Canada the ending had seven extra notes played by David Mason on piccolo trumpet over the final few seconds of the recording. When the record actually reached the shops those seven notes had been trimmed off, which, besides making the radio station copies different, also made them rather valuable.

Baby You're A Rich Man (Lennon–McCartney)   3:07

John Lennon : Clavioline, Piano and Lead Vocal
Paul McCartney : Bass Guitar, Piano and Harmony Vocal
George Harrison : Tambourine and Harmony Vocal
Ringo Starr : Drums and Maraccas
Studio Engineer : Vibes

This started life as two different songs—One Of The Beautiful People (a song that John had written for a possible Sgt. Pepper Volume II album) and Baby, You're A Rich Man written by Paul. Although both songs were apparently recorded, neither has ever been issued in its original form. The two songs were joined together in a similar way to A Day In The Life with John singing the opening part of the song and then joining Paul and George for the Baby You're A Rich Man section.

The strange 'pipes of Pan' sound is a keyboard instrument called a clavioline. This is a rather strange device with a mind of its own and which will only play one note at a time.

John manages to play it and also piano. Paul plays his bass guitar and adds a second piano while an obliging engineer adds some vibes. The track in its present form was originally intended for the *Yellow Submarine* film, but was hurriedly included as the B-side of All You Need Is Love.

All You Need Is Love (Lennon–McCartney) 3:57

John Lennon : Harpsichord and Lead Vocal
Paul McCartney : Arco String Bass, Bass Guitar and Backing Vocal
George Harrison : Violin, Lead Guitar and Backing Vocal
Ringo Starr : Drums
George Martin : Piano
Chorus : Includes Mick Jagger, Marianne Faithfull, Keith Richard, Gary
  Brooker and Keith Moon
Session Musicians : Four Violins, two Cellos, two Trumpets, two
  Trombones, two Saxophones and one Accordion

The BBC invited the Beatles to represent the UK in a worldwide television broadcast called *Our World*, which was part of the Canadian EXPO 67 festival. The Beatles were to be seen recording their new single All You Need Is Love. The recording was not all made live; the rhythm section was pre-recorded earlier in the day and simply played back at the time of the broadcast, although the Beatles were seen playing their guitars. All other parts of the song, the vocals, the backing vocals and the orchestra, were recorded at the time of broadcast, before an audience of approximately 200 million people. A second recording of the song, made during rehearsals for the broadcast, is included on the Yellow Submarine album. The day before the broadcast, the Beatles decided that they would release All You Need Is Love as soon as possible after the show. After listening to the playback, John's vocals were re-recorded and copies of the master tape were then flown all over the world and the record was on sale within weeks of being broadcast.

The Beatles asked the orchestra to dress in white dinner suits for the broadcast, and also invited a few of their friends along to join in on the backing vocals; these included Mick Jagger, Marianne Faithfull, Keith Richard, Gary Brooker from Procol Harum and Keith Moon. As it was to be a worldwide broadcast, the Beatles wanted to have an international flavour. George Martin suggested that they use the *Marseillaise* (the French national anthem) for the beginning, and for the ending he included Greensleeves and Glen Miller's In The Mood in the orchestral arrangement. Unfortunately, George had used Miller's own arrangement, not then out of copyright, and as soon as the record was released EMI was approached by the copyright holders. However, EMI agreed to pay and all was sorted out.

The initial rhythm track the Beatles recorded for All You Need Is Love ran for just over ten minutes and included John playing a harpsichord, Paul an Arco string bass with a bow, George a violin and Ringo on drums. For the actual broadcast the Beatles played their usual instruments, except John who just sang. The orchestra, conducted by Mike Vickers, consisted of 13 musicians playing four violins, two cellos, two saxophones, two trombones, two trumpets and an accordion; even George Martin joined in on piano. At the end, John comes in with an off-key rendition of She Loves You. The recording lasted for approximately six minutes, although it was later trimmed down to just under four. The broadcast took place on 25 June 1967 and the record, which was to become the international anthem for a generation, was on sale in Great Britain by 7 July 1967, and ten days later in the USA.

THE BEATLES (2 L.P.s)
Apple PMC 7067-8; PCS 7067-8
Producer : George Martin
Release Date : 22 November 1968
Running Time : 93:33

The BEATLES

SIDE ONE: Back In The U.S.S.R.; Dear Prudence; Glass Onion; Ob-La-Di, Ob-La-Da; Wild Honey Pie; The Continuing Story Of Bungalow Bill; While My Guitar Gently Weeps; Happiness Is A Warm Gun.
SIDE TWO: Martha My Dear; I'm So Tired; Blackbird; Piggies; Rocky Racoon; Don't Pass Me By; Why Don't We Do It In The Road?; I Will; Julia.

SIDE THREE: Birthday; Yer Blues; Mother Nature's Son; Everybody's Got Something To Hide Except Me And My Monkey; Sexy Sadie; Helter Skelter; Long, Long, Long.
SIDE FOUR: Revolution 1; Honey Pie; Savoy Truffle; Cry Baby Cry ; Can You Take Me Back; Revolution 9; Good Night.

This album, more widely known as The White Album (although its working title was A Dolls House) was the Beatles' first album on their then newly formed Apple label which had made its first appearance three months earlier on 30 August 1968 with the single Hey Jude/Revolution (Apple R5722). Both tracks were recorded during the sessions for this album. With this album the Beatles appeared to return to the Revolver album of 1966, before their flight of fantasy into psycedelia during 1967.

Most of the 30 tracks on this double album were written during the Beatles' stay at the Maharishi Mahesh Yogi's Academy of Meditation just outside of the town of Rishikesh in northern India in early 1968. They show the Beatles' ever-increasing ability to write and perform all types of music from hard rock (Helter Skelter) to ballads (Blackbird and Mother Nature's Son) including a Hollywood-type number (Goodnight) sendups of previously recorded songs (Glass Onion and Revolution 1) and the nightmarish Revolution 9.

The widening gap between John and Paul's writing styles begins to show on this album. John's lyrics are hard hitting and caustic, while Paul tends to write pleasant inoffensive ballads and love songs. Although these songs are jointly credited as being Lennon — McCartney compositions, the only track they did co-write on this album is Birthday. From this album on all Lennon—McCartney credited songs can be more clearly defined as being written by the lead vocalist on the individual tracks. George Harrison, whose song-writing ability progressed with time, had four new songs on this album, While My Guitar Gently Weeps, Piggies, Long, Long, Long and Savoy Truffle, and Ringo had one, Don't Pass Me By.

At the time of recording this album, the Beatles were beginning to be disillusioned with the group; John wanted to leave, and Ringo did leave for a period of two weeks, but was eventually coaxed back. With the creation of APPLE the Beatles had gone from being just musicians to being businessmen. This, along with the death of Brian Epstein in 1967 and the arrival of Yoko Ono, all contributed to the beginning of the end of the Beatles. The tension of continual business meetings, musical differences and John's growing interest in working with Yoko, were all contributory factors to the break-up. When the sessions for this album were eventually finished the rift between the Beatles had grown so wide that none of them had much interest in what they had recorded. The Beatles had decided to issue two albums mainly to fulfil their contract with EMI as soon as possible, so they sifted through the tracks, of which there were approximately 40, and rejected ten of them. Amongst the tracks rejected was What's The New Mary Jane, which was continually reported as being their next single. To date this has not seen the light of day.

After the elaborate Sgt Pepper sleeve the Beatles decided to have the simplest possible plain white sleeve, hence the unofficial title of The White Album. The outer part of the sleeve has only the title plus the catalogue number printed down the spine, with the words 'The Beatles' embossed into the cardboard on the front. The inner part of the sleeve gives the barest of information with song titles on one side and four black and white photographs of the Beatles on the other. The sleeve contains four separate colour photographs and a poster with a hodge podge of photographs — rather like a visual version of Revolution 9. On the back of the poster are the complete lyrics to all the songs.

SIDE ONE

Back In The U.S.S.R. (Lennon – McCartney) 2:45

John Lennon : Six-String Bass and Backing Vocal
Paul McCartney : Lead Guitar, Piano and Lead/Backing Vocal
George Harrison : Bass Guitar and Backing Vocal
Ringo Starr : Drums

The opening track, originally titled I'm Backing The U.S.S.R., fades in with the sound of a plane landing then goes straight into a great rock and roll song heavily influenced by Chuck Berry's Back In The U.S.A. Paul is on lead vocals with a Beach Boys style backing from both John and Paul. The lead guitar is played by Paul, as is the rocking piano. John can be heard playing a six-string bass and, for the first time on a Beatles' record, George plays a bass guitar. The Beatles also add handclapping to the backing for the first time since approximately 1964. The track ends in much the same way as it began, with the sound of an aircraft, which then fades into the following track.

Dear Prudence (Lennon – McCartney) 4:00

John Lennon : Lead Guitar, Tambourine and Lead/Backing Vocal
Paul McCartney : Bass Guitar, Piano, Flugelhorn and Backing Vocal
George Harrison : Acoustic Guitar and Backing Vocal
Ringo Starr : Drums
Mal Evans : Tambourine

As Back In The U.S.S.R. fades out to the sound of jet engines, Dear Prudence fades in with the sound of a rather persistent acoustic guitar which continues throughout the recording. The gentle beginning builds up into an extravagant and interesting climax that includes a complicated drumbeat from Ringo, with Paul on bass guitar, piano and flugelhorn. The lead vocal on this recording is a multi-tracked John Lennon with a three-part backing vocal from John, Paul and George. The song could almost be made up of two songs joined together, rock song and ballad, although there is no evidence to confirm this. John's lead vocal is double-tracked for the main lyrics with a further over-dubbing in places — an extremely interesting combination. The song was written by John for Prudence Farrow (sister of Mia Farrow) while the Beatles were in India. Prudence spent most of her day meditating in spite of John's attempts to persuade her to do otherwise.

Glass Onion (Lennon – McCartney) 2:10

John Lennon : Acoustic Guitar and Solo Vocal
Paul McCartney : Bass Guitar, Piano and Flute
George Harrison : Lead Guitar
Ringo Starr : Drums and Tambourine
Session Musicians : Orchestra

John's nonsensical lyrics are basically a series of unconnected comments, which include references to Strawberry Fields Forever, Fixing A Hole, The

Fool On The Hill, Lady Madonna and I Am The Walrus. The track features an unusual combination of a Rain-style drumbeat, with an Eleanor Rigby-style orchestration and an All My Loving stop-start structure. The song sends up all those who tried to explain the Beatles' lyrics, and John includes a line especially for them: 'well, here's a clue for you all.'

Ob-La-Di, Ob-La-Da (Lennon—McCartney) 3:10

John Lennon : Maraccas and Backing Vocal
Paul McCartney : Piano, Bass Guitar and Lead Vocal
George Harrison : Acoustic Guitar and Backing Vocal
Ringo Starr : Drums
Session Musicians : Brass

On this lively track the Beatles, having attempted many forms of music, now tried their hand at reggae. Paul is on piano and lead vocals, with John and George joining in for the chorus. The recording also features some Jamaican style brass. Paul took the expression 'ob-la-di, ob-la-da life goes on, bra' from a Jamaican friend, Jimmy Scott, who had been using the expression for years and had a band called Jimmy Scott and his Ob-La-Di, Ob-La-Da Band. At the time of release of this album Paul McCartney wanted to issue this track as a single but both John and George voted against.

Wild Honey Pie (Lennon—McCartney) 1:02

John Lennon : Not Present
Paul McCartney : Guitars, Drums and All Vocals
George Harrison : Not Present
Ringo Starr : Not Present

This bouncy semi-instrumental was written and performed solely by Paul. In addition to repeating the line 'honey pie' throughout the track he also plays drums, lead, bass and acoustic guitars. This was originally an experimental recording of a spontaneous sing-a-long, that Paul had thought up while the Beatles were staying in India, not intended for release, but Jane Asher, Paul's girl friend, liked it so much that Paul edited it to its present length. The full track has yet to see the light of day.

The Continuing Story Of Bungalow Bill
(Lennon—McCartney) 3:05

John Lennon : Acoustic Guitar, Organ and Lead Vocal
Paul McCartney : Bass Guitar and Backing Vocal
George Harrison : Acoustic Guitar and Backing Vocal
Ringo Starr : Drums, Tambourine and Backing Vocal
Yoko Ono : Harmony Vocal
Chris Thomas : Mellotron
Chorus : Includes Yoko Ono and Maureen Starkey

The track opens with a Spanish/Mexican style acoustic guitar solo which leads straight into the sing-a-long chorus of 'Hey Bungalow Bill, what did you Kill? Bungalow Bill'. The song, written by John who also sings lead, sounds rather like an updated version of Yellow Submarine. It's a pleasant track with, for the first and only time on a Beatles' record, harmony vocals from Yoko Ono on the third verse and also on chorus (where she was joined by Ringo's wife Maureen). The Beatles are also joined by assistant Chris Thomas, who adds the Mellotron near the end. The track doesn't fade out but is linked to the following track with an 'Eh up' introduction from John.

While My Guitar Gently Weeps (Harrison)   4:46

John Lennon : Acoustic Guitar, Organ and Harmony Vocal
Paul McCartney : Bass Guitar, Piano and Harmony Vocal
George Harrison : Acoustic Guitar, Lead Guitar and Lead Vocal
Ringo Starr : Drums, Castanets and Tambourine
Eric Clapton : Lead Guitar

The first of four tracks written by George, who seemed at this stage to have given up using Indian instruments on Beatles' recordings although he issued a solo album called Wonderwall consisting mainly of Indian instrumentals. Here he enlists the help of his long-time friend Eric Clapton to play the lead guitar. The lead vocal is by George, who double-tracks in part and John and Paul join in on the chorus. The track has an extremely long fade-out which is really a showcase for Eric Clapton's lead guitar.

Happiness Is A Warm Gun (Lennon–McCartney)   2:47

John Lennon : Lead Guitar, Tambourine and Lead/Backing Vocal
Paul McCartney : Bass Guitar and Backing Vocal
George Harrison : Lead Guitar and Backing Vocal
Ringo Starr : Drums

This title is an interesting collage consisting of three separate songs which John had written but decided to join together into one song. The track begins as a gentle ballad with solo vocal from John who interweaves nonsensical one-line comments into the lyrics. The song slowly changes into a semi-rock song which builds up with the repetitive 'Mother Superior jumped the gun'. The third and final section has John shouting out the lyrics over a 'bang, bang — shoot, shoot' backing vocal which he recorded with Paul. John had the idea for the third section of the song after George Martin showed him an advertisement in a magazine proclaiming 'Happiness is a warm gun'.

SIDE TWO

Martha My Dear (Lennon–McCartney)   2:28

John Lennon : Bass Guitar
Paul McCartney : Piano and Solo Vocal
George Harrison : Lead Guitar
Ringo Starr : Drums
Session Musicians : Strings and Brass

This is a Paul McCartney thirties-influenced song written about his old

English sheepdog. It features an orchestral/danceband backing and has a solo vocal from Paul who also plays piano.

I'm So Tired (Lennon—McCartney)   2:01

John Lennon :   Acoustic Guitar, Lead Guitar, Organ and Lead Vocal
Paul McCartney :   Bass Guitar and Harmony Vocal
George Harrison :   Lead Guitar and Rhythm Guitar
Ringo Starr :   Drums

Written by John about Yoko, this song features a lead vocal from John who also plays acoustic guitar and organ. Paul harmonises in places. The recording is structured in a similar way to Happiness Is A Warm Gun. It starts, builds up and then stops, only to start up again. The track finishes with a few seconds of nonsensical gibberish that has been interpreted as Ringo saying 'Paul is dead, man, miss him, miss him' backwards.

Blackbird Lennon—McCartney)   2:20

John Lennon :   Not Present
Paul McCartney :   Acoustic Guitar, Bongos and Solo Vocal
George Harrison :   Not Present
Ringo Starr :   Not Present

This gentle song with inoffensive lyrics has a solo vocal from Paul who double tracks his lead vocal in part and backs it himself with an acoustic guitar. A metronomic beat is tapped out on what sounds like half of a set of bongos. Like several tracks on the album, this stops and starts up again, but here with the addition of a blackbird singing sweetly over the encore.

Piggies (Harrison)   2:04

John Lennon :   Sound Effects
Paul McCartney :   Bass Guitar
George Harrison :   Acoustic Guitar and Solo Vocal
Ringo Starr :   Tambourine
Chris Thomas :   Harpsichord
Session Musicians :   Strings

This song is a sarcastic swipe at the greedy, the 'piggies', always out to make money, and in particular out of the Beatles. Lead vocal is from George with double-tracking in parts. Chris Thomas plays harpsichord and the sound of grunting, snorting pigs is used to good effect.

Rocky Racoon (Lennon—McCartney)   3:33

John Lennon :   Harmonium, Harmonica and Backing Vocal
Paul McCartney :   Acoustic Guitar and Lead Vocal
George Harrison :   Bass Guitar and Backing Vocal
Ringo Starr :   Drums
George Martin :   Piano

Written by Paul during one of his visits to India, this has a country-folk flavour, like his earlier I've Just Seen A Face, on Help! He sings lead vocal, and backing vocals are a three-part harmony from himself plus John and George. A harmonica is used, although sparingly, for the first time since the earlier recordings; a honky-tonk, bar-room style piano is added by George Martin and a harmonium by John.

Don't Pass Me By (Starkey)   3:52

John Lennon : Acoustic Guitar and Tambourine
Paul McCartney : Bass Guitar
George Harrison : Violin
Ringo Starr : Piano, Drums and Solo Vocal

After years of performing songs specially written for him by John and Paul, and co-writing only one song, What Goes On? on Rubber Soul, Ringo finally sings solo on a self-penned song which he wrote in 1963, five years previously. The very bouncy backing includes a violin reputed to have been played by George Harrison, and the solid drum beat of course is provided by Ringo. This excellent first song from Ringo proved he too could write.

Why Don't We Do It In The Road? (Lennon–McCartney)   1:42

John Lennon : No Present
Paul McCartney : Lead Guitar, Bass Guitar, Piano, Drums and Solo Vocal
George Harrison : Not Present
Ringo Starr : Not Present

Another multi-tracked solo vocal from Paul who sings and plays every instrument on this regrettably short track: piano, drums, lead and bass guitars. In 1971 Paul re-styled and re-recorded it as Oh Woman, Oh Why.

I Will (Lennon–McCartney)   1:46

John Lennon : Not Present
Paul McCartney : Acoustic Guitar, Bass Guitar and Solo Vocal
George Harrison : Not Present
Ringo Starr : Drums, Bongos and Maraccas

This ballad is also a rather short track. Paul sings solo vocal and supplies a minimum backing with an acoustic guitar. Bongos are supplied by Ringo, together with drums and maraccas.

Julia (Lennon–McCartney)   2:57

John Lennon : Acoustic Guitar and Solo Vocal
Paul McCartney : Not Present
George Harrison : Not Present
Ringo Starr : Not Present

This beautiful song, written by John, helped by Yoko, is mainly about his love for his dead mother. A reference to his love for Yoko is included with the words 'ocean child' (an English translation of Yoko is 'child of the ocean'). John sings solo vocal and backs himself with two acoustic guitars.

SIDE THREE

Birthday (Lennon–McCartney)   2:40

John Lennon : Lead Guitar and Lead Vocal
Paul McCartney : Piano and Lead Vocal
George Harrison : Bass Guitar and Tambourine
Ringo Starr : Drums
Chorus : Includes Yoko Ono and Patti Harrison

This is the only track on the two albums to have been co-written by John and Paul. It is basically an up-dated, noisier re-write of the traditional 'Happy Birthday' and was written in India for Patti Harrison, George's wife, who was celebrating her birthday. It races along with a heavy drumbeat from Ringo, a persistent lead guitar riff from George and a jangling piano (phased in places) from Paul. The lead vocal, also from Paul, is double-tracked onto each channel of the stereo (an effect not used since Revolver). John sings lead in places but is mainly confined to backing, with Yoko Ono and Patti Harrison.

Yer Blues (Lennon–McCartney)   4:01

John Lennon : Lead Guitar and Solo Vocal
Paul McCartney : Bass Guitar
George Harrison : Lead Guitar
Ringo Starr : Drums

This is John Lennon's send-up of the flourishing British electric blues scene of the late sixties. The music and lyrics are just as powerful as John's vocals and the stabbing, attacking lead guitar from George with Ringo's insistent drumbeat suit the track perfectly.

Mother Nature's Son (Lennon–McCartney)   2:46

John Lennon : Not Present
Paul McCartney : Acoustic Guitar, Bongos, Timpani and Solo Vocal
George Harrison : Not Present
Ringo Starr : Not Present
Session Musicians : Horns

Paul McCartney set his vision of country life to pleasantly simple music. His solo vocal is backed by himself on acoustic guitar with a secondary acoustic guitar, bongos and a very distant timpani being over-dubbed also by himself. Some unobtrusive, pleasant horns are added by session musicians.

Everybody's Got Something To Hide Except Me And My Monkey (Lennon–McCartney)   2:25

John Lennon : Lead Guitar, Maraccas and Lead Vocal
Paul McCartney : Bass Guitar and Backing Vocal
George Harrison : Rhythm Guitar and Firebell
Ringo Starr : Drums

This track was written by John in reply to a drawing depicting Yoko as a monkey sitting on his shoulders, digging long talons into his back, supposedly draining him of his talent. John dismissed it with this song, saying 'we've got nothing to hide, Yoko inspires me, she doesn't destroy my ability to write good songs'. This is a great piece of rock and roll with John on lead vocal, and backing vocals (in places) from John and Paul. It features a prominent lead guitar riff and extensive use of a fire bell. The song began life with the working title of Come On, Come On.

Sexy Sadie (Lennon–McCartney)   3:15

John Lennon : Acoustic Guitar, Rhythm Guitar, Organ and Lead/Backing Vocal
Paul McCartney : Piano, Bass Guitar and Backing Vocal
George Harrison : Lead Guitar and Backing Vocal
Ringo Starr : Drums and Tambourine

Written by John about the Maharishi, who, during the Beatles' stay at his academy of meditation in India, had made a very non-mystical approach to Mia Farrow, proving to John that he was not all he made out to be. John originally intended to write the song as 'Mararishi What Have You Done, You Made A Fool of Everyone' but in the end decided against it. The track features a lead vocal from John, who joins Paul and George for the partly phased backing vocals, which produce an unusual effect. John plays acoustic guitar, Paul piano and George a distorted lead guitar.

Helter Skelter (Lennon–McCartney)   4:30

John Lennon : Bass Guitar, Lead Guitar, Saxophone and Backing Vocal
Paul McCartney : Bass Guitar, Lead Guitar and Lead Vocal
George Harrison : Rhythm Guitar and Backing Vocal
Ringo Starr : Drums
Mal Evans : Trumpet

This is the heaviest sound that the Beatles produced, a sound first tried out in 1966 with tracks such as Rain and And Your Bird Can Sing.
   Paul's lead vocals are screamed out of the speakers; the backing vocals from John and Paul add to the overall excited sound of the recording which includes various unexplainable bleeps and squeaks. At one point the guitars run down the musical scale and then dissolve into distorted feedback. Ringo starts the track up again with his drums but it fades out to a few seconds of silence and the recording seems to finish — but no, back it comes with all its heaviness then fades slightly only to reappear with Ringo Starr's famous statement 'I've got blisters on my fingers'. John plays saxophone and Mal

Evans, one of the Beatles' roadies, plays trumpet. This recording was originally 25 minutes long but the Beatles realised that at that length it would take up an entire album side so it was edited to 4:30.

After the Charles Manson murders in 1969 — reportedly inspired, in part, by this song — John Lennon later appeared in court to defend the recording, saying that it was simply about a fairground slide and nothing else.

Long, Long, Long (Harrison) 3:08

John Lennon : Acoustic Guitar and Piano
Paul McCartney : Bass Guitar and Hammond Organ
George Harrison : Acoustic Guitar and Solo Vocal
Ringo Starr : Drums

George Harrison's third offering on the album is reminiscent of a funeral dirge. George's double-tracked lead vocal is mixed so far back that it's difficult to hear the lyrics above the acoustic guitar. The recording includes a very dramatic drumbeat from Ringo and features Paul playing both piano and Hammond organ. It ends with a rather unearthly screech which sounds as though it might have come from Yoko.

SIDE FOUR

Revolution 1 (Lennon–McCartney) 4:13

John Lennon : Lead Guitar, Acoustic Guitar and Lead/Backing Vocal
Paul McCartney : Bass Guitar, Acoustic Guitar, Piano and Backing Vocal
George Harrison : Rhythm Guitar and Backing Vocal
Ringo Starr : Drums
Session Musicians : Brass

This recording is a slower, almost acoustic version of the song issued as the B-side of the Hey Jude single, issued two or three months before the album. The double-tracked lead vocal is by John. The track has a false start and when it does begin the lead guitar, instead of being on the right-hand channel, as it is on the faster version, is on the left-hand channel. There is a do-wop backing which makes it sound rather like a send-up. Additional features are a brass section and Paul playing piano.

Honey Pie (Lennon–McCartney) 2:42

John Lennon : Lead Guitar
Paul McCartney : Piano and Solo Vocal
George Harrison : Bass Guitar
Ringo Starr : Drums
Session Musicians : 15-Piece Band

Like When I'm Sixty-Four and Your Mother Should Know this song is influenced by the music of the twenties. Paul wrote it, sings lead vocal and plays piano. John plays lead guitar and George (as on several tracks of this album) bass guitar. Ringo, of course, is on drums, and 15 session musicians add the danceband-type backing.

Savoy Truffle (Harrison) 2:55

John Lennon : Lead Guitar
Paul McCartney : Bass Guitar
George Harrison : Lead Guitar, Organ and Solo Vocal
Ringo Starr : Drums and Tambourine
Session Musicians : Brass

This song is dedicated to Eric Clapton's sweet tooth! George makes an uncomfortable reference to Ob-La-Di, Ob-La-Da which does not fit in with the other lyrics but rhymes with the following line. The recording has a solid brass backing, rather reminiscent of Got To Get You Into My Life.

Cry Baby Cry (Lennon–McCartney) 2:34

John Lennon : Acoustic Guitar, Piano, Organ and Solo Vocal
Paul McCartney : Bass Guitar
George Harrison : Lead Guitar
Ringo Starr : Drums and Tambourine
George Martin : Harmonium

John Lennon demonstrates his versatility on this track by playing almost every instrument. He plays guitar, piano and organ with help from George Martin on harmonium. The guitars at the beginning are phased and John experiments with the stereo, so that the verses appear in the centre while the chorus appears on the left-hand channel. John was inspired to write the song by a television commercial and his original verse was to have been 'make your mother buy' but he changed his mind and added more nonsensical lyrics.

Can You Take Me Back (Lennon–McCartney) 0:27

John Lennon : Not Present
Paul McCartney : Acoustic Guitar, Drums, Maraccas, Bongos and Solo
  Vocal
George Harrison : Not Present
Ringo Starr : Not Present

This short track links Cry Baby Cry with Revolution 9, and possibly was originally intended to be part of one of these songs. The lyrics are not printed on the back of the poster with those of other songs on the album. The solo vocal is from Paul with backing provided by an acoustic guitar, drums and maraccas (presumably all played by Paul). It does not seem to be an intro to Revolution 9 because it fades out completely before that track begins. It sounds rather like a first take which was initially dismissed, then included at the last moment.

Revolution 9 (Lennon—McCartney)   8:15

John Lennon : Voice, Mixing and Editing
Paul McCartney : Piano
George Harrison : Voice
Ringo Starr : Voice
Yoko Ono : Voice
George Martin : Mixing and Editing

What can be said about a Beatles recording that doesn't feature any music?
The recording starts with a snatch of overheard conversation. A piano
(played by Paul) begins, then an anonymous voice repeats 'Number 9,
Number 9, Number 9'. From here the recording becomes a mixture of
backward-running tapes, discordant sounds, laughter, snatches of
conversation between John and George and crowd noises. It sounds rather
like the memory of a nightmare portrayed in sound. This is one of John's
experimental avant-garde recordings, many of which are featured on his
Two Virgins album. It was created solely by John and Yoko, was rejected
initially by the other three, but eventually included.

Good Night (Lennon—McCartney)   3:14

John Lennon : Not Present
Paul McCartney : Not Present
George Harrison : Not Present
Ringo Starr : Solo Vocal
Session Musicians : 30-Piece Orchestra , Harp and Choir

This was written by John specifically for Ringo and only him. The thirties,
Hollywood-style backing is supplied by the George Martin orchestra, with a
sweet-sounding female choir. One cannot resist the feeling that this track is
a Lennon send-up.

YELLOW SUBMARINE
Apple PMC 7070; PCS 7070
Producer : George Martin
Release Date : 17 January 1969
Running Time : 20:34 Side One*;
17:41 Side Two**

*The Beatles
**The George Martin Orchestra

SIDE ONE: Yellow Submarine; Only A Northern Song; All Together Now; Hey Bulldog; It's All Too Much; All You Need Is Love.

SIDE TWO: Contains incidental music by George Martin and Orchestra as played in the film.

This is the soundtrack album for the feature-length cartoon film of the same name based loosely around the lyrics of Yellow Submarine.

The contract for the film and album, signed by Brian Epstein, stipulated that the Beatles were to supply at least three previously unreleased recordings for use in the soundtrack. The Beatles, who felt Brian Epstein had let them down, initially wanted nothing to do with the project, but eventually decided to supply songs that would not normally have been seriously considered for release. One song, however, Baby You're A Rich Man, originally recorded for inclusion on this album, was issued six months previously as the B-side to All You Need Is Love (see the Magical Mystery Tour album).

The four songs eventually given, albeit reluctantly, for use in the film (Only A Northern Song, All Together Now, Hey Bulldog and It's All Too Much) were considered by the Beatles to be 'throwaway' recordings. The original plan was to release the four new tracks as an E.P., but after consideration it seemed that an album would sell better. Unfortunately, for Beatles' fans this turned out to be a one-sided Beatles' album with George Martin's orchestral score of the film's incidental music on the second side. The Beatles' previous soundtrack albums, when issued in Britain, had included on the second sides tracks not used in the respective films and it was a great pity that this album was not compiled in the same way.

The film soundtrack has these six album tracks plus parts or complete recordings of Sgt. Pepper's Lonely Hearts Club Band, With A Little Help From My Friends, Lucy In The Sky With Diamonds, Within You, Without You, When I'm Sixty-Four, A Day In The Life, Eleanor Rigby, Nowhere Man, Baby You're A Rich Man, Think For Yourself and Love You Too.

SIDE ONE

Yellow Submarine (Lennon–McCartney) 2:40

John Lennon : Acoustic Guitar and Backing Vocal
Paul McCartney : Acoustic Guitar and Backing Vocal
George Harrison : Tambourine and Backing Vocal
Ringo Starr : Drums and Lead Vocal
Chorus : Includes George Martin, Patti Harrison, Mal Evans, Neil Aspinall and Geoff Emerick
Session Musicians : Brass Band

Previously issued on Revolver, this is an eternally fresh song which does not seem to have dated at all.

Only A Northern Song (Harrison) 3:23

John Lennon : Piano and Various Discordant Instruments
Paul McCartney : Bass Guitar and Various Discordant Instruments
George Harrison : Organ, Various Discordant Instruments and Solo Vocal
Ringo Starr : Drums and Various Discordant Instruments

This track seems to reflect George Harrison's displeasure with the project. His one-line comments are thinly linked together into what can be loosely described as a song. The ironical title was also a sarcastic jibe at the publishing company, Northern Songs. The backing is a cacophonous 'tune-up' reminiscent of Tomorrow Never Knows and Revolution 9. Ringo's drums and Paul's bass guitar are the only musical parts of the backing. The organ intro is good, but gets lost amidst the continual burps and interruptions of off-key instruments. As this is a mono recording, it is difficult to tell if it continues throughout the recording. The track is not at present available anywhere in the world in stereo.

All Together Now (Lennon – McCartney) 2:08

John Lennon : Banjo and Backing Vocal
Paul McCartney : Acoustic Guitar, Bass Guitar and Lead Vocal
George Harrison : Harmonica and Backing Vocal
Ringo Starr : Drums and Finger Cymbals

Paul's contribution also sounds rather half-hearted. His lead vocal, with backing from John and George, seems to lack real enthusiasm, although it comes across reasonably well and is still enjoyable.

Hey Bulldog (Lennon-McCartney) 3:09

John Lennon : Piano, Lead Guitar and Lead Vocal
Paul McCartney : Bass Guitar and Harmony Vocal
George Harrison : Lead Guitar and Tambourine
Ringo Starr : Drums

John's sole contribution was, as he described it himself, 'a filler track for the album'. The recording was not intended for use in the film, as the contract demanded only three new songs, but it was finally included. John's lead vocal without sounding over-enthusiastic, manages to give the recording power and excitement. He insisted on this title for the song, rather than the more obvious You Can Talk To Me, although nowhere in his original lyrics was there any reference to a bulldog. He then decided to include the words 'Hey Bulldog' right at the end of the song.

It's All Too Much (Harrison) 6:27

John Lennon : Lead Guitar and Harmony Vocal
Paul McCartney : Bass Guitar and Harmony Vocal
George Harrison : Lead Guitar, Organ and Lead Vocal
Ringo Starr : Drums and Tambourine
Session Musicians : Two Trumpets

George's lead vocals on this, his second contribution to Yellow Submarine, sound more enthusiastic than his first—probably because it was not recorded with the project in mind. This, and the recording used in the soundtrack (which has a verse not included here) are reputed to have been edited from a thirty-minute recording, although this has never been verified. George includes two rather odd lines. One is a line previously used in the Mersey's hit record Sorrow; the second is the mysterious line in which he sings 'we are dead'.

All You Need Is Love (Lennon–McCartney)   3:47

John Lennon : Harpsichord and Lead Vocal
Paul McCartney : Arco String Bass, Bass Guitar and Backing Vocal
George Harrison : Violin, Lead Guitar and Backing Vocal
Ringo Starr : Drums
George Martin : Piano
Chorus : Includes Mick Jagger, Marianne Faithfull, Keith Richard, Gary Brooker and Keith Moon
Session Musicians : Four Violins, two Cellos, two Trumpets, two Trombones, two Saxophones and one Accordion

This is a completely different version of the track included on the Magical Mystery Tour album. This recording, although using the same pre-recorded rhythm track as the single, recorded during the *Our World* broadcast on 25 June 1967, has a different main track and lead vocal from John. This recording is also ten seconds shorter than the single and is in stereo whereas the single is in mono.

SIDE TWO

The George Martin Orchestra

Pepper Land (Martin) 2:18 , **Sea Of Time** (Martin) 2:58 ; **Sea Of Holes** (Martin)   2:14 ; **Sea Of Monsters** (Martin)   3:35 ; **March of the Meanies** (Martin)   2:16 ; **Pepper Land Laid Waste** (Martin)   2:09 ; **Yellow Submarine in Pepper Land** (Lennon–McCartney —arr. Martin)   2:10

ABBEY ROAD
Apple PCS 7088
Producer : George Martin
Release Date : 26 September 1969
Running Time : 46:54

SIDE ONE: Come Together; Something; Maxwell's Silver Hammer; Oh! Darling; Octopus's Garden; I Want You (She's So Heavy).

SIDE TWO: Here Comes The Sun; Because; You Never Give Me Your Money; Sun King; Mean Mr Mustard; Polythene Pam; She Came In Through The Bathroom Window; Golden Slumbers; Carry That Weight; The End; Her Majesty.

The Beatles were on the verge of splitting up after the bad feeling created during the ill-fated Get Back session (see also Chapter 19 Let It Be). Still trying to hold the group together, they briefly settled their personal and musical differences long enough to record Abbey Road, which was to be their last studio-recorded album. The tension that had grown within the Beatles since the death of Brian Epstein had now reached the point that they could no longer agree on anything, particularly their music. John's concept of Abbey Road was that it should be a basic rock and roll album like Get Back. Paul envisaged a 'pop opera' of different songs edited into one long medley. In the end they both got their way.

Side one of the album fulfills John's concept of individual tracks, which in the main are basically rock and roll. He contributes Come Together and I Want You (She's So Heavy), Paul his gutsy Oh! Darling and Maxwell's Silver Hammer, while George and Ringo contribute Something and Octopus's Garden, respectively.

Side two has Paul's now famous 'Pop Opera' of ten different songs (of which only eight are listed) edited along with George's Here Comes The Sun and John's Because to form a 16-minute medley.

The album contains some of the Beatles' most technically perfect recordings, and includes the use of a synthesiser. George suggested the instrument after he had recorded the album Electronic Sound using only a synthesiser. That album and his other solo venture Wonderwall (a soundtrack album consisting almost entirely of Indian music) showed that George's musical interests were no longer fitting into the framework of the Beatles. John, too, now discontented with being a Beatle, had also begun to pursue a solo career. With the help of Yoko Ono he had recorded Two Virgins and Life With The Lions, two albums consisting entirely of avant-garde sound. He had also issued a solo single Give Peace A Chance under the name of the Plastic Ono Band. He was to continue his solo career by issuing The Wedding Album, a third album of avant-garde sound; Live Peace in Toronto, a live recording of the Plastic Ono Band; and Cold Turkey—all within weeks of the release of Abbey Road. In fact, John had wanted the Beatles to record Cold Turkey as a new single, but neither Paul nor George was interested. John, along with Ringo, Eric Clapton and Klaus Voorman (the first real line-up of the Plastic Ono Band), recorded Cold Turkey and it was issued in direct competition with the Something/Come Together single (the first Beatles single issued in Britain from an album *after* the album had been issued).

Abbey Road, named after the location of the recording studios where the Beatles made most of their recordings, including this one, was the first Beatles' album to be issued solely in stereo. All previous Beatles' albums up to and including Yellow Submarine had been issued in both mono and stereo. This decision was made because the Beatles felt that their music should be heard in stereo and that the mono versus stereo argument that had raged through the late fifties and early sixties was now over, with most people accepting stereo. Other record companies soon followed suit and the mono versions of albums quickly disappeared. During the sessions for Abbey Road the Beatles recorded six other tracks including re-recordings of What's The New Mary Jane and Not Guilty, which were originally recorded during the White Album sessions. All six tracks were eventually rejected.

What's The New Mary Jane

John was planning to use this as a single under the name of the Plastic Ono
Band because the other Beatles kept rejecting it as a Beatles' single.
However, this time it was rejected by John.

Junk

This song eventually ended up on Paul's solo album McCartney.

Not Guilty

A George Harrison song of which where there were several versions, all of
which were rejected by the Beatles. It was eventually re-recorded by
George in 1979 and included on his George Harrison album.
    The other three songs—When I Come To Town, Four Nights In Moscow
and the oddly titled I Should Like To Live Up A Tree—have, along with
What's The New Mary Jane, yet to see the light of day.

The sleeve of the album shows the   Beatles walking across a zebra
crossing in Abbey Road, walking *away* from the recording studio. This, with
the album's closing track The End, was regarded by many as being a cryptic
message from the Beatles saying 'this is it, we've finished recording our final
album, we're walking away and splitting up'. An announcement to that effect
was to be made by Paul on 10 April 1970, almost six months after the release
of this album.

SIDE ONE

Come Together (Lennon—McCartney)   4:16

John Lennon : Lead Guitar, Electric Piano and Lead Vocal
Paul McCartney : Bass Guitar and Harmony Vocal
George Harrison : Lead Guitar
Ringo Starr : Drums and Maraccas

Written by John, this was originally intended to be a campaign song for
Timothy Leary, who was at one time proposing to run for the post of
Governor of California. The idea was dropped after Leary decided not to
run, and John changed the style of the song. It was eventually the subject of a
law suit as Maurice Levy, owner of the American music publishers Big
Seven Music, who hold the publishing rights to Chuck Berry's song You
Can't Catch Me, claimed that John had used two of the song's lines in Come
Together. To save months of legal arguments John agreed to record You
Can't Catch Me and Sweet Little Sixteen (also Berry's composition and
published by Maurice Levy's company) for his Rock and Roll solo album.
John had another problem with the song; the BBC banned it, because of a
reference to Coca Cola which they deemed to be advertising. The
recording features a lead vocal from John with harmonies in places from
Paul. Two lead guitars are used, one played by John, the other by George.

Something (Harrison) 2:59

John Lennon : Lead Guitar
Paul McCartney : Bass Guitar
George Harrison : Lead Guitar, Organ and Solo Vocal
Ringo Starr : Drums
Session Musicians : Strings

George sings solo vocal on this dramatic rendition of his own song which was inspired by his wife Patti. The orchestration is by the George Martin Orchestra. The song (which uses the title of James Taylor's Something In The Way She Moves as its opening line) ranks alongside some of the best Lennon—McCartney compositions as a very fine Beatle song.

Shortly after the album's release it was issued as the A-side of a single which had Come Together as its B-side. This was the first time a George Harrison song was used as an A-side (although previously, two of George's songs, The Inner Light and Old Brown Shoe had been issued as B-sides to Lady Madonna and The Ballad of John and Yoko, respectively). This was the first British Beatles' single since Penny Lane that failed to reach number one—its highest position was number four.

Maxwell's Silver Hammer (Lennon—McCartney) 3:24

John Lennon : Lead Guitar and Harmony/Backing Vocal
Paul McCartney : Bass Guitar, Piano and Lead/Backing Vocal
George Harrison : Acoustic Guitar and Synthesiser
Ringo Starr : Anvil and Drums

Paul's first song on the album features himself on lead vocal with harmonies in places from John; they also get together for the backing vocals. The track includes Paul on piano, Ringo banging a hammer on an anvil and for the first time on the album George plays a synthesiser. On the song's final line, 'silver hammer man', all four Beatles can be heard singing. The Beatles can be seen rehearsing this song in the film *Let It Be*.

Oh! Darling (Lennon—McCartney) 3:28

John Lennon : Backing Vocal
Paul McCartney : Bass Guitar, Piano and Lead/Backing Vocal
George Harrison : Lead Guitar and Synthesiser
Ringo Starr : Drums

Before recording the vocals for this dramatic track, Paul spent a week going early to the studios to practice and make his voice as harsh and gutsy as possible. The backing includes Paul on piano, a stabbing lead guitar from George that jumps out of the speakers and a wordless backing vocal from John and Paul. Paul re-wrote this for his 1973 album Band On The Run and called it Let Me Roll It.

Octopus's Garden (Starkey)   2:49

John Lennon : Lead Guitar and Backing Vocal
Paul McCartney : Bass Guitar, Piano and Backing Vocal
George Harrison : Lead Guitar and Synthesiser
Ringo Starr : Drums and Lead Vocal

This is the second song written by Ringo to be included on a Beatles' album—the first, Don't Pass Me By, was included twelve months earlier on the double album The Beatles. Although he found it difficult to write songs both are bouncy with infectious chorus lines. This song is reminiscent of Yellow Submarine particularly as it uses the same sound effects of water being swirled around in a bucket and bubbles being blown into water. Another interesting sound effect is the section of 'gargling' backing vocals. Ringo sings lead vocal with backing from John and Paul. As on the album's opening track Come Together, two lead guitars are played by John and George. Paul can be heard playing piano and George adds a synthesiser.

I Want You (She's So Heavy) (Lennon–McCartney)   7:49

John Lennon : Lead Guitar, Organ and Lead Vocal
Paul McCartney : Bass Guitar and Harmony Vocal
George Harrison : Rhythm Guitar, Synthesiser and White Noise Generator
Ringo Starr : Drums

With the exception of Revolution 9 this is the longest recording issued by the Beatles—even 38 seconds longer than Hey Jude, which clocks in at 7:11. The track is really two separate songs, I Want You and She's So Heavy, joined together, but without a link. Each is sung in segments throughout the recording with I Want You, sung repeatedly, predominating, and She's So Heavy inserted twice. Lead vocal and blues-style lead guitar are from John with Paul harmonising here and there. The ending features a persistent guitar riff being repeated maddeningly. Then George Harrison adds a synthesiser and a white noise generator building up the sound seemingly for ever until suddenly it stops.

SIDE TWO

Here Comes The Sun (Harrison)   3:40

John Lennon : Acoustic Guitar and Backing Vocal
Paul McCartney : Bass Guitar and Backing Vocal
George Harrison : Acoustic Guitar, Synthesiser and Lead Vocal
Ringo Starr : Drums
Session Musicians : Strings

To escape from the pressures of work, George took a day off from the recording session and sat in Eric Clapton's garden on one of the first days of spring and wrote this song. It's his second song on this album—he sings lead vocal and plays synthesiser and acoustic guitar. Harmonies and backing vocals are from John and Paul. The intro starts on the left-hand channel with an acoustic guitar and synthesiser, then floats across the stereo to the

108

right-hand channel as George begins to sing. This recording features the same instrumental break as Badge, a song co-written by George Harrison and Eric Clapton and recorded by Clapton's group Cream. The song is also structured in a similar way to an earlier George Harrison composition, If I Needed Someone.

Because (Lennon–McCartney)   2:45

John Lennon : Lead Guitar, Harpsichord and Lead Vocal
Paul McCartney : Bass Guitar and Lead Vocal
George Harrison : Synthesiser
Ringo Starr : Not Present

John got the idea for this song when he heard Yoko play Beethoven's Moonlight Sonata. John suggested that she play it backwards, which she did. He then slightly re-structured it and added the lyrics. It features a close-harmony vocal from John and Paul with John also playing harpsichord and George adding a cleverly programmed synthesiser. A section of this track can be heard on John and Yoko's Wedding Album.

You Never Give Me Your Money (Lennon–McCartney)   3:57

John Lennon : Lead Guitar and Backing Vocal
Paul McCartney : Piano, Bass Guitar and Lead/Backing Vocal
George Harrison : Rhythm Guitar
Ringo Starr : Drums and Tambourine

This is a medley of four separate songs written by Paul. The first, You Never Give Me Your Money, features Paul singing solo and backing himself on piano. It was written about the boardroom squabbles at Apple and the arguments between the Beatles themselves. The second song, That Magic Feeling, features a honky-tonk style backing piano and Paul's vocals sound rougher—more like his Little Richard style. The third song, One Sweet Dream, is linked to That Magic Feeling by a wordless chorus from John and Paul. This is another up-beat rock and roll song featuring Paul in fine voice. The fourth song comes in only as the track fades, John and Paul repeat 'one-two-three- four-five-six-seven, all good children go to heaven'. These four songs have been successfully welded to form one. The track has a long fade-out overlapping the intro of the following track.

Sun King (Lennon–McCartney)   2:31

John Lennon : Lead Guitar, Maraccas and All Vocals
Paul McCartney : Bass Guitar and Harmonium
George Harrison : Lead Guitar
Ringo Starr : Drums and Bongos
George Martin : Organ

John, who wrote this song, originally intended to call it Los Paranoios, claiming that it came to him in a dream. This might explain the lyrics which are a mixture of Spanish, Italian, French and nonsense. The sound of crickets chirping opens the track with a bluesy lead guitar. John's vocals are double-tracked for the lead, then multi-tracked to produce his own harmonies. In addition to their usual instruments John plays maraccas, Paul harmonium and Ringo bongos. George Martin joins them on organ.

Mean Mr Mustard (Lennon–McCartney)   1:06

John Lennon : Piano and Lead Vocal
Paul McCartney : Fuzz Bass Guitar and Harmony Vocal
George Harrison : Lead Guitar
Ringo Starr : Drums and Tambourine

John wrote this when he was meditating in India. Nevertheless his strong Liverpudlian accent gives his lead vocal a local flavour. Paul harmonises here and there and also plays fuzz bass guitar for the first time since 1965 when he played on George Harrison's Think For Yourself on Rubber Soul.

Polythene Pam (Lennon–McCartney)   1:13

John Lennon : Acoustic Guitar, Lead Guitar and Lead Vocal
Paul McCartney : Bass Guitar, Lead Guitar and Harmony Vocal
George Harrison : Rhythm Guitar and Tambourine
Ringo Starr : Drums and Maraccas

Written in India, by John, about a mythical prostitute in Liverpool. The track is based on a persistent lead guitar riff. A second version lasting approximately three minutes was recorded but has yet to be issued.

She Came In Through The Bathroom Window
(Lennon–McCartney)   1:58

John Lennon : Acoustic Guitar and Harmony/Backing Vocal
Paul McCartney : Lead Guitar and Lead/Backing Vocal
George Harrison : Bass Guitar and Tambourine
Ringo Starr : Drums and Maraccas

This song harks back to the days of the Beatles' early sixties American tours, when fans would literally do anything to see their idols. One in particular, undaunted by the fact that the Beatles were staying on the upper floors of a hotel, scaled a drainpipe and broke into Paul's suite through the bathroom window. Paul sings lead vocal and joins John for the backing vocals.

Golden Slumbers (Lennon–McCartney)   1:31

John Lennon : Not Present
Paul McCartney : Bass Guitar, Piano and Solo Vocal
George Harrison : Not Present
Ringo Starr : Drums
Session Musicians : Strings

During a stay at his father's house in Heswall, not far from Liverpool, Paul wrote this lilting melody with dramatic overtones. He took the lyrics (originally from a 400-year-old poem written by Thomas Dekker) from his step-sister's music book. As he could not read the music to accompany himself on piano he improvised his own version.

Carry That Weight (Lennon–McCartney)   1:37

John Lennon : Bass Guitar and Lead Vocal
Paul McCartney ; Piano and Lead Vocal
George Harrison : Lead Guitar and Lead Vocal
Ringo Starr : Drums and Lead Vocal
Session Musicians : Strings and Brass

Paul McCartney wrote this song about the responsibility of keeping the Beatles together after Brian Epstein's death in 1967. The first section has a four-part harmony from the Beatles; the second section is the second verse of You Never Give Me Your Money, which appears earlier on the album. This part features Paul McCartney on lead vocal backed by himself on piano and George Martin and orchestra. The track then returns to the original melody of Carry That Weight, with all four Beatles on vocals.

The End (Lennon–McCartney)   2:04

John Lennon : Lead Guitar and Backing Vocal
Paul McCartney : Bass Guitar, Piano and Lead/Backing Vocal
George Harrison : Rhythm Guitar and Backing Vocal
Ringo Starr : Drums
Session Musicians : Strings

This track is made up of four parts. It begins with Paul McCartney singing one verse of a song unconnected with the rest of the track. A 16-second drum solo by Ringo follows (his first on a Beatles' record). The track then changes into a jam session reminiscent of the instrumental break in Good Morning, Good Morning on Sgt. Pepper, with John, Paul and George alternating lead guitar solos, while a monotonous 'love you', sung by John, Paul and George is repeated 24 times. As this section, which lasts for just under a minute, stops the piano begins and John and Paul duet on the final verse. There is a break of 18 seconds' silence before the last short track.

Her Majesty (Lennon–McCartney)   0:23

John Lennon : Not Present
Paul McCartney : Acoustic Guitar and Solo Vocal
George Harrison : Not Present
Ringo Starr : Not Present

With a certain tongue-in-cheek irony, this could be regarded as a re-written version of the British National Anthem with Paul on solo vocal and acoustic guitar. It is the last track on the last Beatles' album.

HEY JUDE
Parlophone PCS 7184
Producer : George Martin
Release Date : May 1979
Running Time : 32:59

SIDE ONE: Can't Buy Me Love; I Should Have Known Better; Paperback Writer; Rain; Lady Madonna; Revolution.

SIDE TWO: Hey Jude; Old Brown Shoe; Don't Let Me Down; The Ballad Of John And Yoko.

Previously only available on import from the USA, this album was not issued in Britain until 1979, although it is one of the best compilations of previously issued Beatles' tracks. These include singles issued between 1968 and 1969, both sides of the Paperback Writer single issued in 1966, Can't Buy Me Love and I Should Have Known Better. The last two are out of sequence recordings included in preference to The Inner Light and Get Back even though their respective A- and B-sides Lady Madonna and Don't Let Me Down are included.

SIDE ONE

Can't Buy Me Love (Lennon–McCartney)   2:15

John Lennon : Rhythm Guitar
Paul McCartney : Bass Guitar and Solo Vocal
George Harrison : Lead Guitar
Ringo Starr : Drums

Previously reviewed on the A Hard Day's Night album.

I Should Have Known Better (Lennon–McCartney)   2:42

John Lennon : Acoustic Guitar, Harmonica and Solo Vocal
Paul McCartney : Bass Guitar
George Harrison : Lead Guitar
Ringo Starr : Drums

Previously reviewed on the A Hard Day's Night album.

Paperback Writer (Lennon–McCartney)   2:25

John Lennon : Rhythm Guitar and Backing Vocal
Paul McCartney : Bass Guitar and Lead Vocal
George Harrison : Lead Guitar and Backing Vocal
Ringo Starr : Drums

Recorded during the sessions for Revolver and issued as a single just prior to its release, this song, written by Paul, was inspired by John Lennon's two books *In His Own Write* and *Spaniard In The Works*, and tells of Paul's wish to become a writer too. It begins with an a capella introduction, followed by one of the best instrumental backings on any Beatles' record. The guitar sound on this record could be regarded as a foretaste of heavy metal. The lead vocal comes from Paul, who also joins John and George for the three-part-harmony backing vocals, which are a repetition of the title, with the curious inclusion of 'Frere Jaques'.

Rain (Lennon–McCartney)   2:59

John Lennon : Rhythm Guitar and Lead Vocal
Paul McCartney : Bass Guitar and Backing Vocal
George Harrison : Lead Guitar and Backing Vocal
Ringo Starr : Drums and Tambourine

Previously issued as the B-side to Paperback Writer, this track features a stronger heavy guitar sound than the A-side, making the latter sound rather tame. The sound was to influence artists such as The Who, Cream and Jimi Hendrix. The guitars attack from the beginning; Ringo's superb drumbeat accentuates the heaviness of the sound and John's laconic sententious lead vocal grinds out of the left-hand channel. At the end of this recording one line of John's vocal is played backwards. 'Rain, when the rain comes they run and hide their heads'. (Note the substitution of 'when' for 'if'.) Apparently, John took a copy of the master tape home and accidentally played it backwards, liked it, and included it on the final record. After this experiment backwards-playing tapes were also included on I'm Only Sleeping and Tomorrow Never Knows on Revolver.

Lady Madonna (Lennon–McCartney) 2:17

John Lennon : Backing Vocal
Paul McCartney : Bass Guitar, Piano and Lead Vocal
George Harrison : Lead Guitar and Backing Vocal
Ringo Starr : Drums
Ronnie Scott : Saxophone
Harry Klein : Saxophone
Bill Povey : Saxophone
Bill Jackman : Saxophone

This was the last single issued by the Beatles on the Parlophone label in 1968, before the dream of Apple became a reality later that year. It is written and sung by Paul, who also plays piano in true rock and roll style, showing the influence of Little Richard, Jerry Lee Lewis and Elvis Presley. The song is rather like a rock version of his earlier Eleanor Rigby with loneliness again as the main theme. The backing includes saxophones played by Ronnie Scott, Harry Klein, Bill Povey and Bill Jackman. The saxophone solo in the middle was originally some 15–20 seconds longer, but was edited.

Revolution (Lennon–McCartney) 3:22

John Lennon : Lead Guitar and Solo Vocal
Paul McCartney : Bass Guitar, Organ and Piano
George Harrison : Lead Guitar
Ringo Starr : Drums

This track was previously issued as the B-side to the Beatles' first Apple single Hey Jude in August 1968. The sound of a distorted guitar, played by John, is heard at the beginning of the record. Ringo joins in with an electronically compressed drumbeat giving the recording a solid 'heavy' sound. John's lead vocals were recorded several times, as he was not satisfied with them. Then as an experiment he lay down on the floor and recorded them once more. This was the sound that he wanted.

Later in the recording John is joined by Paul on piano, and George playing a second, distorted guitar. The lyrics and distorted guitar sound made this one of the Beatles' most controversial recordings.

SIDE TWO

Hey Jude (Lennon—McCartney) 7:11

John Lennon : Acoustic Guitar and Backing Vical
Paul McCartney : Bass Guitar, Piano and Lead Vocal
George Harrison : Lead Guitar and Backing Vocal
Ringo Starr : Drums and Tambourine
Session Musicians : 40 Piece Orchestra

This was the A-side of the first single issued by the Beatles on their own Apple label, in August 1968. It was the longest single issued to that date, totalling with its B-side Revolution, 10 minutes and 33 seconds, which made the record very good value for the money. Written by Paul, the song had started out as Hey Jules, about John's son Julian. Paul sings lead vocal and accompanies himself on piano with backing vocals from John and George. The song starts simply, the main part lasting three minutes and 11 seconds, but builds up until it finally explodes into a 4-minute fade-out-the longest on a Beatles' record. The fade consists of all four Beatles plus a 40-piece orchestra playing and singing along to a one-line chorus 'na-na-na-na'.

Old Brown Shoe (Harrison) 3:16

John Lennon : Backing Vocal
Paul McCartney : Bass Guitar, Piano and Backing Vocal
George Harrison : Lead Guitar and Lead Vocal
Ringo Starr : Drums
Billy Preston : Organ

Originally issued as the B-side to a 1969 single the Ballad of John and Yoko, this was the second George Harrison song used as the B-side of a Beatles' single. The first was The Inner Light on the B-side of Lady Madonna in 1968. Reputed to have been recorded during the Get Back sessions in January 1969, it features George on lead vocals and lead guitar, with John and Paul adding harmony vocals. Paul adds piano, and the organ is widely believed to have been played by Billy Preston, who joined the Beatles for the Get Back sessions.
This was quite an up-tempo song from George, who during the previous two years had been writing either Indian mantras or slower more doleful songs like While My Guitar Gently Weeps and Blue Jay Way.

Don't Let Me Down (Lennon—McCartney) 3:34

John Lennon : Lead Guitar and Lead Vocal
Paul McCartney : Bass Guitar and Harmony Vocal
George Harrison : Rhythm Guitar
Ringo Starr : Drums
Billy Preston : Organ

Previously issued as the B-side to the Get Back single in April 1969, this recording features an extremely raw lead vocal from John Lennon, with harmony vocals from Paul McCartney. The Beatles are joined by Billy

Preston on backing and some interesting solo organ passages. The lyrics are minimal with John simply repeating the title. This is a powerful blues-influenced track.

The Ballad Of John And Yoko (Lennon—McCartney)   2:58

John Lennon : Acoustic Guitar, Lead Guitar and Lead Vocal
Paul McCartney : Bass Guitar, Drums, Piano, Maraccas and Harmony Vocal
George Harrison : Not Present
Ringo Starr : Not Present

This was released as a single on 20 May 1969 two months after John and Yoko married in Gibraltar. John and Paul play all instruments, with John on lead vocal, acoustic and lead guitars and Paul on bass guitar, drums, piano and maraccas plus harmony vocals. The song tells the story of John and Yoko's wedding and their subsequent week-long bed-in for peace at the Amsterdam Hilton, where they recorded the classic anthem Give Peace A Chance. In return for Paul's help in recording The Ballad Of John and Yoko, John gave him joint writer credits on Give Peace A Chance, although Paul had little to do with either its writing or its production.

LET IT BE
Apple PXS 1/PCS 7096
Producer : George Martin and
Phil Spector
Release Dates : 8 May 1970;
6 November 1970
Running Time : 35:07

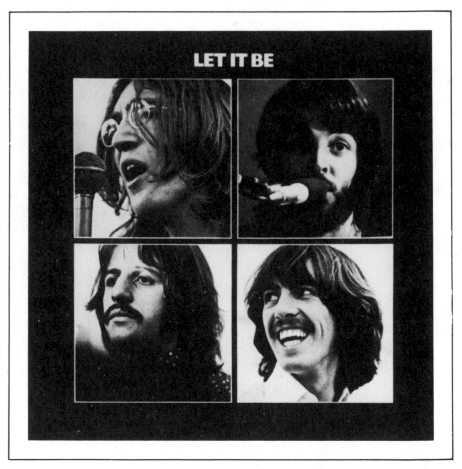

SIDE ONE: Two Of Us; Dig A Pony; Across The Universe; I Me Mine; Let It Be; Maggie Mae.

SIDE TWO: I've Got A Feeling; One After 909; The Long And Winding Road; For You Blue; Get Back.

It is interesting that Abbey Road was recorded *after* this album. Let It Be was originally called Get Back and intended as the soundtrack for a television film of the same name. It was to have been the official follow-up to the double album, The Beatles.

The idea originally came from John, who wanted to record an album that was not necessarily reliant upon techninal tricks, overdubs or electronic wizardry. What he wanted was an album of up-to-date but basic Beatle music, without studio effects. Paul then suggested that they make a film showing the Beatles in the studio recording the album—and so recording and filming began on 2 January 1969 and finished on 30 January 1969 with the now famous concert on the roof of the Apple Office in Londons Saville Row.

The album and film were not finally released until a year later, as they were delayed by Allen Klein, the Beatles' financial adviser. When released, the title was changed to Let It Be.

Klein had been called in originally by John against Paul's wishes to manage the Beatles' affairs, but initially proved valuable when he re-negotiated the contract with EMI to give the Beatles a higher royalty payment from their records. Now, with his eye on a better commercial proposition, he suggested that the proposed television film made originally in 16mm should be blown up to 35mm and marketed as a new Beatles' cinema film.

As this would take time, and as the Get Back single had been released already, in April 1969, Klein suggested that film and album be re-scheduled and retitled Let It Be and that a single of the same name be issued to promote both.

The Get Back album, which got as far as being pressed and sent to radio stations in both the USA and Canada, was never released to record stores because Klein felt that it could be improved. Originally it consisted of the following tracks: One After 909, Save The Last Dance For Me, Don't Let Me Down, Dig A Pony, I've Got A Feeling, Get Back, For You Blue, The Walk, Teddy Boy, Two Of Us, Maggie Mae, Dig It, Let It Be, The Long And Winding Road and Get Back.

Klein also wanted the 'live' recordings of Get Back and Don't Let Me Down scrapped and replaced with studio recordings although the first made it through to the Let It Be album.

Because of the delay between recording and release of the final album, the Beatles lost interest in the possibility of themselves improving the original album, so John invited Phil Spector (who had worked with him on Instant Karma, and who was to work with both John and George later) to produce the album as Let It Be. Spector sifted through 24 hours of recorded material in which there were many different versions of each song. He eventually salvaged the album, which he remixed and overdubbed strings on Let It Be, Across The Universe and I Me Mine, and strings *and* a heavenly choir on The Long And Winding Road to the apparent dissatisfaction of Paul McCartney who had envisioned the recording with only himself on vocals and piano, and John on bass guitar.

This was the first album since the Beatles signed with EMI for which George Martin did not have complete responsibility. Although he had produced the original recordings, the final production was left to Spector whose syrupy technique did little to hide the Beatles' sloppy playing. One wonders if he really did choose the best possible versions of each track as the inevitable bootlegs, such as Sweet Apple Tracks, include far better alternatives.

The album was packaged as a boxed set complete with book (exactly as had been planned for Get Back). It was also given the catalogue number held for the original Get Back album package (PXS 1). It went on sale in Britain on 8 May 1970 at £1 more than other albums, and sold poorly. After six months the album was re-issued on 6 November 1970, separately, without the book (as PCS 7096), but because of the time lag it did not sell well although it picked up sales at Christmas.

From 96 hours of recorded film, *Let It Be* finally emerged as a 90-minute semi-documentary, about the recording of the Get Back album. The film is as embarrassing to watch as the album is to listen to. It shows four rather unhappy looking individuals involved in petty squabbles. After one scene, where Paul and George are seen arguing over a guitar riff, George left for three days and filming had to be halted until he returned. It is a sad spectacle, showing the public break-up of one of the world's greatest pop groups. One can only hope that one day enough will be salvaged from the remaining 94½ hours of footage to make a second movie. Certainly the Beatles were captured on film performing many rock and roll standards and reworkings of a number of their old songs. The most exciting surviving part of the film, shown at the end of the movie, is the impromptu concert on the roof of the Apple office in London's Saville Row. This shows the stunned and excited reaction of lunchtime shoppers and office workers in the area to the unbelievable noise of a Beatles' concert drifting down from the roof to the streets below. The Beatles manage to perform five songs (I Dig A Pony, I've Got A Feeling, One After 909, Don't Let Me Down and Get Back) before the arrival of the police to stop the concert.

An interesting postscript is that Get Back was not the only album to be planned from the material but which never reached the shops. There were two more, which although taken to the final stages were never given working titles. The second was to have been re-recordings of old Beatles' tracks. Love Me Do, Norwegian Wood and She Said, She Said were announced as prospective tracks. The third album was to have consisted of 14 old rock and roll standards without any Beatle-written songs. Tracks recorded for this included Shake Rattle and Roll, All Shook Up, Good Golly Miss Molly and Johny B. Goode.

It is also interesting to document the events which followed Let It Be. After the recording sessions for Abbey Road (after this album) finished in August 1969 both Paul and Ringo began work on their first solo albums (John and George had already done so). Ringo's first solo album, Sentimental Journey, a run-through of 12 old standards, was issued on 27 March 1970 and Paul McCartney's album, McCartney, a selection of left-over Beatles' songs and instrumentals, was issued on 17 April 1970, a few weeks prior to the release of the Let It Be album. John, George and Ringo were not pleased that Paul was about to issue a solo album in competition with a Beatles' album. As he could not be persuaded otherwise, Ringo was sent by John to try and change his mind. On 10 April 1970, exactly one week prior to the release of the McCartney album, Paul announced that he was leaving the Beatles, a statement that shook and saddened all Beatles' fans. Many also thought that Paul's statement was a little too well timed to tie in with the release of his first solo album.

After Paul left the group John, George and Ringo considered recruiting Klaus Voormann (on bass) and forming The Ladders. This line-up did get together once in 1973 with Billy Preston when they recorded the track I'm The Greatest for Ringo's solo album Ringo (Apple PCTC 252).

SIDE ONE

Two Of Us (Lennon–McCartney) 3:33

John Lennon : Acoustic Guitar and Lead Vocal
Paul McCartney : Acoustic Guitar and Lead Vocal
George Harrison : Lead Guitar
Ringo Starr : Drums

Just before this track begins a snatch of studio conversation is included and John proclaims 'I dig a pygmy by Charles Hawtrey and the Deaf Aids—Phase one, in which Doris gets her oats'. Two Of Us was written by Paul as a duet for himself and John, possibly as a reaction to the arrival of Yoko Ono who was claiming all of John's attention. When the song was originally recorded it was called On Our Way Home. After the Get Back album was scrapped Paul gave the song to one of Apple's latest signings, a New York trio called Mortimer, who recorded the song under its original title in May 1969. The recording, produced by Paul, never appeared and nothing has been heard of Mortimer since.

   The track is a close harmony duet between John and Paul (who also play acoustic guitars) with Paul soloing in places. George adds lead guitar with Ringo on drums (memories of the 'three guitars and drums' sound of the early sixties). The song is featured twice in the film Let It Be; first, in rehearsal, slightly up-tempo when John and Paul ad-lib the lyrics, and secondly, when they play the complete song which is the version issued on this album.

Dig A Pony (Lennon–McCartney) 3:55

John Lennon : Lead Guitar and Lead Vocal
Paul McCartney : Bass Guitar and Harmony Vocal
George Harrison : Rhythm Guitar
Ringo Starr : Drums
Billy Preston : Organ

The first of the four 'live' recordings (taken from the 30 January 1969 rooftop concert) included on the album, this was written by John as two separate songs, All I Want Is You and Dig A Pony. When the track listing for the Get Back album was announced, this track was called All I Want Is You, but when the album was compiled the title was changed to Dig A Pony. It has a false start then a lead vocal from John with harmonies from Paul. The lyrics sound as if they could have been made up on the spot. John makes references to the Rolling Stones and Johnny and The Moondogs (one of the Beatles' earlier names). At the end of the recording John can be heard complaining that his hands are cold. The recording sounds rough both in instrumentation and the falsetto harmonies from John and Paul.

   It should be noted that the album's American sleeve lists this track as I Dig A Pony.

Across The Universe (Lennon–McCartney) 3:51

John Lennon : Acoustic Guitar, Lead Guitar, Organ (With George Martin) and Solo Vocal
Paul McCartney : Piano
George Harrison : Sitar
Ringo Starr : Maraccas
George Martin : Organ (With John)
Session Musicians : (Overdubbed) Strings and Choir

The original recording of this song, which appears on the charity album No One's Gonna Change Our World (Regal Starline SRS 5018) is a far superior version (see the Rarities album). Unfortunately Phil Spector's heavenly choirs and slushy orchestras, over-dubbed in March 1970, have destroyed the original simplicity of the song. This recording is slightly slower than the original, as if it has been deliberately slowed down from its recorded speed, which unfortunately gives John's voice a whining quality. The original recording featured backing vocals from Paul and two female singers (See Rarities album); these are not included in this version.

I Me Mine (Harrison) 2:25

John Lennon : Lead Guitar and Harmony Vocal
Paul McCartney : Piano and Harmony Vocal
George Harrison : Acoustic Guitar and Lead Vocal
Ringo Starr : Drums
Billy Preston : Organ
Session Musicians : (Overdubbed) Strings

Reputedly, this was recorded on 3 January 1970, and is therefore the last recording made by the Beatles. Bearing a distinct resemblance to Harrison's earlier Savoy Truffle on The White Album, it opens with a dramatic organ from Billy Preston with George on acoustic guitar, Paul on piano, John on lead guitar and Ringo on drums. The vocals are mainly a solo from George with John and Paul joining on chorus. This track also has an over-dubbed orchestra, but thankfully Phil Spector has not mixed them too far forward.

Dig It (Lennon–McCartney–Harrison–Starkey) 0:51

John Lennon : Solo Vocal
Paul McCartney : Piano
George Harrison : Lead Guitar
Ringo Starr : Drums
Billy Preston : **Organ**

The original recording of this track lasts for nearly five minutes, and was included in its entirety on the Get Back album. This short extract fades in with John singing odd, unconnected lines held together with the insistent chorus of 'dig it'. Billy Preston is on organ, Paul on piano and Ringo on drums. As the track fades John announces 'that was "can you dig it" by Georgie Wood now we'd like to do" Ark the Angels Come ";' Let It Be then begins.

Let It Be (Lennon–McCartney)   4:01

John Lennon : Lead Guitar
Paul McCartney : Piano and Solo Vocal
George Harrison : Bass Guitar
Ringo Starr : Drums
Billy Preston : Organ
Session Musicians : (Overdubbed) Horns and Organ

The song is dedicated to Paul's late mother, Mary, and includes a reference to 'Mother Mary' (also with religious implications, reminiscent of Lady Madonna) in the lyrics.

A different version was issued as a single two months earlier on 6 March 1970 (Apple R5833). Both feature the same line-up of Paul on lead vocal and piano, John on lead guitar, Ringo on drums, with Billy Preston on organ.

This is a lot sloppier than the single version, especially John's lead guitar. Phil Spector's overdub of brass and choir ruins the original arrangement and his mixing is disastrous; near the end Paul battles with John's lead guitar which has been mixed too far forward.

Maggie Mae (Trad. Arr.–Lennon–McCartney–Harrison–Starkey)   0:39

John Lennon : Acoustic Guitar and Lead Vocal
Paul McCartney : Acoustic Guitar and Harmony Vocal
George Harrison : Bass Guitar and Harmony Vocal
Ringo Starr : Drums

Here, the Beatles interpret a traditional old Liverpudlian song. John is on lead vocal with Paul and George harmonising. John and Paul play acoustic guitars and Ringo, drums. The Beatles quite often did short renditions of songs like this to 'warm up' their recordings sessions. This is one of only a few such tracks and to be released (see Chapter 44 *Unreleased Tracks*).

SIDE TWO

I've Got A Feeling (Lennon–McCartney)   3:38

John Lennon : Lead Guitar and Lead Vocal
Paul McCartney : Bass Guitar and Lead Vocal
George Harrison : Rhythm Guitar
Ringo Starr : Drums
Billy Preston : Organ

The second 'live' recording on the album taken from the rooftop concert on 30 January 1969 sounds as rough as the previous live track, Dig A Pony, on side one. George's heavily distorted rythm guitar provides the intro. The verses are split between John and Paul with Paul on lead vocal for the first two. John leads on the second two and finally there is an interesting interchange between stereo channels, with Paul on the left, repeating the first two verses, and John on the right-hand channel, repeating the third and fourth verses. The line-up is John on lead guitar, Paul on bass guitar, George on rhythm guitar, Ringo on drums and Billy Preston on organ.

One After 909 (Lennon – McCartney)   2:52

John Lennon : Lead Guitar and Lead Vocal
Paul McCartney : Bass Guitar and Lead Vocal
George Harrison : Rhythm Guitar
Ringo Starr : Drums
Billy Preston : Organ

This is one of John's earliest songs, which he revived especially for the Get Back project. Again this is a rough-sounding recording, also taken from the rooftop concert. The vocals are a duet between John and Paul with John singing solo for one verse.

At the end of the track John goes into an off-the-cuff rendition of Danny Boy, not credited on either record label or sleeve.

The Long And Winding Road (Lennon – McCartney)   3:40

John Lennon : Bass Guitar
Paul McCartney : Piano and Solo Vocal
George Harrison : Not Present
Ringo Starr : Not Present
Session Musicians : (Overdubbed) Choir, Strings, Harp and Drums

Paul McCartney's ballad is overlaid with Spector's choirs and orchestras. Originally, Paul backed himself on piano while John provided the accompaniment on bass guitar.

For You Blue (Harrison)   2:33

John Lennon : Steel Guitar
Paul McCartney : Bass Guitar and Piano
George Harrison : Acoustic Guitar and Solo Vocal
Ringo Starr : Drums

Prior to this track another snatch of studio chat can be heard from John: 'the Queen says no to pot smoking FBI members'. Musically this is quite good, but at the same time it still seems like a rehearsal recording. It features a lead vocal from George who also plays acoustic guitar, with John on a steel guitar, Paul on bass and Ringo on drums. Although the Beatles' music changed between 1962 and 1970 the return to a basic four-instrument sound is quite evident on this recording. Curiously, although this track is called For You Blue, the title is not mentioned anywhere in the lyrics.

Get Back (Lennon – McCartney)   3:09

John Lennon : Lead Guitar and Harmony Vocal
Paul McCartney : Bass Guitar and Lead Vocal
George Harrison : Rhythm Guitar
Ringo Starr : Drums
Billy Preston : Organ

The recording starts with Paul saying 'Rosetta, Oh Rosetta' which prompts

John to launch into 'Sweet Rosetta Fart, she thought she was a cleaner, but she was a frying pan'. Although a live recording, the quality is comparable with the studio version issued as a single instead of this one as planned. The track features a lead vocal from Paul, who wrote the song, with harmonies in places from John. This recording omits the final verse of the song which is included on the studio version. The track ends with John saying poignantly 'I'd like to say "thank you" on behalf of the group and ourselves. I hope we've passed the audition.'

THE BEATLES 1962-1966 (2 L.P.s)
Apple PCSP 717
Producer : George Martin
Release Date : 20 April 1973
Running Time : 61:26

The Beatles / 1962-1966

SIDE ONE: Love Me Do; Please Please Me; From Me To You; She Loves You; I Want To Hold Your Hand; All My Loving; Can't Buy Me Love.
SIDE TWO: A Hard Day's Night; And I Love Her; Eight Days A Week; I Feel Fine; Ticket To Ride; Yesterday.

SIDE THREE: Help!; You've Got To Hide Your Love Away; We Can Work It Out; Day Tripper; Drive My Car; Norwegian Wood (This Bird Has Flown).
SIDE FOUR: Nowhere Man; Michelle; In My Life; Girl; Paperback Writer; Eleanor Rigby; Yellow Submarine.

THE BEATLES 1967-1970 (2 L.P.s)
Apple PCSP 718
Producers : George Martin and
Phil Spector
Release Date : 20 April 1973
Running Time : 99:01

SIDE ONE: Strawberry Fields Forever;
Penny Lane; Sgt. Pepper's Lonely Hearts
Club Band; With A Little Help From My
Friends; Lucy In The Sky With Diamonds; A
Day In The Life; All You Need Is Love.
SIDE TWO: I Am The Walrus; Hello
Goodbye; The Fool On The Hill; Magical
Mystery Tour; Lady Madonna; Hey Jude;
Revolution.

SIDE THREE: Back In The U.S.S.R.; While My
Guitar Gently Weeps; Ob-La-Di, Ob-La-Da;
Get Back; Don't Let Me Down; The Ballad Of
John And Yoko; Old Brown Shoe.
SIDE FOUR: Here Comes The Sun; Come
Together; Something; Octopus's Garden; Let
It Be; Across The Universe; The Long And
Winding Road.

Although it was three years after the Let It Be album of May 1970 before the next Beatles' album was released, it was worth waiting for. It was not one album but four, compiling the Beatles' greatest hits, selected by themselves. Although its release was planned to combat the ever-growing numbers of bootleg compilations it is excellent, nonetheless. The four albums, as the titles suggest, trace the Beatles' recording history from the first single Love Me Do in 1962 to 1970 and Let It Be. All the Beatles' number one hit songs are included, plus all the A-sides of the singles and a fair selection of tracks from almost every L.P. released. Every one of the 54 tracks is Beatle-written, either by Lennon and McCartney, George Harrison or Ringo Starr. In a way, it is sad that one or two of the 24 non-Beatle written tracks were not included, but as they wrote so many highly commercial songs, there just wasn't room for any songs they didn't write. Similarly, although the Beatles' solo material was also considered, there was not sufficient space.

The first double album, The Beatles 1962 – 1966, contains all the A-sides of the Beatles' singles issued on Parlophone up to the end of 1966, plus a selection of album tracks from the same period, namely, All My Loving from With The Beatles, Eight Days A Week from Beatles For Sale, Yesterday from Help! and Norwegian Wood and Michelle from Rubber Soul. These two albums consist solely of Lennon-McCartney songs.

The second double album, The Beatles 1967 – 1970, compiles the remaining A-sides of singles, plus a further selection of album tracks issued during that period. Of the 28 tracks, three (While My Guitar Gently Weeps, Old Brown Shoe and Something) are written by George Harrison. Octopus's Garden is written by Ringo and the remaining 24 tracks are written by Lennon and McCartney.

The sleeves of these two double albums show two photographs, taken eight years apart, of the Beatles in the same pose. The first is that used in 1963 for the Please Please Me album; the second taken in 1969 had been planned for the unreleased Get Back album. It was good that this was not scrapped as the two make an effective pair. They differ in their coloured borders—the first is red, the second blue, reputedly picked by the Beatles themselves for their Liverpool fans to show the colours of Liverpool's two football clubs, Liverpool and Everton. In the late 1970s when coloured vinyl records became popular, these two double albums were re-issued on coloured vinyl, the first on red, the second on blue. To date, these are the only Beatles' albums available in Britain on coloured vinyl, although other albums are available elsewhere in the world in varying colours. Because of this they have the additional letters R and B (for Red and Blue) in their catalogue number prefixes. They make interesting (although expensive if you already own the black vinyl copies) additions to a Beatles collection

THE BEATLES 1962-1966

Side One

Love Me Do   2:19
Please Please Me   2:00
From Me To You   1:55
She Loves You   2:18
I Want To Hold Your Hand   2:24
All My Loving   2:04
Can't Buy Me Love   2:15

Side Two

A Hard Day's Night   2:32
And I Love Her   2:27
Eight Days A Week   2:43
I Feel Fine   2:19
Ticket To Ride   3:03
Yesterday   2:04

Side Three

James Bond Theme (Monty
   Norman)   0:16*
Help!   2:16
You've Got To Hide Your Love
   Away   2:08
We Can Work It Out   2:10
Day Tripper   2:37
Drive My Car   2:25
Norwegian Wood (This Bird Has
   Flown)   2:00
The George Martin Orchestra (U.S. copies only)

Side Four

Nowhere Man   2:40
Michelle   2:42
In My Life   2:23
Girl   2:26
Paperback Writer   2:25
Eleanor Rigby   2:11
Yellow Submarine   2:40

THE BEATLES 1967 - 1970

Side One

Strawberry Fields Forever   4:05
Penny Lane   3:00
Sgt. Pepper's Lonely Hearts
   Club Band   1:59
With A Little Help From My
   Friends   2:46
Lucy In The Sky With Diamonds   3:25
A Day In The Life   5:03
All You Need Is Love   3:57

Side Two

I Am The Walrus   4:35
Hello Goodbye   3:24
The Fool On The Hill   3:00
Magical Mystery Tour   2:48
Lady Madonna   2:17
Hey Jude   7:11
Revolution   3:22

Side Three

Back In The U.S.S.R.   2:45
While My Guitar Gently Weeps
   (Harrison)   4:46
Ob-La-Di, Ob-La-Da   3:10
Get Back   3:11
Don't Let Me Down   3:34
The Ballad of John And Yoko   2:58
Old Brown Shoe (Harrison)   3:16

Side Four

Here Comes The Sun (Harrison)   3:04
Come Together   4:16
Something (Harrison)   2:59
Octopus's Garden (Starkey)   2:49
Let It Be   3:50
Across The Universe   3:51**
The Long And Winding Road   3:40**
**Produced by George Martin / Phil Spector; all
others produced by George Martin.*

All Lennon—McCartney songs except where stated.

ROCK AND ROLL MUSIC (2 L.P.s)
Parlophone PCSP 719
Producers : George Martin and
Phil Spector
Release Date : 11 June 1976
Running Time : 72:44

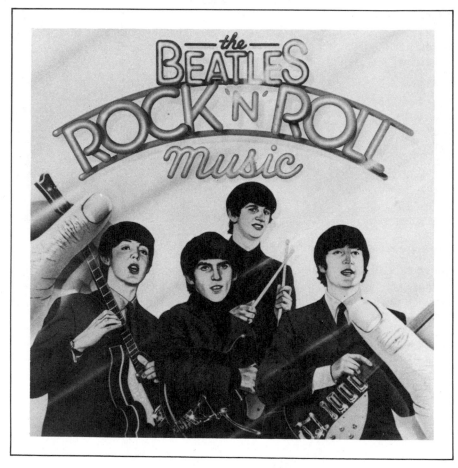

SIDE ONE: Twist And Shout; I Saw Her Standing There; You Can't Do That; I Wanna Be Your Man; I Call Your Name ; Boys; Long Tall Sally.
SIDE TWO: Rock And Roll Music; Slow Down; Kansas City; Money; Bad Boy; Matchbox; Roll Over Beethoven.

SIDE THREE: Dizzy Miss Lizzy; Anytime At All; Drive My Car; Everybody's Trying To Be My Baby; The Night Before; I'm Down; Revolution.
SIDE FOUR: Back In The U.S.S.R.; Helter Skelter; Taxman; Got To Get You Into My Life; Hey Bulldog; Birthday; Get Back.

After the release of the four-album set, but prior to the release of this album the Beatles' contract expired and EMI decided, in 1976 to re-issue every Beatles' single — at the same time! This obviously caused chaos in the British record charts. No less than six reached the top 40: Help (37), Strawberry Fields Forever (32), Paperback Writer (23), Hey Jude (12), Get Back (28) and a specially issued single of Yesterday (8). As could be expected, other record companies were irate as this was spoiling the chanches of newer artists.

Decca Records, the Rolling Stones record company throughout the sixties, replied by re-promoting the Rolling Stones' singles with advertisements stating 'The Rolling Stones singles, are, and always have been available: none have ever been deleted'. Although this seemed like a 'Battle of the Giants' created by the two record companies of the sixties none of the Rolling Stones singles were placed a second time in the top forty in 1976 (although their new single Fool To Cry: RS19131, issued on their own label reached number 6 on 1 May 1976).

It seemed hopeful that after the re-release of the old Beatles' singles that some of the unreleased tracks would then be issued. Instead, the idea for this album Rock and Roll Music came from Bhaskar Menon, the head of Capitol Records in the U.S.A. Menon, after trying unsuccessfully to contact one or all of the Beatles for approval of the track listing for this new double album, eventually gave up and contacted George Martin, their producer. When Martin was told of the plan to release this compilation of old Beatles' tracks as a new album he flew to the Hollywood offices of Capitol.

After hearing some of the older tracks with bad background noise and poor stereo Martin was appalled at the prospect of their reissue and set about filtering and remixing every track included on this album. On some of the older tracks, such as Twist and Shout and I Saw Her Standing There he reversed the stereo and brought the vocal track away from the edge into the centre, adding a slight echo for a more modern sound. He also filtered out the bass from the rhythm track and placed that also in the centre of the stereo. On newer tracks Martin reversed the stereo, and with the aid of filters and equalisers gave the recordings a crisper sound.

When he had finished his work, Martin took a copy of these tapes back to EMI Records in Britain, but the Company was horrified as the Beatles had issued official instructions that the tapes must not be 'touched, added to, edited or mutilated in any way'. EMI Records took this edict rather too literally, i.e. that if they were to be re-issued, the tapes should be exactly as originally recorded. Thus George Martin's remixed and filtered versions of the original tracks were not included on the Rock and Roll Music album when released in Britain.

In 1980, however, EMI Records relented and decided to issue the remixed recordings. They split the two albums, put them into new sleeves (after receiving numerous complaints about the original sleeve) and issued them on the Music For Pleasure label as Rock and Roll Music, Volumes 1 and 2 MFP 50506 and 50507. These two albums are worth buying if only to compare the original recordings with the re-mixes.

The following track listing, complete with timings, applies to both the original double album *and* the two remixed Music For Pleasure albums Rock and Roll Music Volumes 1 and 2 (MFP50506 and 50507) issued in 1980. All are Lennon — McCartney songs except where stated.

Side One

Twist And Shout
  (Medley — Russell)   2:32
I Saw Her Standing There   2:50
You Can't Do That   2:33
I Wanna Be Your Man   1:59
I Call Your Name   2:02
Boys (Goffin — King)   2:24
Long Tall Sally
  (Johnson — Penniman — Blackwell)   1:58

Side Two

Rock and Roll Music (Berry)   2:02
Slow Down (Williams)   2:54
Kansas City (Lieber — Stoller)/Hey Hey
  Hey Hey (Penniman)   2:30
Money (Bradford — Gordy)   2:47
Bad Boy   (Williams)   2:17
Matchbox (Perkins)   1:37
Roll Over Beethoven (Berry)   2:44

Side Three

Dizzy Miss Lizzy (Williams)   2:51
Anytime At All   2:10
Drive My Car   2:25
Everybody's Trying To Be My Baby
  (Perkins)   2:24
The Night Before   2:33
I'm Down   2:30
Revolution   3:22

Side Four

Back In The U.S.S.R.   2:45
Helter Skelter   4:30
Taxman (Harrison)   2:36
Got To Get You Into My Life   2:31
Hey Bulldog   3:09
Birthday   2:40
Get Back - Version Two   3:09*

Produced by George Martin and Phil Spector; all others produced by George Martin.

THE BEATLES AT THE HOLLYWOOD BOWL
Parlophone EMTV 4
Producers : Voyle Gilmore
              George Martin
Release Date : 6 May 1977
Running Time : 33:50

SIDE ONE: Twist And Shout; She's A Woman; Dizzy Miss Lizzy; Ticket To Ride; Can't Buy Me Love; Things We Said Today; Roll Over Beethoven.

SIDE TWO: Boys; A Hard Day's Night; Help!; All My Loving; She Loves You; Long Tall Sally.

The release of a 'live' album by the Beatles recorded at the Hollywood Bowl had been announced in the music press at various intervals during the 1970s. In 1972 it was announced to combat the increasing number of bootleg albums appearing on the market. Eighteen months later the album was announced again. Details were given that the album would be a live recording of the Hollywood Bowl concert on 23 August 1964, with the following tracks:

Side One : Twist And Shout, You Can't Do That, All My Loving, She Loves You, Things We Said Today, Roll Over Beethoven.

Side Two : Can't Buy Me Love, If I Fell, I Want To Hold Your Hand, Boys, A Hard Days Night, Long Tall Sally.

However, once again the album did not appear.

In 1977 the release of a live album by the Beatles was announced yet again. This time it was to include some of the recordings from the 1964 concert with some from a second concert held on 29 August 1965. The album did appear this time and was worth waiting for. The excitement of a Beatles' concert is captured perfectly, complete with the sound of 17,000 screaming Beatles' fans, the only disadvantage being that because of the noise, the album is neither technically nor musically perfect. Of the 13 tracks, six (All My Loving, She Loves You, Things We Said Today, Roll Over Beethoven, Boys and Long Tall Sally) are from the 1964 concert. The remaining seven (Twist and Shout, She's A Woman, Dizzy Miss Lizzy, Ticket To Ride, Can't Buy Me Love, A Hard Day's Night, and Help!) are from the 1965 concert. They have been edited together successfully by George Martin to make a highly enjoyable live album.

Because the original recordings were made on old fashioned three-track machines, it was necessary to first transfer them onto sixteen-track tape before George Martin and his studio engineer, Geoff Emerick, could filter, equalise and edit them. The major problem was that with continual use the tape heads of these old machines overheated and melted the magnetic tape. The resourceful Martin hit on the idea of using hair dryers, blowing cold air, to cool down the tape heads.

As a postscript, it is interesting to note that the biggest concert ever given by the Beatles was neither of these Hollywood Bowl concerts but was one given two weeks previously at New York's Shea Stadium on 15 August 1965 before 65,000 fans. It was recorded and also filmed. Nine months after the concert, on 1 May 1966, the BBC premiered the film on British television. Unlike the recording of the Hollywood Bowl Concert, the Shea Stadium Concert has never been officially released, although it is available on bootleg albums.

In the full track listing of The Beatles At The Hollywood Bowl album given below, the timing given for each side is the full playing time including various introductions and crowd noises.

Side One   17:57

Twist And Shout
   (Medley–Russell)   1:20
She's A Woman   2:45
Dizzy Miss Lizzy (Williams)   3:00
Ticket To Ride   2:18

Can't Buy Me Love   2:08
Things We Said Today   2:07
Roll Over Beethoven (Berry)   2:10

Side Two   15:53

Boys (Dixon–Farrell)   1:57
A Hard Day's Night   2:30
Help!   2:16
All My Loving   1:55
She Loves You   2:10
Long Tall Sally
   (Johnson–Penniman–Blackwell) 1.54

LOVE SONGS (2 L.P.s)
Parlophone PCSP 721
Producers : George Martin and
Phil Spector
Release Date : 28 November 1977
Running Time : 59:25

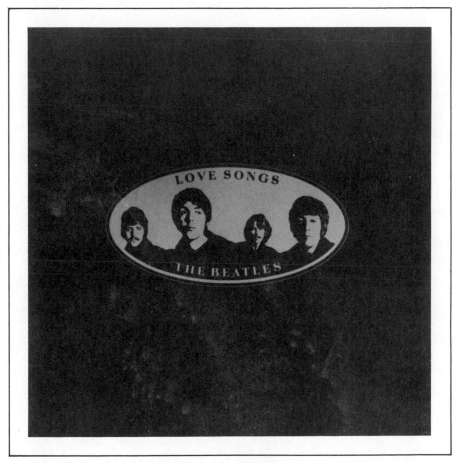

SIDE ONE: Yesterday; I'll Follow The Sun; I
Need You; Girl; In My Life; Words Of Love;
Here, There And Everywhere.
SIDE TWO: Something; And I Love Her; If I
Fell; I'll Be Back; Tell Me What You See; Yes
It Is.

SIDE THREE: Michelle; It's Only Love; You're
Going To Lose That Girl; Every Little Thing;
For No One; She's Leaving Home.
SIDE FOUR: The Long And Winding Road;
This Boy: Norwegian Wood (This Bird Has
Flown); You've Got To Hide Your Love Away;
I Will; P.S. I Love You.

This album is mainly a compilation of tracks previously available on other Beatles' albums. The only two not previously issued on British albums are This Boy and Yes It is and these are simply mono recordings re-channelled into fake stereo, even though This Boy is available in stereo on a Canadian single.

The album was issued just in time for Christmas, 1977 so sales were guaranteed to a certain extent. In addition to taking these buyers for a ride, the record of course exploited dedicated fans and collectors who always bought Beatles' albums. To add insult to injury there were many other tracks available, which would have made a far better compilation album. One good feature of the album package is the inclusion of the 1967 Richard Avedon poster.

Side One

Yesterday   2:04
I'll Follow The Sun   1:46
I Need You (Harrison)   2:28
Girl   2:26
In My Life   2:23
Words Of Love (Holly)   2:10
Here, There And Everywhere   2:29

Side Two

Something (Harrison)   2:59
And I Love Her   2:27
If I Fell   2:16
I'll Be Back   2:22
Tell Me What You See   2:35
Yes It Is   2:40

Side Three

Michelle   2:42
It's Only Love   1:53
You're Going To Lose That Girl   2:18
Every Little Thing   2:01
For No One   2:03
She's Leaving Home   3:24

Side Four

The Long And Winding Road   3:40*
This Boy   2:11
Norwegian Wood (This Bird Has
   Flown)   2:00
You've Got To Hide Your Love
   Away 2:08
I Will   1:46
P.S. I Love You   2:02

Produced by George Martin/Phil Spector. All others produced by George Martin.

All Lennon – McCartney songs except where stated.

THE BEATLES COLLECTION
Parlophone / Apple BC 13
Producers : George Martin and
Phil Spector
Release Date : 15 December
1978
Running Time : See Individual
Albums

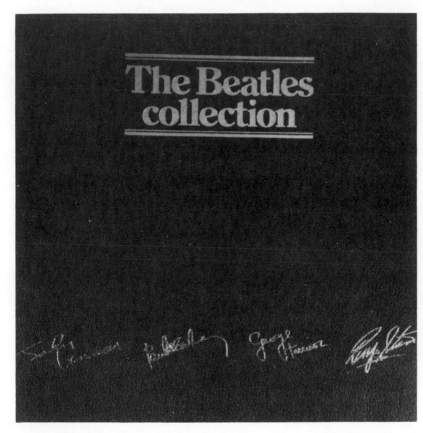

A boxed set containing the following
albums: Please Please Me; With The Beatles;
A Hard Day's Night; Beatles For Sale; Help!;
Rubber Soul; Revolver; Sgt. Pepper's Lonely
Hearts Club Band; The Beatles; Yellow
Submarine; Abbey Road; Let It Be; Rarities.

This collection of the main Beatle's albums as a boxed set was inevitable. Unfortunately, it is by no means a complete collection of the Beatles' recordings issued by EMI/Parlophone between 1962 and 1970. Rather it is a collection of the Beatles' studio Albums, issued by EMI in Britain during that period. Curiously, A Collection of Beatles Oldies is excluded, although included is brand new album The Beatles Rarities, (a collection of B-sides from singles, plus a few tracks not previously available on British Beatles' albums).

As usual with a collection of this sort there are a few gaps. The main omissions are Magical Mystery Tour, Hey Jude and The Beatles At The Hollywood Bowl, plus a number of other tracks available on The Beatles 1962 — 1966 and The Beatles 1967 — 1970

Overall it is a good collection for either younger Beatles' fans buying for the first time or older fans who would like to renew their Beatles' albums. For the serious collector, who has bought everything issued since 1962, the only thing of interest is the box.

The Beatles Collection comes neatly packaged in a dark blue box, with the title and the four Beatles' autographs printed in gold on the front. It consists of stereo versions of twelve albums plus the Rarities album.

Please Please Me (PCS 3042)
With The Beatles (PCS 3045)
A Hard Day's Night (PCS 3058
Beatles For Sale (PCS 3062)

Help! (PCS 3071)
Rubber Soul (PCS 3075)
Revolver (PCS 7009)
Sgt. Pepper's Lonely Hearts Club Band (PCS 7027)
The Beatles (PCS 7067/8)
Yellow Submarine (PCS 7070)
Abbey Road (PCS 7088)
Let It Be (PCS 7096)
Rarities (PSLP 261)

THE BEATLES' "RARITIES"
Parlophone PSLP 261; PCM 1001
Producer : George Martin
Release Date : October 1979
Running Time : 43:29

SIDE ONE: Across The Universe; Yes It Is; This Boy; The Inner Light; I'll Get You; Thank You Girl; Komm, Gib Mir Deine Hand; You Know My Name (Look Up The Number); Sie Liebt Dich.

SIDE TWO: Rain; She's A Woman; Matchbox; I Call Your Name; Bad Boy; Slow Down; I'm Down: Long Tall Sally.

Originally included as a free addition to the 1978 boxed set, The Beatles Collection, this album was issued separately in 1979 after EMI had received complaints that the only way of obtaining this 'free' album was to pay for the box and its duplicate copies of Beatles' albums. For most British fans the album contains very little in the way of rarities, as the title suggests. The only rare tracks are Across The Universe, previously abailable only on the now deleted charity album No-one's Gonna Change Our World, and the German language versions of She Loves You and I want to Hold Your Hand, previously unavailable in Britian. The sleeve notes proclaim that the remaining 14 tracks which are a collection of B-sides and E.P. tracks were not available on earlier British Beatles' albums. In fact eight of the 17 tracks were previously available (Long Tall Sally, I Call Your Name, Slow Down, Matchbox and I'm Down already on the Rock and Roll Music, Yes It Is and This Boy on 'Love Songs and Rain on Hey Jude).

Although the album contains very little in the way of rare tracks, it is a useful compilation of some of the material on B-sides, E.P.s and foreign releases. There are, however, still sufficient tracks left to fill three more volumes.

British fans who search this album for the long-awaited stereo versions of various B-sides will be disappointed. Only four of the 17 tracks are in stereo. I was informed by the albums' compiler, Mike Heatley from EMI's International Division, that this is due to a mix-up in the recordings. It was EMI's intention to issue the stereo versions but the mono versions of Rain, Long Tall Sally, I Call Your Name, Slow Down, Matchbox and I'm Down were mistakenly used although already available on other British Beatles' albums in stereo. This album is a good start and is cheaper than buying all the singles but an album of *real* rarities would be much more exciting.

SIDE ONE

Across The Universe (Lennon – McCartney)   3:41

John Lennon : Acoustic Guitar, Lead Guitar, Organ and Lead Vocal
Paul McCartney : Piano and Harmony Vocal
George Harrison : Sitar
Ringo Starr : Maraccas
George Martin : Organ
Lizzie Bravo : Backing Vocal
Gayleen Pease : Backing Vocal

This recording, eventually released in December 1969 as part of the charity compilation album No-one's Gonna Change Our World (Regal Starline SRS 5013), was recorded in 1968 and considered for release as the A-side of a single, but it never made it as Lady Madonna was chosen instead. The track re-surfaced in early 1969 when it was considered for inclusion on the Get Back album—again it never made it altough as it turned out the Get Back album itself did not reach the shops. In late 1969 it was finally given to the World Wildlife Fund who included it on the charity album No-One's Gonna Change Our World. A different recording of Across The Universe then appeared four months later on the Let It Be album.

The track begins with the sound of birds which then "flies" across the stereo. When it fades the track proper begins. John sings lead vocal on his own song, with Paul harmonising in places. The backing vocals were added by two women, Lizzie Bravo and Gayleen Pease. Apparently Paul stated that he would never have female voices on a Beatles' record but it seems that John and Paul invited these two into the studio, from Abbey Road where they had been waiting to see the Beatles.

The lyrics to this song are some of John's most imaginative with his incessant chorus line 'Nothing's gonna change my world' accentuating their dreamy effect. The backing includes John on lead guitar, Paul on piano, George on sitar and John and George Martin duetting on organ.

Yes It Is (Lennon—McCartney)   2:40

John Lennon : Acoustic Guitar and Lead Vocal
Paul McCartney : Bass Guitar and Backing Vocal
George Harrison : Lead Guitar and Backing Vocal
Ringo Starr : Drums

Originally released in 1965 as the B-side to Ticket To Ride, this makes its second appearance on a British Beatles' album. The first was in 1977 on the Love Songs album, when it was electronically faked into bad stereo. Here it is in mono; the true stereo version has yet to appear. The vocals are a three-part harmony from John, Paul and George, with John singing solo in parts over a whining background guitar. This whining effect was achieved with a volume/tone control pedal with which George had been experimenting at the time. A few other tracks recorded during 1965 have a similar effect.

This Boy (Lennon—McCartney)   2:11

John Lennon : Acoustic Guitar and Lead Vocal
Paul McCartney : Bass Guitar and Harmony Vocal
George Harrison : Lead Guitar and Harmony Vocal
Ringo Starr : Drums

This must be the Beatles' biggest selling, forgotten track. It was released in 1963 as the B-side to their multi-million seller I Want To Hold Your Hand. Like the previous track, This Boy was included on the Love Songs album in fake stereo and here in mono. The stereo version has been released, however. In 1976 it was made available in both Canada and Australia on re-issued singles, and in 1981 it was included on the British E.P. The Beatles. The song is dominated by a close harmony from John, Paul and George, with a powerful solo vocal from John.

The Inner Light (Harrison)   2:36

John Lennon : Not Present
Paul McCartney : Not Present
George Harrison : Solo Vocal
Ringo Starr : Not Present
Session Musicians : All Instruments

Issued originally in 1968 as the B-side of Lady Madonna, this was George's first song to be released on a Beatles' single. It is the last of three Beatles' tracks by George Harrison featuring almost entirely Indian instrumentation. The previous two were Love You Too, included on Revolver and Within You, on Sgt. Pepper's Lonely Hearts Club Band. The instrumental track was recorded in January 1968, with some of India's virtuoso musicians, during the recording of George's music for the *Wonder Wall* film sound-track album. The lyrics were inspired by a Japanese poem by Roshi, translated into English by R. H. Bluth. George used extracts of the English translation as the basis for the lyrics. Again, this is in mono here although it is in stereo on the E. P. The Beatles.

I'll Get You (Lennon–McCartney)   2:04

John Lennon : Rhythm Guitar, Harmonica and Lead Vocal
Paul McCartney : Bass Guitar and Harmony Vocal
George Harrison : Lead Guitar and Harmony Vocal
Ringo Starr : Drums

Originally considered as an A-side for the follow up to From Me To You, this was released in 1963 as the B-side to She Loves You. The song is reminiscent of She Loves You with the opening 'Oh yeah' and the duet by John and Paul on lead vocals. John's over-dubbed harmonica is prominent at the beginning and ending but it is mixed back during the rest of the track. This recording makes its first appearance here on any British Beatles' album, although it had been available since 1964 on the American album The Beatles Second Album. Neither here nor on the American album is the recording in stereo although no doubt a stereo version exists somewhere.

Thank You Girl (Lennon–McCartney)   2:01

John Lennon : Acoustic Guitar, Harmonica and Lead Vocal
Paul McCartney : Bass Guitar and Lead Vocal
George Harrison : Lead Guitar
Ringo Starr : Drums

This exciting track dates back to April 1963 when it was originally released as the B-side of the Beatles' third Parlophone single From Me To You. It has a predominant harmonica from John and the usual John and Paul lead vocal duet featured on most of their 1963 singles. This recording sounds as old as it is. The significantly different stereo version of Thank You Girl has yet to be released in Britain, but is currently available on the American The Beatles Second Album (Capitol ST 2080).

Komm, Gib Mir Deine Hand
(Lennon–McCartney–Nicolas–Hellmer)   2:24

John Lennon : Rhythm Guitar and Lead Vocal
Paul McCartney : Bass Guitar and Lead Vocal
George Harrison : Lead Guitar
Ringo Starr : Drums

The German language versions of I Want To Hold Your Hand and She Loves

You were not recorded, as many thought, as a tribute to the Beatles' early days in Hamburg, but in answer to a request from EMI in Germany, who wanted authentic versions for the German market. The Beatles were far from enthusiastic but George Martin eventually persuaded them to record the tracks in the EMI studios in Paris, where they were at the time. They were subsequently released in Germany as a double A-sided single in January 1964. The German lyrics of both songs were written by two German songwriters, one of whom was present at the recording session to ensure that the songs were sung with the correct accent. Komm, Gib Mir Deine Hand was released for the first time in Britain as part of this album although it had been available since 1964 in the USA on the deceptively titled Something New album.

You Know My Name (Look Up The Number)
(Lennon–McCartney)   4:20

John Lennon : Maraccas and Lead Vocal
Paul McCartney : Piano, Double Bass and Lead Vocal
George Harrison : Xylophone and Backing Vocal
Ringo Starr : Drums, Bongos and Lead Vocal
Brian Jones : Saxophone
Mal Evans : Backing Vocal

This intriguing track was recorded during the sessions for the album The Beatles in 1968, but not issued until 1970, as the B-side of Let It Be. It was once considered for release as an A-side but the idea was dropped. In December 1969 John decided to release the recording as a single under the banner of the Plastic Ono Band, but at the last minute it was withdrawn without explanation, and Instant Karma was released in its place. The Plastic Ono Band single was to have been You Know My Name (Look Up The Number)/ What's The New Mary Jane, with the catalogue number of Apples 1002. In fact this number is stamped in the run-off groove of the British single. This was repeatedly rumoured to be the Beatles next single after it was recorded in 1968, but it never emerged, either as a Beatles' single or as a Plastic Ono Band single.
    The lyrics are simply a repetition of the title, with various additional comments. The jazz piano is supplied by Paul McCartney and a saxophone solo by Brian Jones of the Rolling Stones.

Sie Liebt Dich (Lennon–McCartney–Nicolas–Montague)   2:18

John Lennon : Rhythm Guitar and Lead Vocal
Paul McCartney : Bass Guitar and Lead Vocal
George Harrison : Lead Guitar
Ringo Starr : Drums

This German language version of She Loves You shares the same history as Komm, Gib Mir Deine Hand. Although it had been available in America and Germany since 1964 as a mono single, it was issued for the first time in Britain in stereo on this album.

SIDE TWO

Rain (Lennon–McCartney) 2:59

John Lennon : Rhythm Guitar and Lead Vocal
Paul McCartney : Bass Guitar and Backing Vocal
George Harrison : Lead Guitar and Backing Vocal
Ringo Starr : Drums and Tambourine

Originally released as the B-side to Paperback Writer in 1966, this song was included in stereo in 1970 on the Hey Jude album. (See discussion of that album for review.) The version included here is in mono, although the original stereo version is available.

She's A Woman (Lennon–McCartney) 2:57

John Lennon : Rhythm Guitar
Paul McCartney : Bass Guitar, Piano and Solo Vocal
George Harrison : Lead Guitar
Ringo Starr : Drums and Maraccas

This great chunk of syncopated rock and roll, written by Paul McCartney, was originally released as the B-side of I Feel Fine in 1964. This is the first appearance on a British album although it had been available on the American album Beatles '65. Both album tracks are in mono, and the stereo track was eventually released in Britain on Record 2 of the Beatles Box.

Matchbox (Perkins) 1:37

John Lennon : Rhythm Guitar
Paul McCartney : Bass Guitar
George Harrison : Lead Guitar
Ringo Starr : Drums and Solo Vocal
George Martin : Piano

Ringo sings a rousing lead vocal on this track, the first of four on this album originally released in 1964 as part of the E.P. Long Tall Sally, and then in 1976 on the album Rock and Roll Music. The song was originally written and recorded by Carl Perkins, who was reputed to have been present at the session when this and some of his other songs were recorded by the Beatles. It is a great pity that this album track is in mono, when the previous album features a stereo recording.

I Call Your Name (Lennon–McCartney)   2:02

John Lennon : Rhythm Guitar and Solo Vocal
Paul McCartney : Bass Guitar
George Harrison : Lead Guitar
Ringo Starr : Drums

Billy J. Kramer and The Dakotas recorded this as the B-side to another Lennon-McCartney composition Bad To Me. It was then recorded by the Beatles themselves with John on lead vocals and included in stereo, on the Long Tall Sally E.P. In 1964 and in stereo on the album Rock and Roll Music in 1976. The song has a similar feel to You Can't Do That both musically and vocally.

Bad Boy (Williams)   2:17

John Lennon : Rhythm Guitar, Hammond Organ and Solo Vocal
Paul McCartney : Bass Guitar
George Harrison : Lead Guitar
Ringo Starr : Drums and Tambourine

Previously included on the A Collection Of Beatles Oldies album.

Slow Down (Williams)   2:54

John Lennon : Rhythm Guitar and Solo Vocal
Paul McCartney : Bass Guitar
George Harrison : Lead Guitar
Ringo Starr : Drums
George Martin : Piano

The third track from the Long Tall Sally E.P. shares the same history as Matchbox and I Call Your Name. This mono track features John on lead vocal with an extremely enthusiastic rendition of this little-known Larry Williams song. It was included in stereo, on the Rock and Roll Music album.

I'm Down (Lennon–McCartney)   2:30

John Lennon : Hammond Organ and Backing Vocal
Paul McCartney : Bass Guitar and Lead Vocal
George Harrison : Lead Guitar and Backing Vocal
Ringo Starr : Drums and Bongos

Paul seems to have re-written Long Tall Sally as this song, which rattles along at an incredible pace. He shouts out the lyrics in true Little Richard style while John hammers away at the Hammond organ. Originally issued as the B-side of Help! in 1965, this brilliant Beatles' track was not included on an L.P. until the Rock and Roll Music album in 1976, where it appeared in stereo, although here, sadly, it is mono.

Long Tall Sally (Johnson—Penniman—Blackwell)   1:58

John Lennon : Rhythm Guitar
Paul McCartney : Bass Guitar, Piano and Solo Vocal
George Harrison : Lead Guitar
Ringo Starr : Drums

This final album track, the last of the four from the Long Tall Sally E.P., was originally recorded by Little Richard, who also co-wrote it. Here, Paul's lead vocals sound just as enthusiastic and spontaneous as John's on the classic Twist And Shout. The Beatles had used both songs for years during their live performances, which invariably opened with Twist And Shout and closed with Long Tall Sally — a format they were to continue in their later, larger scale concert performances. Again, the track here is disappointingly in mono, although available in stereo on the album Rock and Roll Music.

THE BEATLES BALLADS — 20 Original Tracks
Parlophone PCS 7214
Producers : George Martin and
                Phil Spector
Release Date : October 1980
Running Time : 58:29

SIDE ONE: Yesterday; Norwegian Wood (This Bird Has Flown); Do You want To Know A Secret; For No One; Michelle; Nowhere Man; You've Got To Hide Your Love Away; Across The Universe; All My Loving; Hey Jude.

SIDE TWO: Something; The Fool On The Hill; Till There Was You; The Long And Winding Road; Here Comes The Sun; Blackbird; And I Love Her; She's Leaving Home; Here, There And Everywhere; Let It Be.

When I enquired of EMI why this album was issued, the reply was that it was for those people who did not buy Love Songs. Although a better compilation album than Love Songs, it contains nothing new — no previously unreleased tracks or even stereo versions of former mono recordings. A remixed version of Norwegian Wood **is** included with the backing track now on the right-hand channel instead of the left and the vocals mixed into the centre. Also, someone in the depths of EMI seems to have confused and reversed the stereo on Yesterday, You've Got To Hide Your Love Away, She's Leaving Home and Here, There and Everywhere.

The possible permutations of material for compilation albums boggles the mind. We have had the rock and roll music, the love songs, and on this album the ballads. Presumably one album still to be compiled is The Songs The Beatles Didn't Write. After all, there are 24 of them. There could even be four separate albums — John Lennon and the Beatles, Paul McCartney and the Beatles, George Harrison and the Beatles, and Ringo Starr and the Beatles. This is not such a ridiculous idea when you consider that the album The Best of George Harrison (Parlophone PAS 10011) has on side one Something, If I Needed Someone, Here Comes The Sun, Taxman, Think For Yourself, For You Blue and While My Guitar Gently Weeps.

Side One

Yesterday 2:04
Norwegian Wood (This Bird Has
  flown) 2:00
Do You Want To Know A Secret 1:55
For No One 2:03
Michelle 2:42
Nowhere Man 2:40
You've Got To Hide Your Love
  Away 2:08
Across The Universe — Version
One 3:41
All My Loving 2:04
Hey Jude 7:11

Side Two

Something (Harrison) 2:59
The Fool On The Hill 3:00
Till There Was You (Willson) 2:12
The Long And Winding Road★ 3:40
Here Comes The Sun (Harrison) 3:40
Blackbird 2:20
And I Love Her 2:27
She's Leaving Home 3:24
Here, There And Everywhere 2:29
Let It Be 3:50

★Produced by George Martin/Phil Spector. All others produced by George Martin.

All Lennon—McCartney songs except where stated.

REEL MUSIC
Parlophone PCS 7218
Producers : George Martin and
Phil Spector
Release Date : 12 March 1982
Running Time : 42:03

SIDE ONE: A Hard Day's Night; I Should Have Known Better; Can't Buy Me Love; And I Love Her; Help!; You've Got To Hide Your Love Away; Ticket To Ride; Magical Mystery Tour.

SIDE TWO: I Am The Walrus; Yellow Submarine; All You Need Is Love; Let It Be; Get Back; The Long And Winding Road.

Rock And Roll Music, Love Songs, The Beatles Ballads . . . . Now we have a further compilation, Reel Music, a selection of songs from the Beatles' films.

The album features four songs from A Hard Day's Night, three from Help!, two from Magical Mystery Tour, two from Yellow Submarine and three from Let It Be. Unfortunately, from the way the album is arranged, there is no real sense of 'flow' to the Reel Music. For a Beatles' album to have Ticket to Ride followed by Magical Mystery Tour and I Am The Walrus followed by Yellow Submarine suggests some peculiar criteria for selection of tracks.

The album cover, which depicts the Beatles — in their five different roles as film stars, arriving at a film theatre — reflects the album's contents, indicating a rapidly produced piece of merchandise.

The sleeve notes, consist of a six — paragraph potted history of the Beatles and their film career. These words are aimed mainly at the newer, younger Beatles fans, many of who were not even born when the 'fab four' broke up. For the fans' benefit, the sleeve also credits the individual Beatles as composers, the first album to do so since With The Beatles in 1963.

The album is complete with a 12 - page 'Souvenir Program' which contains a brief resumé of each of the five Beatles movies along with selected stills. The inner sleeve has a further selection of stills and other photographs.

Following the 1981-82 worldwide success of the Stars on 45 medley by the Dutch 'Beatles soundalike' group Starsound (a medley which contained some very believable John Lennon - sounding vocals), Capitol Records decided to put together their own Beatle medley using the original Beatles' master tapes. The record, entitled The Beatles Movie Medley, contains excerpts from Magical Mystery Tour, All You Need Is Love, You've Got To Hide Your Love Away, I Should Have Known Better, A Hard Day's Night, Ticket To Ride and Get Back. The recording was issued as both a 12 inch and 7 inch single (Capitol B-5107) on 30 March 1982.

The editing, which is questionable, was carried out by John Palladino of Capitol Records. Unfortunately, the inclusion of You've Got To Hide Your Love Away within the medley seems to spoil the rhythm of the medley as a whole, which has a running time of 3 mins 56 secs.

When the first promotional copies of this record were pressed the B-side contained an edited press conference interview from 1964. When the record reached the stores, the B-side had been changed to I'm Happy Just To Dance With You.

In Britain, EMI Records decided that the editing of Beatles' recordings was unacceptable and withheld release of the record (but still allocated it a catalogue number, just in case). Demand for imported copies of the U.S. record was so high that EMI conceded and eventually issued it on 25 May 1982 (Parlophone R6055).

Side One		Side Two	
A Hard Day's Night	2:32	I Am The Walrus	4:35
I Should Have Known Better	2:42	Yellow Submarine	2:40
Can't Buy Me Love	2:15	All You Need Is Love	3:47
And I Love Her	2:27	Let It Be	4:01*
Help!	2:16	Get Back	3:09*
You've Got To Hide Your Love Away	2:08	The Long And Winding Road	3:40*
Ticket To Ride	3:03		
Magical Mystery Tour	2:48		

*Produced by George Martin and Phil Spector, all others produced by George Martin.

All Lennon—McCartney songs.

THE BEATLES BOX
Parlophone/World Records
SM 701 — 8
Producers : George Martin and
                       Phil Spector
Release Date : October 1980
Running Time : See Individual
                          Albums

     Track listings for the eight albums in the box are given on the following pages.

This collection is a must for any Beatles' fan or collector. A masterpiece, it spans the entire recording career of the Beatles from Love Me Do to Let It Be and is even better than The Beatles 1962-66 and 1967-70 albums.

The eight albums that make up The Beatles Box contain 124 tracks of what can definitively be classed as the Beatles' greatest hits — a tribute to the group's achievement, as there cannot be many artists whose 'greatest hits' would fill eight albums. Another good point is that The Beatles Box consists of eight *new* albums not re-packages like The Beatles Collection issued in 1978. Amongst the 124 tracks are ten of particular interest.

The first is the original single version of Love Me Do with Ringo on drums (this is *not* the version included on the Please Please Me album). All My Loving in this version was previously only available on the German album Beatles Greatest (Odeon SMO 83991) and features a six-tap hi-hat intro. It makes its first appearance on a British Beatles' album here. And I Love Her, as heard here was previously unavailable in Britain but was on the German album Something New (Odeon 1C 072-04 600). The final riff is repeated here six times whereas on the album A Hard Day's Night, it is repeated only four times. She's A Woman was previously only available in Britain in mono. This is the stereo version which had been available only on the East Asian/Australian album The Beatles Greatest Hits Vol. 2 (Parlophone LPEA 1002). I Feel Fine is the much talked about 'whispering version' previously included on the album The Beatles 1962-66. It is the same stereo recording as on the album A Collection Of Beatles Oldies but includes two seconds of mysterious whisperings at the beginning. Day Tripper is a different stereo mix from that available on the album A Collection Of Beatles Oldies. Previously available only on the American album Yesterday ... And Today (Capitol ST 2553) it has the guitar intro mixed into the left-hand channel instead of across the stereo. Paperback Writer is the re-mixed version from Hey Jude with the stereo reversed and the backing vocals mixed further forward than on A Collection Of Beatles Oldies. Penny Lane in this version was previously unavailable anywhere in the world. It was distributed to radio stations in America and Canada prior to the release of the single. It features seven extra piccolo trumpet notes played over the ending of the recording which had been edited out by the time the record reached the stores. Baby, You're A Rich Man is in stereo for the first time in Britain. I Am The Walrus, previously unavailable anywhere in the world in this format, is included in full, combining the oddities of three previous versions. The British single features the organ intro repeated four times, the stereo version on the Magical Mystery Tour two E.P. set, six times, and the American single with the organ intro repeated four times also has a few extra beats in the middle between the lines 'I'm Crying' and 'Yellow Matter Custard'. These are missing from both British versions but are combined here.

Other tracks of interest are the stereo version of Long Tall Sally, I Call Your Name, Matchbox, Slow Down and I'm Down. Previously included on the rather messy compilation album Rock and Roll Music, these five tracks are presented here in a far superior way. On record six, All You Need Is Love is the original mono single not the re-recorded version from Yellow Submarine. Get Back, Let It Be and Across The Universe are the recordings from the album Let It Be, and not, in the case of the first two, the versions released as singles.

The eight albums, complete with individual sleeve notes, come packaged in a cardboard box looking rather like a wooden crate. This album set is only available through EMI's mail order division, World Records.

THE BEATLES BOX – RECORD 1
**Parlophone / World Records
SM 701**
Producer : George Martin
Running Time : 31:57

THE BEATLES BOX – Record 1

Side One

Love Me Do   2:22
P.S. I Love You   2:02
I Saw Her Standing There   2:50
Please Please Me   2:00
Misery   1:43
Do You Want To Know A Secret   1:55
A Taste Of Honey (Marlow – Scott)   2:02
Twist And Shout
   (Medley – Russell)   2:32

Side Two

From Me To You   1:55
Thank You Girl   2:01
She Loves You   2:18
It Won't Be Long   2:11
Please Mister Postman (Holland)   2:34
All My Loving   2:07
Roll Over Beethoven (Berry)   2:44
Money (Bradford – Gordy)   2:47

All Lennon – McCartney songs except
where stated.

THE BEATLES BOX – RECORD 2
**Parlophone / World Records
SM 702**
Producer : George Martin
Running Time : 38:13

THE BEATLES BOX – Record 2

Side One

I Want To Hold Your Hand   2:24
This Boy   2:11
Can't Buy Me Love   2:15
You Can't Do That   2:33
A Hard Day's Night   2:32
I Should Have Known Better   2:42
If I Fell   2:16
And I Love Her   2:36

Side Two

Things We Said Today   2:35
I'll Be Back   2:22
Long Tall Sally
   (Johnson – Penniman – Blackwell)   1:58
I Call Your Name   2:02
Matchbox (Perkins)   1:37
Slow Down (Williams)   2:54
She's A Woman   2:57
I Feel Fine   2:19

All Lennon – McCartney songs except
where stated.

THE BEATLES BOX – RECORD 3
Parlophone / World Records
SM 703
Producer : George Martin
Running Time : 38:12

Side One

Eight Days A Week   2:43
No Reply   2:15
I'm A Loser   2:31
I'll Follow The Sun   1:46
Mr Moonlight (Johnson)   2:35
Every Little Thing   2:01
I Don't Want To Spoil The Party   2:33
Kansas City (Lieber – Stoller) /Hey Hey
   Hey Hey (Penniman)   2.30

Side Two

Ticket To Ride   3:03
I'm Down   2:30
Help!   2:16
The Night Before   2:33
You've Got To Hide Your Love
   Away   2:08
I Need You (Harrison)   2:28
Another Girl   2:02
You're Gonna To Lose That Girl   2:18

All Lennon – McCartney songs except
where stated.

THE BEATLES BOX – RECORD 4
Parlophone / World Records
SM 704
Producer : George Martin
Running Time : 38:49

Side One

Yesterday   2:04
Act Naturally (Morrison – Russell)   2:27
Tell Me What You See   2:35
It's Only Love   1:53
You Like Me Too Much (Harrison)   2:34
I've Just Seen A Face   2:04
Day Tripper   2:37
We Can Work It Out   2:10

Side Two

Michelle   2:42
Drive My Car   2:25
Norwegian Wood (This Bird Has
   Flown)   2:00
You Won't See Me   3:19
Nowhere Man   2:40
Girl   2:26
I'm Looking Through You   2:20
In My Life   2:23

All Lennon – McCartney songs except
where stated.

THE BEATLES BOX – RECORD 5
Parlophone / World Records
SM 705
Producer : George Martin
Running Time : 34:13

Side One

Paperback Writer   2:25
Rain   2:59
Here, There And Everywhere   2:29
Taxman (Harrison)   2:36
I'm Only Sleeping   2:58
Good Day Sunshine   2:08
Yellow Submarine   2:40

Side Two

Eleanor Rigby   2:11
And Your Bird Can Sing   2:02
For No One   2:03
Dr. Robert   2:14
Got To Get You Into My Life   2:31
Penny Lane   3:00
Strawberry Fields Forever   4:05

All Lennon – McCartney songs except
where stated.

THE BEATLES BOX – RECORD 6
Parlophone / World Records
SM 706
Producer : George Martin
Running Time : 47:07

Side One

Sgt. Pepper's Lonely Hearts Club
   Band   1:59
With A Little Help From My
   Friends   2:46
Lucy In The Sky With Diamonds   3:25
Fixing A Hole   2:33
She's Leaving Home   3:24
Being For The Benefit of Mr. Kite   2:36
A Day In The Life   5:03

Side Two

When I'm Sixty-Four   2:38
Lovely Rita   2:43
All You Need Is Love   3:57
Baby, You're A Rich Man   3:07
Magical Mystery Tour   2:48
Your Mother Should Know   2:33
The Fool On The Hill   3:00
I Am The Walrus   4:35

All Lennon – McCartney songs.

154

THE BEATLES BOX — RECORD 7
Parlophone / World Records
SM 707
Producer : George Martin
Running Time : 48:17

Side One
Hello Goodbye   3:24
Lady Madonna   2:17
Hey Jude   7:11
Revolution   3:22
Back In The U.S.S.R.   2:45
Ob-La-Di, Ob-La-Da   3:10
While My Guitar Gently Weeps
   (Harrison)   4:46

Side Two
The Continuing Story Of Bungalow
   Bill   3:05
Happiness Is A Warm Gun   2:47
Martha My Dear   2:28
I'm So Tired   2:01
Piggies (Harrison)   2:04
Don't Pass Me By (Starkey)   3:52
Julia   2:57
All Together Now   2:08

All Lennon — McCartney songs except
where stated.

THE BEATLES BOX — RECORD 8
Parlophone / World Records
SM 708
Producers : George Martin and
                        Phil Spector
Running Time : 52:11

Side One
Get Back   3:09
Don't Let Me Down   3:34
The Ballad Of John And Yoko   2:58
Across The Universe   3:51
For You Blue (Harrison)   2:33
Two Of Us   3:33
The Long And Winding Road   3:40
Let It Be   4:01

Side Two
Come Together   4:16
Something (Harrison)   2:59
Maxwell's Silver Hammer   3:24
Octopus's Garden (Starkey)   2:49
Here Comes The Sun (Harrison)   3:04
Because   2:45
Golden Slumbers   1:31
Carry That Weight   1:37
The End   2:04
Her Majesty   0:23

All Lennon — McCartney songs except
where stated.

THE SONGS LENNON AND McCARTNEY GAVE AWAY
EMI Nut 18
Producer : Various (See
individual tracks)
Release Date : April 1979
Running Time : 46:14

SIDE ONE: I'm The Greatest (Ringo Starr); One And One Is Two (The Strangers with Mike Shannon); From A Window (Billy J. Kramer and The Dakotas); Nobody I Know (Peter and Gordon); Like Dreamers Do (The Applejacks); I'll Keep You Satisfied (Billy J. Kramer and The Dakotas); Love Of The Loved (Cilla Black); Woman (Peter and Gordon); Tip Of My Tongue (Tommy Quickly); I'm In Love (The Fourmost).

SIDE TWO: Hello Little Girl (The Fourmost); That Means A Lot (P.J. Proby); It's For You (Cilla Black); Penina (Carlos Mendes); Step Inside Love (Cilla Black); World Without Love (Peter and Gordon); Bad To Me (Billy J. Kramer and The Dakotas); I Don't Want To See You Again (Peter and Gordon); I'll Be On My Way (Billy J. Kramer and The Dakotas); Catcall (The Chris Barber Band).

This album is a collection of Beatle-written songs written by other artists. Although most were also recorded by the Beatles, either as demonstration recordings for the final artists or as possible releases by themselves. Only one of the songs on this album did not come from the Beatles' collective recording career — I'm The Greatest, a song written by John Lennon for Ringo's 1973 album Ringo. The 20 tracks performed by ten artists range from extremely good to very bad and cover the Beatles' career from 1963 to 1969. Most were not written specifically for the artists who recorded them, with the exceptions of Step Inside Love written for Cilla Black by Paul McCartney in 1968 and the Peter and Gordon songs on the album, also written for them by McCartney.

Seven other songs, written betwenn 1963 and 1969, by either Lennon, McCartney, or both — and recorded by other artists — are mentioned at the end of the album listing here. These are relevant although they do not appear on the album. I have not commented on any of these tracks but simply given credits plus details of their initial UK and USA releases. However, as I'm the Greatest features John, George and Ringo, it is worth mentioning briefly.

Written by John for the album Ringo in 1973, the lyrics refer to Sgt. Pepper and the music has snatches reminiscent of I Want You (She's So Heavy), Golden Slumbers, Being For The Benefit of Mr Kite, Revolution and Cry Baby Cry. Ringo is on lead vocals and drums, John Lennon on guitar and harmony vocals, George Harrison on lead guitar, Klaus Voorman on bass guitar and Billy Preston on organ.

SIDE ONE

I'm The Greatest (John Lennon/Ringo Starr)   3:23
Producer : Richard Perry
UK Release : Apple PCTC 252 (L.P. Ringo)
US Release : Apple SWAL 3414 (L.P. Ringo)

John Lennon : Piano and Harmony Vocal
Paul McCartney : Not Present
George Harrison : Lead Guitar
Ringo Starr : Drums and Lead Vocal
Klaus Voormann : Bass Guitar
Billy Preston : Organ

One and One Is Two
(Lennon – McCartney) The Strangers with Mike Shannon   2:10
Producer : Unknown
UK Release : 8 May 1964 Phillips BF 1335
No US Release

From A Window
(Lennon – McCartney)   Billy J. Kramer and The Dakotas   1:55
Producer : George Martin
UK Release : 17 July 1964 Parlophone R5156
US Release : 12 August 1964 Imperial 66051

Nobody I Know (Lennon – McCartney) Peter and Gordon   2:27

Producer : John Burgess
UK Release : 27 May 1964 Columbia DB 7292
US Release : 15 June 1964 Capitol 5211

Like Dreamers Do
(Lennon – McCartney) The Applejacks   2:30
Producer : Mike Smith
UK Release : 5 May 1964 Decca F11916
US Release : 6 July 1964 London 9681

I'll Keep You Satisfied
(Lennon—McCartney) Billy J. Kramer
and The Dakotas   2:04
Producer : George Martin
UK Release : 1 November
1963   Parlophone R5073
US Release : 11 November
1963   Liberty 55643

Love Of The Loved
(Lennon—McCartney)   Cilla
Black   2:00
Producer : George Martin
UK Release : 27 September 1963
No US Release.

Woman (Paul McCartney as B.
Webb)   Petter and Gordon   2:21
Producer : John Burgess
UK Release : 11 February
1966   Columbia DB 7834
US Release : 10 January 1966   Capitol
5579

Tip Of My Tongue
(Lennon—McCartney)   Tommy
Quickly   2:02
Producer : Les Reed
UK Release : 30 July 1963   Piccadilly
7N 35137
No US Release

**I'm In Love (Lennon—McCartney) The
Fourmost**   2:07
Producer : George Martin
UK Release : 15 November
1963   Parlophone R5078
UK Release : 10 February 1964 Atco
6285

SIDE TWO

**Hello Little Girl (Lennon—McCartney)
The Fourmost**   1:50
Producer : George Martin
UK Release : 30 August
1963   Parlophone R5056
US Release : 15 November 1963 Atco
6280

**That Means A Lot (Lennon—McCartney)
P.J.Proby**   2:31
Producer : Ron Richards
UK Release : 17 September 1965
Liberty LBF 10215

US Release : 23 August 1965 Liberty
LST 7421
(L.P. P.J. Proby)

**It's For You (Lennon—McCartney) Cilla
Black**   2:20
Producer : George Martin
UK Release : 31 July 1964   Parlophone
R5162
US Release : 17 August 1964   Capitol
5258

Penina (Paul McCartney) Carlos
Mendes   2:36
Producer : Unknown
UK Release : 1969, Portugal only, no UK
release
No US Release

Step Inside Love (Lennon—McCartney)
Cilla Black   2:20**Producer** : George
Martin
UK Release : 8 March 1968 Parlophone
R5674
US Release : 6 May 1968 Bell 726

World Without Love
(Lennon—McCartney) Peter and
Gordon   2:38
Producer : Norman Newell
UK Release : 28 February 1964
Columbia DB 7225
US Release : 27 April 1964 Capitol 5175

**Bad To Me (Lennon—McCartney) Billy J.
Kramer and The Dakotas**   2:18
Producer : George Martin
UK Release : 26 July 1963 Parlophone
R5049
US Release : 23 September 1963
Liberty 55626

**I Don't Want To See You Again
(Lennon—McCartney) Peter and
Gordon**   1:59
Producer : Norman Newell
UK Release : 11 September 1964
Columbia DB 7356
US Release : 21 September 1964
Capitol 5272

I'll Be On My Way
(Lennon—McCartney) Billy J. Kramer
and The Dakotas   1:38
Producer : George Martin
UK Release : 26 April 1963 Parlophone
R5023

158

US Release : 10 June 1963 Liberty 55586

Catcall (Paul McCartney) The Chris
   Barber Band   3:05
Producers : Chris Barber, Giorgio
   Gomelsky, Reggie King
UK Release : 20 October 1967
   Marmalade 598-005
No US Release

The seven relevant songs written by Lennon and/or McCartney, recorded
by other artists up to the end of 1969, but not included on this album, are:

Thingumy Bob (Paul McCartney) John
   Fosters and Sons Ltd. Black Dyke
   Mills Band   1:51
Producer : Paul McCartney
UK Release : 6 September 1968 Apple 4
US Release : 28 August 1968 Apple 1800

Goodbye (Lennon – McCartney) Mary
   Hopkin   2:23
Producer : Paul McCartney
UK Release : 28 March 1969
   Apple 10
US Release : 7 April 1969
   Apple 1806

Theme From The Family Way (Paul
   McCartney) The George Martin
   Orchestra   2:05
Producer : George Martin
UK Release : 23 December 1966 United
   Artists UP 1165
No US Release

Love In The Open Air (Paul McCartney)
   The George Martin Orchestra   2:18
Producer : George Martin
UK Release : 23 December 1966 United
   Artists UP 1165

US Release : 24 April 1967 United
   Artists UA 50148

Give Peace A Chance
   (Lennon – McCartney) The Plastic
   Ono Band   4:49
Producers : John Lennon and Yoko Ono
UK Release : 4 July 1969
   Apple 13
US Release : 7 July 1969
   Apple 1809

Cold Turkey (John Lennon) The Plastic
   Ono Band   4:59
Producers : John Lennon and Yoko Ono
UK Release : 24 October 1969 Apple
   1001
US Release : 20 October 1969 Apple
   1813

Come And Get It (Paul McCartney)
   Badfinger   2:21
Producer : Paul McCartney
UK Release : 5 December 1969 Apple
   20
US Release : 12 January 1970 Apple
   1815

   One further track that could be included here is the 1968 Beach Boys'
recording Bluebirds Over The Mountains, which was written (supposedly)
by one Ersel Hickey and published by Northern Songs. Of course, Northern
Songs was set up in 1963 specifically to publish songs written by John
Lennon and Paul McCartney and whilst they also published some of George
Harrison's earliest songs before he found it Harrisongs, they never
published non-Beatle songs. So who is the mysterious Ersel Hickey and why
was his songs published by Northern Songs?
   One theory is that Ersel Hickey is none other than Paul McCartney under a
pseudonym. When Paul co-produced Vegetables with the Beach Boys for
their 1967 album Smiley Smile, he gave them Bluebirds Over The Mountain

to record at a later date. It is quite possible and there seems to be a precedent.

In 1966, two years before this recording was issued, Paul, using the subsequently admitted pseudonym Bernard Webb, wrote a song entitled Woman and gave it to Peter and Gordon to record.

So did Paul McCartney as Ersel Hickey write Bluebirds Over The Mountain—or does Ersel Hickey actually exist?

THE AMERICAN ALBUMS

MEET THE BEATLES
Capitol ST 2047
Producer : George Martin
Release Date : 20 January 1964
Running Time : 26:43

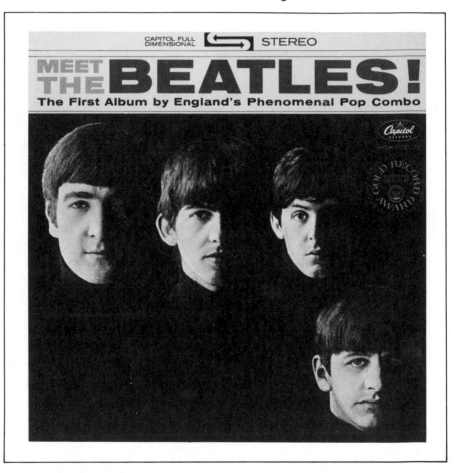

SIDE ONE: I Want To Hold Your Hand; I Saw Her Standing There; This Boy; It Won't Be Long; All I've Got To Do: All My Loving.

SIDE TWO: Don't Bother Me; Little Child; Till There Was You; Hold Me Tight; I Wanna Be Your Man; Not A Second Time.

After almost twelve months of rejecting the Beatles, Capitol Records put together this first 'official' American Beatles' album. Previously, Beatles' records (as issued on Parlophone in the UK) had been issued on a variety of record labels in the USA such as Vee Jay, Tollie and Swan. When Beatlemania swept America, Capitol, fully aware that they had originally rejected the Beatles, were desparate to take up the option of issuing their records.

Meet the Beatles, which has a similar jacket to the British album With The Beatles, also contains nine of the 14 tracks from that album, plus I Saw Her Standing There from Please Please Me and the Beatles' latest British single at the time, I Want To Hold Your Hand/This Boy.

Capitol also issued I Want To Hold Your Hand with the B-side I Saw Her Standing There as a single from this album.

Side One

I Want To Hold Your Hand   2:24
(See A Collection Of Beatles Oldies
    Album PCS 7016)

I Saw Her Standing There   2:50
(See Please Please Me Album PCS 3042)

This Boy   2:11
(See British Rarities Album PCM 1001)

It Won't Be Long   2:11
(See With The Beatles Album PCS 3045)

All I've Got To Do   2:05
(See With The Beatles Album PCS 3045)

All My Loving   2:04
(See With The Beatles Album PCS 3045)

Side Two

Don't Bother Me (Harrison)   2:28
(See With The Beatles Album PCS 3045)

Little Child   1:46
(See With The Beatles Album PCS 3045)

Till There Was You (Willson)   2:12
(See With The Beatles Album PCS 3045)

Hold Me Tight   2:30
(See With The Beatles Album PCS 3045)

I Wanna Be Your Man   1:59
(See With The Beatles Album PCS 3045)

Not A Second Time   2:30
(See With The Beatles Album PCS 3045)

All Lennon — McCartney songs except where stated.

THE BEATLES' SECOND ALBUM
Capitol ST 2080
Producer : George Martin
Release Date : 10 April 1964
Running Time : 26:12

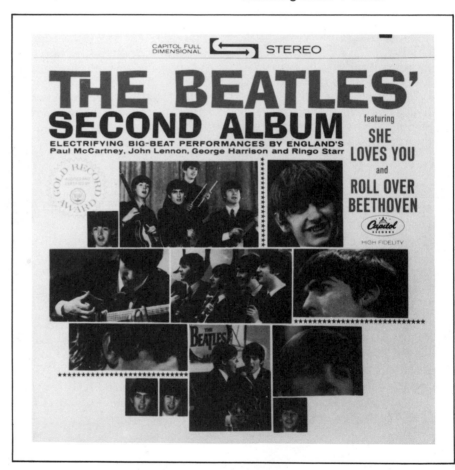

SIDE ONE: Roll Over Beethoven; Thank You Girl; You Really Got A Hold On Me; Devil In Her Heart; Money; You Can't Do That.

SIDE TWO: Long Tall Sally; I Call Your Name; Please Mr. Postman; I'll Get You; She Loves You.

Within four months of issuing Meet The Beatles, Capitol Records, now fully aware of the surge of Beatlemania in America, issued this album which includes the remaining five tracks from With The Beatles. Along with You Can't Do That (the B-side of Can't Buy Me Love which, at the time, was Capitol Records' latest Beatles' single which was also to be included on the soundtrack and album of A Hard Day's Night), She Loves You and I'll Get You (both previously issued as a single by Swan Records for which Capitol had now acquired the rights), Long Tall Sally and I Call Your Name (issued on the E.P. Long Tall Sally in Britain) and the stereo recording of Thank You Girl (yet to be issued in Britain).

Side One

Roll Over Beethoven (Berry)   2:44
(See With The Beatles Album PCS 3045)

Thank You Girl   2:01
(See British Rarities Album PCM 1001)

You Really Got A Hold On Me
   (Robinson)   2:58
(See With The Beatles Album PCS 3045)

Devil In Her Heart (Drapkin)   2:23
(See With The Beatles Album PCS 3045)

Money (Bradford-Gordy)   2:47
(See With The Beatles Album PCS 3045)

You Can't Do That   2:33
(See British A Hard Day's Night Album
   PCS 3058)

Side Two

Long Tall Sally
(Johnson-Penniman-Blackwell)   1:58
(See British Rarities Album PCM 1001)

I Call Your Name   2:02
(See British Rarities Album PCM 1001)

Please Mr. Postman (Holland)   2:34
(See With The Beatles Album PCS 3045)

I'll Get You   2:04
(See British Rarities Album PCM 1001)

She Loves You   2:18
(See A Collection Of Beatles Oldies
Album PCS 7016)

All Lennon — McCartney songs except where stated.

A HARD DAY'S NIGHT
United Artists UAS 6366
Producer : George Martin
Release Date : 26 June 1964
Running Time : 29:21

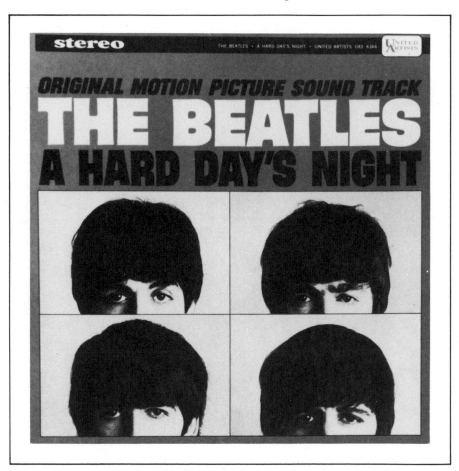

SIDE ONE: A Hard Day's Night; Tell Me Why; I'll Cry Instead; (I Should Have Known Better); I'm Happy Just To Dance With You; (And I Love Her).

SIDE TWO: I Should Have Known Better; If I Fell; And I Love Her; (Ringo's Theme - This Boy); Can't Buy Me Love; (A Hard Day's Night).

The Beatles' first movie soundtrack album bears little resemblance to the British album of the same name, although it does include all the new material used in the film plus George Martin's orchestral contributions. The seven new songs heard in the film are spread between the two album sides (whereas they are all on side one of the British album) with I'll Cry Instead, which was dropped from the film at the last minute.

Side One

A Hard Day's Night   2:28
(See British A Hard Day's Night Album
    PCS 3058)

Tell Me Why   2:04
(See British A Hard Day's Night Album
    PCS 3058)

I'll Cry Instead   2:06
(See British A Hard Day's Night Album
    PCS 3058)

I Should Have Known Better*   2:16

I'm Happy Just To Dance With You   1:59
(See British A Hard Day's Night Album
    PCS 3058)

And I Love Her*   3:42

Side Two

I Should Have Known Better   2:42
(See British A Hard Day's Night Album
    PCS 3058)

If I Fell   2:16
(See British A Hard Day's Night Album
    PCS 3058)

And I Love Her   2:27
(See British A Hard Day's Night Album
    PCS 3058)

Ringo's Theme (This Boy)*   3:06

Can't Buy Me Love   2:15
(See British A Hard Day's Night Album
    PCS 3058)

A Hard Day's Night*   2:00
The George Martin Orchestra*

All Lennon—McCartney songs.

SOMETHING NEW
Capitol ST 2108
Producer : George Martin
Release Date : 20 July 1964
Running Time : 24:23

SIDE ONE: I'll Cry Instead; Things We Said Today; Any Time At All; When I Get Home; Slow Down; Matchbox.

SIDE TWO: Tell Me Why; And I Love Her; I'm Happy Just To Dance With You; If I Fell; Komm Gib Mir Deine Hand.

Although this album claims to be 'something new', five of the eleven tracks were previously issued on the American album A Hard Day's Night. Of the remaining six tracks, three have been extracted from the British album A Hard Day's Night, whilst Slow Down and Matchbox come from the British E.P. Long Tall Sally. The final track, Komm, Gib Mir Deine Hand, is the German language version of I Want To Hold Your Hand, which although issued in both Germany and America was not issued in Britain until 1978 on the Rarities album.

Side One

I'll Cry Instead   1:44
(See British A Hard Day's Night Album
   PCS 3058)

Things We Said Today   2:35
(See British A Hard Day's Night Album
   PCS 3058)

Any Time At All   2:10
(See British A Hard Day's Night Album
   PCS 3058)

When I Get Home   2:14
(See British A Hard Day's Night Album
   PCS 3058)

Slow Down (Williams)   2:54
(See British Rarities Album PCM 1001)

Matchbox (Perkins)   1:37
(See British Rarities Album PCM 1001)

Side Two

Tell Me Why   2:04
(See British A Hard Day's Night Album
   PCS 3058)

And I Love Her   2:27
(See British A Hard Day's Night Album
   PCS 3058)

I'm Happy Just To Dance With You   1:59
(See British A Hard Day's Night Album
   PCS 3058)

If I Fell   2:16
(See British A Hard Day's Night Album
   PCS 3058)

Komm, Gib Mir Deine Hand
   (Lennon—McCartney—Nicolas—
   Hellmer)   2:24
(See British Rarities Album PCM 1001)

All Lennon—McCartney songs except where stated.

THE BEATLES' STORY (2 L.P.s)
Capitol STBO 2222
Producer : Gary Usher and
Roger Christian
Release Date : 23 November
1964
Running Time : 49:54

RECORD ONE: Side One:
On Stage With The Beatles; How
Beatlemania Began; Beatlemania In
Action; Man Behind The Beatles - Brian
Epstein; John Lennon; Who's A Millionaire?
Side Two:
Beatles Will Be Beatles; Man Behind The
Music - George Martin; George Harrison.

RECORD TWO: Side One:
A Hard Day's Night - Their First Film; Paul
McCartney; Sneaky Haircuts And More
About Paul;
Side Two:
The Beatle's Look At Life 'Victims' Of
Beatlemania; Beatle Medley; Ringo
Starr; Liverpool And All The World!

Many Beatles' interview albums appeared in the USA during 1964, and Capitol Records put together this 'biography in sound' of the Beatles. It gives an approximate 50-minute history of the Beatles, from their beginnings in Liverpool as The Quarrymen and their days in Hamburg, to their eventual worldwide success. It is compiled and narrated by John Babcock in association with Al Wiman and Roger Christian of radio station KFWB, Hollywood, California, and (with the exception of the brief snatches of Beatles' records produced by George Martin) is produced by Gary Usher and Roger Christian.

Overall, the album is a rather glossy biography of the Beatles and includes interviews with them and some of their hysterical fans after the 1964 Hollywood Bowl concert (which incidentally is where the 'live' recording of Twist And Shout on side four comes from). Interspersed with the interviews and narration are 14 Beatles' recordings, which are not credited on the album's jacket or record label. In addition to Twist and Shout the remaining 13 tracks are: I Want To Hold Your Hand; Slow Down; This Boy; You Can't Do That; If I Fell; A Hard Day's Night; And I Love Her; Things We Said Today; I'm Happy Just To Dance With You; Little Child; Long Tall Sally; She Loves You; Boys.

Throughout the album the narrators give brief biographies of each of the Beatles, also of Brian Epstein (their Manager) and George Martin (their record producer). They try to explain Beatlemania but somehow don't succeed. Even so the album does manage to capture the spirit and excitement of Beatlemania in America at the height of the Beatles' success.

Side One

On Stage With The Beatles   1:03
How Beatlemania Began   1:18
Beatlemania in Action   2:24
Man Behind the Beatles — Brian
   Epstein   3:01
John Lennon   4:24
Who's A Millionaire?   0:43

Side Two

Beatles Will Be Beatles   7:37
Man Behind The Music — George
   Martin   0:47
George Harrison   4:43

Side Three

A Hard Day's Night — Their First
   Movie   3:45
Paul McCartney   1:55
Sneeky Haircuts and More About
   Paul   3:38

Side Four

The Beatles Look At Life   1:51
'Victims' Of Beatlemania   1:21
Beatle Medley   3:56
Ringo Starr   6:19
Liverpool And All The World!   1:09

BEATLES' 65
Capitol ST 2228
Producer : George Martin (and
in the USA Dave
Dexter Jr.)
Release Date : 15 December
1964
Running Time : 25:10

SIDE ONE: No Reply; I'm A Loser; Baby's In Black; Rock And Roll Music; I'll Follow The Sun; Mr. Moonlight. Honey Don't.

SIDE TWO: I'll Be Back; She's A Woman; I Feel Fine; Everybody's Trying To Be My Baby.

The first side of this album is in essence side one of the British album Beatles For Sale without the last track, Kansas City. The second side contains two further tracks from Beatles For Sale—Honey Don't and Everybody's Trying To Be My Baby, along with the thirteenth and remaining track from the British album A Hard Day's Night, I'll Be Back, plus I Feel Fine and She's A Woman, issued as a single a week after the release of this album.

Side One

No Reply   2:15
(See Beatles For Sale Album PCS 3062)

I'm A Loser   2:31
(See Beatles For Sale Album PCS 3062)

Baby's In Black   2:02
(See Beatles For Sale Album PCS 3062)

Rock And Roll Music (Berry)   2:02
(See Beatles For Sale Album PCS 3062)

I'll Follow The Sun   1:46
(See Beatles For Sale Album PCS 3062)

Mr. Moonlight (Johnson)   2:35
(See Beatles For Sale Album PCS 3062)

Side Two

Honey Don't (Perkins)   2:56
(See Beatles For Sale Album PCS 3062)

I'll Be Back   2:22
(See British A Hard Day's Night Album PCS 3058)

She's A Woman   2:57
(See British Rarities Album PCM 1001)

I Feel Fine   2:20
(See A Collection of Beatles Oldies Album PCS 7016)

Everybody's Trying To Be My Baby (Perkins)   2:24
(See Beatles For Sale Album PCS 3062)

All Lennon—McCartney songs except where stated.

THE EARLY BEATLES
Capitol ST 2309
Producer : George Martin
Release Date : 22 March 1965
Running Time : 25:31

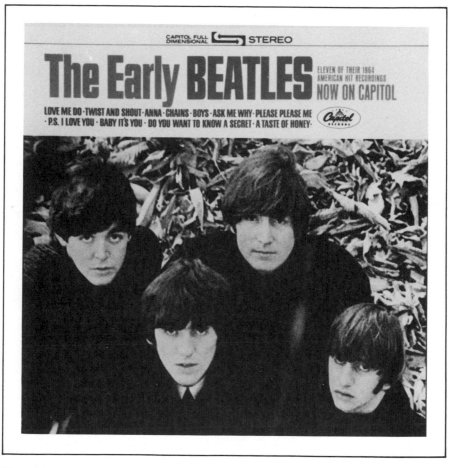

SIDE ONE: Love Me Do; Twist And Shout; Anna (Go To Him); Chains; Boys; Ask Me Why.

SIDE TWO: Please Please Me; P.S. I Love You; Baby It's You; A Taste Of Honey; Do You Want To Know A Secret.

Because Capitol Records rejected the Beatles in 1963, Vee Jay Records issued an album called Introducing The Beatles. When Beatlemania reached its peak at the end of 1964, Capitol acquired the rights to the Vee Jay recordings and issued this album which is a rather truncated version of the British album Please Please Me, without I Saw Her Standing There (already on Capitol's Meet The Beatles album) and without Misery and There's A Place (not to be issued on a Capitol album until 1980).

Side One

Love Me Do   2:19
(See Please Please Me Album PCS 3042)
Twist And Shout (Medley—Russell)   2:32
(See Please Please Me Album PCS 3042)
Anna (Go To Him) (Alexander)   2:56
(See Please Please Me Album PCS 3042)
Chains (Goffin—King)   2:21
(See Please Please Me Album PCS 3042)
Boys (Dixon—Farrell)   2:24
(See Please Please me Album PCS 3042)
Ask Me Why   2:24
(See Please Please Me Album PCS 3042)

Side Two

Please Please Me   2:00
(See Please Please Me Album PCS 3042)
P.S. I Love You   2:02
(See Please Please Me Album PCS 3042)
Baby It's You (David—Bacharach—
   Williams)   2:36
(See Please Please me Album PCS 3042)
A Taste Of Honey (Marlow—Scott)   2:02
(See Please Please Me Album PCS 3042)
Do You Want To Know A Secret   1:55
(See Please Please Me Album PCS 3042)

All Lennon—McCartney songs except where stated.

BEATLES VI
Capitol ST 2358
Producer : George Martin
Release Date : 14 June 1965
Running Time : 27:24

SIDE ONE: Kansas City/Hey Hey Hey Hey; Eight Days A Week; You Like Me Too Much; Bad Boy; I Don't Want To Spoil The Party; Words Of Love.

SIDE TWO: What You're Doing; Yes It Is; Dizzy Miss Lizzy; Tell Me What You See; Every Little Thing.

With Beatlemania still at its height in America, Capitol Records came up with Beatles VI, a compilation of the remaining six tracks left over from the British album Beatles For Sale, plus three tracks pulled from the British Help! album. They also put the B-side (Yes It Is) of the current single (Ticket To Ride) on this album, leaving the A-side which is featured in the film *HELP!* for that album. The only curio on this album is Bad Boy, which although obviously recorded in 1965 was not released in Britain until some eighteen months later when it was included on the album A Collection Of Beatles Oldies.

Side One

Kansas City/Hey Hey Hey Hey
   (Leiber–Stoller) 2:30
(See Beatles For Sale Album PCS 3062)

Eight Days A Week 2:43
(See Beatles for Sale Album PCS 3062)

You Like Me Too Much (Harrison) 2:34
(See British Help! Album PCS 3071)

Bad Boy (Williams) 2:17
(See A Collection of Beatles Oldies Album
   PCS 7016)

I Don't Want to Spoil The Party 2:23
(See Beatles For Sale Album PCS 3062)

Words of Love (Holly) 2:10
(See Beatles For Sale Album PCS 3062)

Side Two

What You're Doing 2:30
(See Beatles For Sale Album PCS 3062)

Yes It Is 2:40
(See British Rarities Album PCM 1001)

Dizzy Miss Lizzy (Williams) 2:51
(See British Help! Album PCS 3071)

Tell Me What You See 2:35
(See British Help! Album PCS 3071)

Every Little Thing 2:01
(See Beatles For Sale Album PCS 3062)

All Lennon–McCartney songs except where stated.

HELP!
Capitol SMAS 2386
Producer : George Martin (and
in the USA Dave
Dexter Jr.)
Release Date : 13 August 1965
Running Time : 28:40

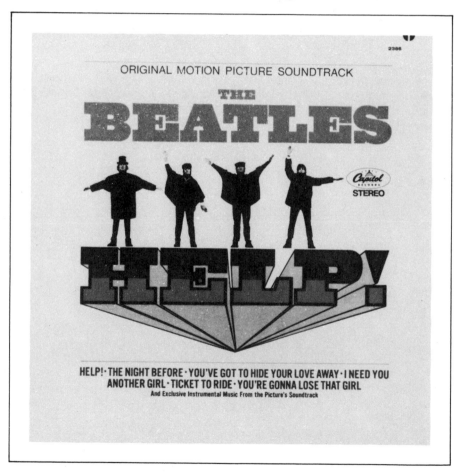

SIDE ONE: (The James Bond Theme); Help!;
The Night Before; (From Me To You Fantasy);
You've Got To Hide Your Love Away; I Need
You; (In The Tyrol).

SIDE TWO: Another Girl; (Another Hard Day's
Night); Ticket To Ride; (The Bitter End/You
Can't Do That; You're Gonna Lose That
Girl; (The Chase).

The soundtrack of the Beatles' second movie includes not only the new songs specially written for the film, but also the incidental music played by the George Martin Orchestra. When this album was released in the USA many fans were annoyed to find that it had been issued as a de-luxe package (thereby increasing the price) but included only seven Beatles' tracks. On the sleeve, the four photographs of the Beatles have been inadvertently rearranged so that the semaphore message spells out a nonsensical H-P-E-L!'. Also, unlike the British track listing, this album cover offers the version You're Gonna Loose That Girl; this spelling only occurs elsewhere on Record 3 of the Beatles Box.

Side One

The James Bond Theme
(Norman)*   0:16

Help!   2:16
(See British Help! Album PCS 3071)

The Night Before   2:33
(See British Help! Album PCS 3071)

From Me To You Fantasy*   2:03

You've Got To Hide Your Love
    Away   2:08
(See British Help! Album PCS 3071)

I Need You (Harrison)   2:28
(See British Help! Album PCS 3071)

In The Tyrol (Wagner – Arr.
    Thorne)*   2:21

Side Two

Another Girl   2:02
(See British Help! Album PCS 3071)

Another Hard Day's Night*   2:28

Ticket To Ride   3:03
(See British Help! Album PCS 3071)

The Bitter End (Thorne)/You Can't Do
    That*   2:20

You're Gonna Lose That Girl   2:18
(See British Help! Album PCS 3071)

The Chase (Thorne)*   2:24

*The George Martin Orchestra

All Lennon – McCartney songs except where stated.

RUBBER SOUL
Capitol ST 2442
Producer : George Martin
Release Date : 6 December 1965
Running Time : 28:46

SIDE ONE: I've Just Seen A Face; Norwegian Wood; You Won't See Me; Think For Yourself; The Word; Michelle.

SIDE TWO: It's Only Love; Girl; I'm Looking Through You; In My Life; Wait; Run For Your Life.

Although the title and sleeve of the American Rubber Soul album are the same as the British, the contents are different. As the American Help! album had used only seven tracks from the British album, leaving four over, two of these (I've Just Seen A Face and It's Only Love) were included on the American Rubber Soul plus ten tracks from the British Rubber Soul. (The remaining tracks from the British albums—two from Help! and four from Rubber Soul — were issued on yet another album by Capitol, Yesterday...and Today.)

Side One

I've Just Seen A Face   2:04
(See British Help! Album PCS 3071)
Norwegian Wood (This Bird Has
   Flown)   2:00
(See British Rubber Soul Album PCS
   3075)
You Won't See Me   3:19
(See British Rubber Soul Album PCS
   3075)
Think For Yourself (Harrison)   2:16
(See British Rubber Soul Album PCS
   3075)
The Word   2:42
(See British Rubber Soul Album PCS
   3075)
Michelle   2:42
(See British Rubber Soul Album PCS
   3075)

Side Two

It's Only Love   1:53
(See British Help! Album PCS 3071)
Girl   2:26
(See British Rubber Soul Album PCS
   3075)
I'm Looking Through You   2:27
(See British Rubber Soul Album PCS
   3075)
In My Life   2:23
(See British Rubber Soul Album PCS
   3075)
Wait   2:13
(See British Rubber Soul Album PCS
   3075)
Run For Your Life   2:21
(See British Rubber Soul Album PCS
   3075)

All Lennon—McCartney songs except
where stated.

YESTERDAY ... AND TODAY
Capitol ST 2553
Producer : George Martin (and
in the USA Bill Miller)
Release Date : 20 June 1966
Running Time : 26:40

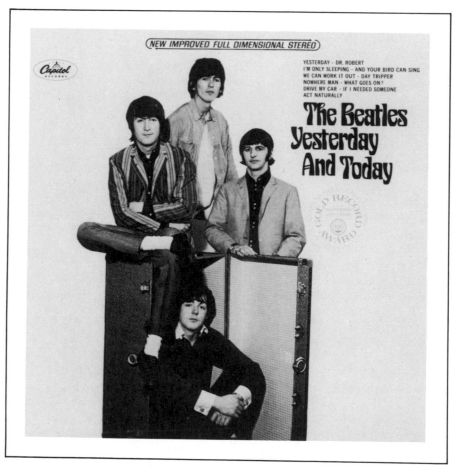

SIDE ONE: Drive My Car; I'm Only Sleeping; Nowhere Man; Dr Robert; Yesterday; Act Naturally.

SIDE TWO: And Your Bird Can Sing; If I Need Someone; We Can Work It Out; What Goes On?; Day Tripper.

When Capitol Records revealed their intention to release this album, the Beatles decided to register a protest against the way their albums had been butchered, and were photographed for the sleeve dressed in butchers' aprons, holding pieces of meat and decapitated baby dolls. (See US Rarities sleeve.)

The public outcry was so great that this sleeve was withdrawn, the present sleeve quickly printed and substituted, and the album reissued. Because so many of the original sleeves had been printed, many simply had the new photograph posted over the offending one. These examples are now quite valuable.

Tracks include Yesterday and Act Naturally from Help!, Drive My Car, Nowhere Man, If I Needed Someone and What Goes On? from Rubber Soul, plus three tracks originally planned for Revolver (and included on the British Revolver album): I'm Only Sleeping, Dr. Robert, and And Your Bird Can Sing. To complete the album Capitol included We Can Work It Out and Day Tripper, issued as a double A-sided single, six months previously.

Side One

Drive My Car   2:25
(See British Rubber Soul Album PCS 3075)

I'm Only Sleeping   2:58
(See British Revolver Album PCS 7009)

Nowhere Man   2:40
(See British Rubber Soul Album PCS 3075)

Dr. Robert   2:14
(See British Revolver Album PCS 7009)

Yesterday   2:04
(See British Help! Album PCS 3071)

Act Naturally (Morrison – Russell)   2:27
(See British Help! Album PCS 3071)

Side Two

And Your Bird Can Sing   2:02
(See British Revolver Album PCS 7009)

If I Needed Someone (Harrison)   2:19
(See British Rubber Soul Album PCS 3075)

We Can Work It Out   2:10
(See A Collection Of Beatles Oldies Album PCS 7016)

What Goes On? (Lennon – McCartney – Starkey)   2:44
(See British Rubber Soul Album PCS 3075)

Day Tripper   2:37
(See A Collection Of Beatles Oldies Album PCS 7016)

All Lennon – McCartney songs except where stated.

REVOLVER
Capitol ST 2576
Producers : George Martin (and
in the USA Bill
Miller).
Release Date : 8 August 1966
Running Time : 27:47

SIDE ONE: Taxman; Eleanor Rigby; Love You Too; Here, There And Everywhere; Yellow Submarine; She Said, She Said.

SIDE TWO: Good Day Sunshine; For No One; I Want To Tell You; Got To Get You Into My Life; Tomorrow Never Knows.

This is the first Beatles album to be issued in the USA bearing any resemblance to its UK equivalent. With the exception of three tracks included on Yesterday ... And Today, the tracks on this album are the same as on the British album. All subsequent albums except Rarities had identical American and British editions.

Side One

Taxman (Harrison)   2:36
(See British Revolver Album PCS 7009)

Eleanor Rigby   2:11
(See British Revolver Album PCS 7009)

Love You Too (Harrison)   3:00
(See British Revolver Album PCS 7009)

Here, There And Everywhere   2:29
(See British Revolver Album PCS 7009)

Yellow Submarine   2:40
(See British Revolver Album PCS 7009)

She Said She Said   2:39
(See British Revolver Album PCS 7009)

Side Two

Good Day Sunshine   2:08
(See British Revolver Album PCS 7009)

For No One   2:03
(See British Revolver Album PCS 7009)

I Want To Tell You (Harrison)   2:30
(See British Revolver Album PCS 7009)

Got To Get You Into My Life   2:31
(See British Revolver Album PCS 7009)

Tomorrow Never Knows   3:00
(See British Revolver Album PCS 7009)

All Lennon—McCartney songs except where stated.

RARITIES
Capitol SHAL 12060
Producer : George Martin
Release Date : 24 March 1980
Running Time : 41:04

SIDE ONE: Love Me Do; Misery; There's A Place; Sie Liebt Dich; And I Love Her; Help; I'm Only Sleeping; I Am The Walrus.

SIDE TWO: Penny Lane; Helter Skelter; Don't Pass Me By; The Inner Light; Across The Universe; You Know My Name (Look Up The Number); Sgt. Pepper Inner Groove.

The contents of this album differ completely from those of the British album with the same basic title.

When Capitol Records decided to compile a rarities album, they originally called it Collectors Items and gave it a catalogue number of SPRO 9462. The contents of that album were: Love Me Do, Thank You Girl, All My Loving, This Boy, Sie Liebt Dich, I Feel Fine, From Me To You, She's A Woman, Help!, I'm Down, Penny Lane, Baby, You're A Rich Man, I Am The Walrus, The Inner Light, Across The Universe, You Know My Name, and Sgt. Pepper Inner Groove.

Capitol then realised that the stereo version of I'm Down had already been issued in the USA on the 1976 album Rock And Roll Music, so they substituted a different stereo mix of Paperback Writer, which although included on the British album A Collection Of Beatles Oldies, had never been issued in America. They also changed the catalogue number to SPRO 9463, and it seemed that this would be the final format for the album. However, for reasons known only to Capitol, Collectors Items was scrapped and all copies were ordered to be destroyed, although an enterprising number of employees at Capitol smuggled them out of the pressing plant and put them on sale. Collectors Items (either pressing) is currently valued at about twice the normal price of a Beatles' album but is unlikely to increase in value as Capitol are currently discussing plans to issue a Rarities II album.

Although details of this are secret, it is highly probable that it will contain the tracks from Collectors Items which were not transferred on to Rarities, plus a few other tracks not included on any Beatles' album issued by Capitol in the USA.

Side One

Love Me Do   2:22
(See Please Please Me Album PCS 3042)

Misery   1:43
(See Please Please Me Album PCS 3042)

There's A Place   1:44
(See Please Please Me Album PCS 3042)

Sie Liebt Dich (Lennon — McCartney — Nicolas — Montague)   2:18
(See British Rarities Album PCM 1001)

And I Love Her   2:36
(See British A Hard Day's Night Album PCS 3058)

Help!   2:16
(See British Help! Album PCS 3071)

I'm Only Sleeping   2:58
(See British Revolver Album PCS 7009)

I Am The Walrus   4:35
(See Magical Mystery Tour Album PCTC 255)

Side Two

Penny Lane   3:00
(See Magical Mystery Tour Album PCTC 255)

Helter Skelter   3:38
(See The Beatles Album PCS 7067-8)

Don't Pass Me By (Starkey)   3:45
(See The Beatles Album PCS 7067-8)

The Inner Light (Harrison)   2:36
(See British Rarities Album PCM 1001)

Across The Universe   3:41
(See British Rarities Album PCM 1001)

You Know My Name (Look Up The Number)   4:20
(See British Rarities Album PCS 1001)

Sgt. Pepper Inner Groove   0:02
(See Sgt. Pepper's.... Album PCS 7027)

All Lennon — McCartney songs except where stated.

This chapter discusses recorded oddities issued by the Beatles—oddities such as more than one recording of the same song or songs available in mono only. There are a number of these 'oddities' which have long been the subject of debate amongst Beatles' fans. I have collected here details of 36 songs involving between them a staggering 76 different recordings. Of these 76, 69 are available in Britain; the remaining 11 are available in either America or Canada but have yet to be issued in Britain.

For each song I have listed all versions, with details of timings, differences, and where each recording can be found. If the same recording is available on more than one record I have given details of its first appearance. I have not included, as separate versions, recordings that feature a premature fade out as do several of the singles, for example, A Hard Day's Night, which is four seconds shorter than the album track. In most cases these singles are purely mono mixing of stereo album tracks. To include all of these would not do justice to the real oddities. This chapter describes the actual recording oddities together with a review of a couple of even rarer Beatles' recordings issued in Italy as part of a four-single set in 1968. The recordings feature two parts of an interview with disc jockey Kenny Everett. Although these are not recording oddities as such, they are nontheless rare recordings and are included on that basis within this chapter.

Finally, there is also included a list of Beatles' recordings that are (at present) only available in mono form.

ACROSS THE UNIVERSE
Version 1   3:41
Previously included on the charity album No One's Gonna Change Our World (Regal Starline SRS 5013) which is now deleted. The track is currently included on the album Rarities (Parlophone PCM 1001).
Version 2   3:51
As included on the Let It Be album (Apple PCS 7096).

Although both recordings of this song feature John on lead vocals, the first had the sound of birds at the beginning and backing vocals from Paul and two girls, Lizzie Bravo and Gayleen Pease, who were invited into the recording session. This is slightly slower than Version 2, which has a solo vocal from John and an orchestral backing.

ALL MY LOVING
Version 1   2:04
As included on With The Beatles (Parlophone PCS 3045).
Version 2   2:07
Previously unavailable in Britain until 1980 when it was included on the eight album set The Beatles Box (Parlophone/World Records SM 701-708). This differs from the first version as it includes six taps of a hi-hat just prior to beginning of the recording.

ALL YOU NEED IS LOVE
Version 1   3:57
As available on the single (Parlophone R5620).

Version 2   3:47
As included on Yellow Submarine (Apple PCS 7070).

Although both of these recordings were made on the same day, they are two entirely different recordings. Version 1 is at present available only in mono. Version 2, in stereo, is not simply a stereo mix of Version 1; it is an entirely different recording. There are slight but significant differences between the lead vocals and also certain sections of the backing. Version 2 is also ten seconds shorter than Version 1.

AND I LOVE HER
Version 1   2:27
As included on the American version of the album A Hard Day's Night (United Artists UAS 6366), this recording is currently unavailable in Britain.
Version 2   2:27
As included on the British version of the album A Hard Day's Night (Parlophone PCS 3058).
Version 3   2:36
Unavailable in Britain until 1980, when it was included in the eight-album set The Beatles Box (Parlophone/World Records SM 701-708).

The three versions are not different recordings, but are different stages of the same recording. Version 1 features Paul's lead vocal, mostly on its own, with only the chorus being double-tracked. Version 2 features Paul's lead vocal double-tracked, and then triple-tracked, for the chorus. Version 3 has the same double-tracked lead vocals as Version 2, but the guitar riff at the ending is repeated six times, rather than four as in Versions 1 and 2.

BLACKBIRD
Version 1   2:20
As included on the mono version of the double album The Beatles (Apple PMC 7067-8).
Version 2   2:20
As included on the stereo version of the double album The Beatles (Apple PCS 7067-8).

Like a number of tracks on the 'White Album' there are slight, almost unnoticeable differences between the mono and stereo mixing with this track. The 'bird' sounds that are included are different on both tracks and are also in slightly different places.

BLUE JAY WAY
Version 1   3:50
As included on the mono version of the Magical Mystery Tour double E.P. set (Parlophone MMT 1).
Version 2   3:50
As included on the stereo version of the Magical Mystery Tour double E.P. set (Parlophone SMMT 1).

Both versions are basically the same, but there are slight differences in that the backing vocals included on the stereo are missing from the mono version.

DAY TRIPPER
Version 1   2:37
As included on the stereo version of A Collection of Beatles Oldies (Parlophone PCS 7016).

Version 2   2:37
Unavailable in Britain until 1980 when it was included on the eight album set The Beatles Box (Parlophone/World Records SM 701-708).

   Although both recordings are the same, Version 1 has the guitar intro double-tracked, with each on a separate stereo channel. Version 2 has the guitar intro single-tracked on the left-hand channel only.

DON'T PASS ME BY
Version 1   3:45
As included on the mono version of the double album The Beatles (Apple PMC 7067-8).
Version 2   3:52
As included on the stereo version of the double album The Beatles (Apple PCS 7067-8).

   With the exception of the violin at the end of the track (probably re-recorded for the mono version) both this and the stereo version are the same although the mono version has been somewhat speeded up, making it seven seconds shorter. This also has the effect of transposing Ringo's voice into a higher key, giving the track a bouncier feel.

FROM ME TO YOU
Version 1   1:55
As available on the single (Parlophone R5015).
Version 2   1:55
As included on the stereo version of A Collection Of Beatles Oldies (Parlophone PCS 7016).

   Although both versions are from the same basic recording, they are noticeably different. The mono version has a harmonica on the intro; the stereo version does not.

GET BACK
Version 1   3:11
As available on the single (Apple R5777).
Version 2   3:09
As included on the album Let It Be (Apple PCS 7096).

   Version 1 is a studio recording including a verse at the end, not featured on Version 2. The latter is a live recording with a spoken intro just prior to the beginning of the track and is quite different. At the end instead of the extra verse we hear John Lennon's classic statement 'I'd like to say "thank you" on behalf of the group and ourselves and I hope we passed the audition'.

HELP!
Version 1   2:16
As available on the single (Parlophone R5305).
Version 2   2:16
As included on the album of the same name (Parlophone PCS 3071).

   The single and album versions have different vocals but the same backing track.

HELTER SKELTER
Version 1   3:38
As included on the mono version of the double album The Beatles (Apple PMC 7067-8).

Version 2   4:30
As included on the stereo version of the double album The Beatles (Apple PCS 7067-8).

Although both mono and stereo versions are, in effect, the same recording, they are mixed and edited differently. The fade-out of the mono version has several notes missing and the drumming is different. When it fades it does not reappear as does the stereo version, thereby missing Ringo's statement 'I've got blisters on my fingers'—words sometimes credited erroneously to John.

I AM THE WALRUS

There are four versions of this song, all slightly different edits of the same recording. This should have made them all slightly different lengths but because each is slowed down or speeded up they are all exactly the same.
Version 1   4:35
As included on the album Magical Mystery Tour (Parlophone PCTC 255). The organ intro here is repeated four times as opposed to six on some other versions.
Version 2   4:35
As available on the American single (Capitol 2056) but currently unavailable in Britain.

Again the organ intro is repeated four times but there are a few extra beats included between the lines 'I'm crying' and 'Yellow matter custard'.
Version 3   4:35
As included on the Magical Mystery Tour double E.P. (Parlophone SMMT 1). The organ intro is repeated six times but the few extra beats are missing from the middle of the recording.
Version 4   4:35
As included on the eight-album set The Beatles Box (Parlophone/World Records SM 701-708.

This fourth and final version includes both the organ intro repeated six times and the few extra beats in the middle of the recording. It is the full version edited from Versions 2 and 3.

I CALL YOUR NAME

Version 1   2:05
As included on the E.P. Long Tall Sally (Parlophone GEP 8913).
Version 2   2:05
As included on the double album Rock And Roll Music (Parlophone PCSP 719).

Although in effect the same recording, on Version 1, in mono, the backing cowbell starts at the beginning of the recording while on Version 2, the stereo mixing, the cowbell does not start until after John sings the opening line 'I call your name'.

I FEEL FINE

Version 1   2:02
As available on the single (Parlophone R5200).
Version 2   2:17
As included on the stereo version of A Collection Of Beatles Oldies (Parlophone PCS 7016).
Version 3   2:19
As included on the double album The Beatles 1962-66 (Apple PCSP 717).

Version 1, in mono, is an entirely different recording from Versions 2 and

3. These two are basically the same except for two seconds of mysterious whispering on Version 3, just before the beginning of the track.

I SHOULD HAVE KNOWN BETTER
Version 1 2:16
As included on the mono version of A Hard Day's Night (Parlophone PMC 1230).
Version 2 2:16
As included on the stereo version of A Hard Day's Night (Parlophone PCS 3058).
   These recordings differ only in the harmonica intro. On the stereo version this cuts out for a few seconds, while on the mono version it is complete.

IF I FELL
Version 1 2:18
As included on the mono version of A Hard Day's Night (Parlophone PMC 1230).
Version 2 2:18
As included on the stereo version of A Hard Day's Night (Parlophone PCS 3058).
   The mono version single-tracks John's lead vocal whereas the stereo version double-tracks it. Both feature a duet between John and Paul. On the stereo version, when they reach, for the second time, 'And I would be sad if our new love, was in vain' Paul's voice gives out on 'vain'. On the mono version, Paul sings the complete line, although on 'vain' his voice sounds strained.

I'LL CRY INSTEAD
Version 1 1:44
As included on the British album A Hard Day's Night (Parlophone PCS 3058).
Version 2 2:06
As included on the American album A Hard Day's Night (United Artists UAS 6366) and currently unavailable in Britain.
   Both versions originate from the same recording. The American version repeats the first verse just before the final verse; the British release does not.

I'M LOOKING THROUGH YOU
Version 1 2:20
As included on the British album Rubber Soul (Parlophone PCS 3075).
Version 2 2:27
As included on the American album Rubber Soul (Capitol ST 2442).
   Although these are from the same basic recording, the American version has two false starts; the rest is the same as the British release.

I'M ONLY SLEEPING
Version 1 2:58
As included on the mono version of the album Revolver (Parlophone PMC 7009).
Version 2 2:58
As included on the stereo version of the album Revolver (Parlophone PCS 7009).
   Only the mono version of this recording features the extra section of backwards guitar during the third verse of the song.

KOMM, GIB MIR DEINE HAND
Version 1 2:24
As included on the British album Rarities (Parlophone PCM 1001).
Version 2 2:24
As included on the American album Something New (Capitol ST 2018), and currently unavailable in Britian.

Although both recordings are the same, the American version has various screams and shouts over the musical intro, which are missing from the version released in Britain.

LET IT BE
Version 1 3:50
As available on the single (Apple R5833).
Version 2 4:01
As included on the album Let It Be (Apple PCS 7096).

Each recording is entirely different—the lead guitar on the album version is sloppier than on the single.

LOVE ME DO
Version 1 2:22
Previously available as a single (Parlophone R4949), this was withdrawn and replaced by Version 2 with the same catalogue number. It is now available on the eight-album set The Beatles Box (Parlophone/World Records SM 701-708).
Version 2 2:19
As included on Please Please Me (Parlophone PCS 3042).

Version 1 has Ringo on drums, while Version 2 features Andy White (a session musician) on drums with Ringo on tambourine. (For the history behind these two recordings see the Please Please Me album.)

MONEY

Version 1 2:47
As included on the mono version of With The Beatles (Parlophone PMC 1206).

Version 2 2:47
As included on the stereo version of With The Beatles (Parlophone PCS 3045).

These are two different recordings. The first, in mono, is slightly slower and has Ringo tapping his drumsticks together in time with the piano intro. Also, John's lead vocal is given more echo than on the stereo version, which does not include the drumstick tapping.

NORWEGIAN WOOD (THIS BIRD HAS FLOWN)
Version 1 2:00
As included on the album Rubber Soul (Parlophone PCS 3075).
Version 2 2:00
As included on The Beatles Ballads (Parlophone PCS 7214).

Although both recordings are the same, Version 2 has been re-mixed, with the backing track moved to the right-hand channel rather than the left, and the vocal track moved into the centre.

OB-LA-DI, OB-LA-DA
Version 1 3:10

As included on the mono version of the double album The Beatles (Apple PMC 7067-8).

Version 2 3:10

As included on the stereo version of the double album The Beatles (Apple PCS 7067-8).

As with two or three other songs, where the stereo recording appears to be the 'finished' version of the mono recording, with Ob-La-Di, Ob-La-Da, the hand clapping included during the piano intro of the stereo mixing is absent from the mono version.

PAPERBACK WRITER
Version 1 2:25

As included on the stereo version of A Collection Of Beatles Oldies (Parlophone PCS 7009).

Version 2 2:25

As included on the album Hey Jude (Parlophone PCS 7184).

Although both recordings are in stereo they are different mixings. Version 2 has the stereo reversed and the backing vocals mixed further forward than on the original mixing.

PENNY LANE
Version 1 3:00

As available on the single (Parlophone R5570).

Version 2 3:00

As included on the eight-album set The Beatles Box (Parlophone/World Records SM 701-708).

Version 2 is a collectors piece and is one of the most sought after Beatles' recordings. It features seven extra notes played on the picolo trumpet over the ending. It was distributed to radio stations in both the USA and Canada in this form, but when the record reached the stores (Version 1) these seven notes had been trimmed away.

PLEASE PLEASE ME
Version 1 2:00

As available on the single (Parlophone R4983).

Version 2 2:00

As included on the album Please Please Me (Parlophone PCS 3042).

At first listening, both the mono and stereo recordings of this song appear to be identical. However, there is a slight difference in both the vocal and lyrics between versions, particularly on the stereo recording when, halfway through the song, John fluffs the lyrics slightly. On the mono single version, the lyrics are sung without fault.

SGT. PEPPER'S LONELY HEARTS CLUB BAND (Reprise)
Version 1 1:20

As included on the mono version of the Sgt. Pepper's Lonely Hearts Club Band album (Parlophone PMC 7027).

Version 2 1:20

As included on the stereo version of the Sgt. Pepper's Lonely Hearts Club Band album (Parlophone PCS 7027).

As with many Beatle recording oddities, the differences between the mono and stereo versions occur during the introduction.

The mono version of this track features a 14 tap introduction (along with an indecipherable comment from John) just before Paul says, 'one, two three, four.'

The stereo version has only a 10 tap introduction and John's background comment is missing. Also the crowd sounds during the drumbeat section of the opening are different; the mono version includes laughter absent from the stereo track.

SEXY SADIE
Version 1   3:15
As included on the mono version of the double album The Beatles (Apple PMC 7067-8).
Version 2   3:15
As included on the stereo version of the double album The Beatles (Apple PCS 7067-8).

On the mono version there is one tambourine tap during the piano intro and on the stereo version there are two taps.

SLOW DOWN
Version 1   2:54
As included on the E.P. Long Tall Sally (Parlophone GEP 8913).
Version 2   2:54
As included on the double album Rock And Roll Music (Parlophone PCSP 719).

These two versions have different lead vocals. The stereo version also includes John shouting 'Ow' just before the last few bars of the track are played.

TELL ME WHY
Version 1   2:06
As included on the mono version of A Hard Day's Night (Parlophone PMC 1230).
Version 2   2:06
As included on the stereo version of A Hard Day's Night (Parlophone PCS 3058).

These recordings are basically the same, except that John's lead vocal is single-tracked on the mono version and double-tracked on the stereo one.

THANK YOU GIRL
Version 1   2:01
As available on the single (Parlophone R5015).
Version 2   2:01
As included on the American The Beatles Second Album (Capitol ST 2080), and currently unavailable in Britain.

These are from the same basic recording, but only the stereo version has the harmonica played twice during the track and also over the last few notes. This is not included on the British single version.

WE CAN WORK IT OUT
Version 1   2:10
As included on the stereo version of A Collection Of Beatles Oldies (Parlophone PCS 7016).
Version 2   2:10
As included on the American album Yesterday.... And Today (Capitol ST

2553), and currently unavailable in Britain.

These are two slightly different stereo mixings of the same track. Version 1 has the stereo split between the two channels without anything mixed into the centre whereas Version 2 has sections of the organ mixed into the centre.

WHY DON'T WE DO IT IN THE ROAD?
Version 1   1:42
As included on the mono version of The Beatles double album (Apple PMC 7067-8).
Version 2   1:42
As included on the stereo version of The Beatles double album (Apple PCS 7067-8).

Included in the intro of this track, along with the drumbeat, is hand clapping absent from the mono version.

In 1968 EMI Italy released a four single set entitled Una Sensazionale Intervista dei Beatles & Tre Dischi Apple. It contained the following records:-

Apple 2 Quelli Erano Giorni/Turn Turn Turn
(Mary Hopkin)
Apple 3 Sour Milk Sea/The Eagle Laughs At You
(Jackie Lomax)
Apple 5 Maybe Tomorrow/And Her Daddy's A Millionaire
Apple DRP 108 Una Sensazionale Intervista Con I Beatles Pts 1 & 2
(The Beatles & Kenny Everett).

The fourth single in this set, which contains an interview with the Beatles, was not issued anywhere else in the world. This four-single set is no longer available in Italy and has become a much sought after collector's item, changing hands for ever increasing sums of money. Below is a brief rundown of what the interview single contains.

A SENSATIONAL INTERVIEW WITH THE BEATLES Part 1   3:27
(UNA SENSAZIONALE INTERVISTA CON I BEATLES—Apple DPR 108).
The recording opens with a perverted version of the Huddie Ledbetter classic, Cottonfields performed tongue-in-cheek by John Lennon, who is then interviewed by that oddball of British television and radio, Kenny Everett. The interview briefly (between the Lennon/Everett offbeat humourous exchanges) touches on such subjects as John's return from India, at which point John breaks into a feigned foreign language, best described as gobbledygook. This is followed by Ringo's first song, Apple and Sgt. Pepper.

For the close of the track, John and Paul perform an improvised song, Goodbye To Kenny Everett.

A SENSATIONAL INTERVIEW WITH THE BEATLES Part 2   3:50
Part two opens with John commenting on Tiny Tim (who had a brief spell of fame singing such songs as Tiptoe Through The Tulips in a falsetto vocal.) John then launches into the third improvised song on this record, Tiny Tim For President. After this Kenny Everett comments about his being

dismissed from the BBC (due to a comment he passed about the wife of the then British Transport Minister having passed her driving test). Ringo, accompanied by drums, then proceeds to sing a further improvised song, Goodbye Kenny, which is followed by a further display of general lunacy. Kenny then asks the Beatles to sing Strawberry Fields Forever in a jazz tempo and with Paul as lead vocalist, they then perform a short acapella version. Paul then goes into a second and falsetto version of Ringo's earlier Goodbye Kenny. The side closes with an unknown announcer commenting on a Beatles' recording session that is taking place in the background.

IN MONO ONLY

As this chapter deals with Beatles' rarities it is the best place to mention the seven recordings that are available only in mono; there are no stereo alternatives of these tracks available anywhere in the world.

Love Me Do and P.S. I Love You were recorded in 1962, before the Beatles made the first album, Please Please Me, and before, stereo was available, but the other five tracks She Loves You, I'll Get You, Yes It is, Only A Northern Song and You Know My Name (Look Up The Number) were recorded at the time when it was standard practice to issue in stereo. Therefore I find it extremely, hard to believe that these tracks exist only in mono, and am certain that somewhere amongst the master tapes, alternative stereo recordings could be found.

One fascinating aspect of the Beatles' recording career is the material recorded, under various circumstances, but never released.

Unfortunately, over the years much of the unreleased material has found its way into the hands of bootleggers who have produced illegal records. It is surprising that this is allowed to continue as the Beatles and their record and publishing companies would benefit if the material was officially issued. I have listened to many of the unreleased recordings and as yet have not heard a bad track. Many fans and collectors would prefer to buy these unreleased tracks as officially issued records rather than as inferior quality bootlegs.

They fall into a minimum of five different categories: auditions, radio broadcasts, rejected tracks from recording sessions, session 'warm-ups' and demonstration recordings —plus the counterfeit records described immediately below.

BOGUS BEATLES

Before listing the unreleased tracks it is important to dispel some rumours and myths which have become associated with the Beatles over the years. A few records were thought by many people to be unreleased Beatles' tracks slipped out on other record labels. The following five records are quite definitely *not the Beatles.*

Have You Heard The Word/Futting Around—Fut (Beacon)

Legend had it that during the late 1960s, after the Beatles had finished Abbey Road and effectively ended their recording career, John Lennon joined the Bee Gees to record this track. Some people thought it was all four Beatles and the Bee Gees: another theory was that it was the Beatles' last recording. It has appeared on a surprising number of bootlegs although it is not the Beatles nor is it the Bee Gees, and the artists are still unknown.

L.S.Bumble Bee/Bee Side—Peter Cooke and Dudley Moore (Decca)

Issued early in 1967 this recording has appeared on many Beatles' bootlegs. It is a send-up of psychedelia which has a vocal sounding slightly like John Lennon. It is in fact Dudley Moore with backing by Peter Cooke.

We Are The Moles Parts I And II—The Moles (Parlophone)

Although released on the Parlophone label, this is not by the Beatles under another name. Mystery surrounded the release of this record in 1968; the master tapes were deposited in a left-luggage locker in a London railway station, and the key, with a mysterious letter, was sent to a leading British music paper, stating that the record was to be issued on the Parlophone label; it also stated that if the record reached the top ten, the identity of the group would be revealed.

Many people assumed that the record was by the Beatles; even so it sold poorly. A few years later The Moles were revealed as Simon Dupree and the Big Sound (later Gentle Giant), who also recorded for the Parlophone label at the time. Again, the recording has appeared on a few Beatles' bootlegs and some people still believe it to be the Beatles.

People Say/I'm Walking—John and Paul (London)
Issued in 1965 at the height of the Beatles' fame, this has appeared on a number of Beatles' bootlegs and has been incorrectly identified as a duet by John Lennon and Paul McCartney. It is not, of course, but although it doesn't even sound like Lennon and McCartney, rumours continue and so does its inclusion on Beatles bootlegs.

Ram You Hard—John Lennon and The Bleechers (Punch)
This reggae record issued in early 1970 may very well feature a John Lennon, but it is not *the* John Lennon.

The following pages describe the real Beatle unreleased tracks.

AUDITIONS
During 1962, when the Beatles were trying to secure a recording contract, they had auditions with both Decca and EMI. All were recorded, and amongst the recordings are some 30 titles which the Beatles never issued. Although they are really quite good it is highly unlikely that they will ever find their way on to official records, as they were audition recordings not made for release. The titles include Beatles' versions of their own Hello Little Girl, Like Dreamers Do and Love Of The Loved, plus versions of other people's material such as Red Sails In The Sunset, Besame Mucho, Memphis Tennessee, Sweet Little Sixteen plus many rock and roll songs that they had performed on stage for years.

RADIO BROADCASTS
Between 1962 and 1965 the Beatles appeared on many BBC radio shows for which they recorded material specifically for broadcast. In addition to alternative versions of material that they did release, there were also 40 tracks recorded and broadcast but never issued. Amongst these are Beatles' versions of many rock and roll songs such as Johnny B Goode, Shake Rattle and Roll and Little Queenie. EMI have been negotiating with the BBC, so it is possible that some of these recordings will one day be released.

ACTUAL UNRELEASED TRACKS
There are reputed to be approximately 60 tracks which although recorded during official sessions have remained unissued for various reasons. A few of the songs were later re-recorded by the individual Beatles—Isolation, Gimme Some Truth and Look At Me by John, Hot As Sun, Junk, Suicide and Teddy Boy by Paul and All Things Must Pass and Sunshine Life For Me by George. The other unreleased tracks include Rubber Soul (recorded as the title track for the album of the same name but rejected at the last minute though the album retained the title), Suzy Parker—a McCartney written rock and roll track so near to being issued that the song was copyrighted, but still didn't come out, and Shakin' In The Sixties—a Lennon-written rocker, dedicated to Dick James, the man who ran the Beatles' music publishers, Northern Songs.
Some tracks were issued in edited form—Mean Mr. Mustard, Polythene Pam and She Came In Through The Bathroom Window were edited together to form part of a medley on the second side of Abbey Road. There is also a five-minute version of Dig It of which only a very small section appears on the Let It Be album.

Many recordings of fifties and sixties songs were rejected, including Blue Suede Shoes, Save The Last Dance For Me, Hippy Hippy Shake, House Of The Rising Sun and How Do You Do It?

Other tracks include new Beatles' songs never issued, with titles such as All Together On The Wireless Machine, Annie, Colliding Circles, Four Nights In Moscow, I Should Like To Live Up A Tree, Indian Rope Trick, In The Old Hillbilly Way, Watching Rainbows and the most famous unreleased track ever recorded by the Beatles, What's The New Mary Jane, which was forever going to be the next Beatles' single, but never was.

RECORDING SESSION 'WARM-UPS'

There are a number of songs the Beatles used to warm-up their recording sessions. Over the years these tracks have found their way onto innumerable Beatles' bootlegs, and are invariably described as 'working versions' of songs. The real truth is that these short tracks were never considered by the Beatles as being serious recordings, nor did they intend to record full versions for release. They were simply tapes of the Beatles messing about in the studio, relaxing and getting ready to record, singing anything that came to mind like Ba Ba Black Sheep, Tea For Two and The Third Man Theme.

These 'warm-up' recordings last anywhere from 30 to 90 seconds and a good example is Maggie Mae on Let It Be.

DEMONSTRATION RECORDINGS

These consist of songs written by Lennon and McCartney and 'given away' to other artists, but demonstrated on record by the Beatles so that the artist involved could hear how the song sounded. With the exception of I'm The Greatest, written after the split-up, the tracks included by other artists on the album The Songs Lennon and McCartney Gave Away were recorded originally by the Beatles in this way. They were never intended to be released as Beatle records and it is improbable that they ever will be.

The following list of 215 titles gives every track generally assumed to have been recorded by the Beatles but not released. It is doubtful that 215 unreleased tracks do exist but only a few people could confirm this. Also included in the listing (at the beginning) are a further five titles which were recorded before the Beatles recorded for either Polydor or EMI Records.

Two of these, That'll Be The Day and In Spite Of All The Danger, were recorded by The Quarrymen. This was John Lennon's first group and at the time these recordings were made the line-up also included Paul McCartney and George Harrison. Made in a small Liverpool recording studio in 1958, there is only one known copy (a 45 rpm single) of these recordings in existence, the master tapes having been destroyed.

The remaining three titles, Fever, September Song and Summertime were recorded by the Beatles' backing Lu Walters bass guitarist and sometime vocalist with another Liverpool group, Rory Storme and The Hurricanes in Akustic Studios, Hamburg, Germany, in September 1960. The recordings also features another member of The Hurricanes who was later to become a Beatle — Ringo Starr. Ringo had sat in on drums because Pete Best, the then Beatles' drummer, was nowhere to be found at the time the recording was due to take place. According to legend there were only four copies of these recordings made, as one-sided 78 rpm records but over the years, they have apparently been lost.

All songs are unpublished individual Beatle or Lennon and McCartney compositions except where stated otherwise.

The Quarrymen (Recorded in Liverpool 1958)
That'll Be The Day (Holly-Petty)
In Spite Of All The Danger

The Beatles With Lu Walters (Recorded In Hamburg 1960)
Fever (John)
September Song (Weil/Anderson)
Summertime (Gershwin)

The Beatles (Recorded In Manchester and London 1962-1970)

After You've Gone (Creamer-Layton) (With Terry Hall, Patsy Ann Noble,
    The Raindrops and The Bert Hayes Octet)
Ain't Nothin' Shakin' (Colacrai—Fontaine—Lambert—Cleveland)
All Along The Watchtower (Dylan)
All Shook Up (Blackwell-Presley)
All Things Must Pass
All Together On The Wireless Machine
Always And Only
Annie
Anything
Aunt Jessie's Nightmare
Ba Ba Blacksheep (Trad.)
Baby, I Don't Care (Leiber—Stoller)
Baby Jane, I'm Sorry
Bad Penny Blues (Lyttleton)
Bad To Me

Beautiful Dreamer (Foster)
Be Bop A Lula (Vincent—Davies)
Be My Baby (Greenwich—Barry—Spector)
Besame Mucho (Velazquez—Shaftel)
Blowin' In The Wind (Dylan)
Blue Suede Shoes (Perkins)
Bound By Love
Bye Bye Love (Bryant—Bryant)

Carol (Berry)
Catcall
Circles
Clarebella (Pingatore)
C'mon Everybody (Cochran—Capehart)
Colliding Circles
Commonwealth Song
Cottonfields (Ledbetter)
Crying, Waiting, Hoping (Holly)

Da Doo Ron Ron (Greenwich—Barry—Spector)
Dig It (Full Version)
Don't Be Cruel (Blackwell—Presley)
Don't Dig No Pakistanis (Get Back, With Entirely Different Lyrics)
Don't Ever Change (Goffin—King)
Dream Baby (Walker)

Early In The Morning (Allison—Petty—Holly)
Echoes Of The Mersey Side
Everybody's Rockin' Tonight
Everybody Needs Someone
Fool Like Me (Clements—Maddox)
Four Nights In Moscow
From A Window
From Us To You

Gimme Some Truth
God Save The Queen (Trad.) (with the entire cast of the 1963 Royal Variety
   Performance)
Goodbye
Good Golly Miss Molly (Blackwell—Marascalco)
Good Rockin' Tonight (Brown)

Hallelujah, I Love Her So (Charles)
Happy Birthday Saturday Club (Trad. Arr. Lennon)
Hare Krishna Mantra (Trad.)
Heather
Hello Little Girl
Hi-Heel Sneakers (Higgenbotham)
Hippy Hippy Shake (Romero)
Hitch Hike
Home
Honeymoon Song (Theodorakis—Sansom)
Hot As Sun
House Of The Rising Sun (Trad)
How Do You Do It (Murray)

I Do Like To Be Beside The Seaside (Dixon)
I Don't Want to See You Again
I Forgot To Remember To Forget (Kesler—Feathers)
I Got A Woman (Charles-Richards)
I Got To Find My Baby (Berry)
I Just Don't Understand (Wilkin—Westberry)
I Lost My Little Girl
I Need You (not as on Help! album)
I Shall Be Released (Dylan)
I Should Like To Live Up A Tree
I Threw It All Away (Dylan)
If You've Got Troubles
I'll Be On My Way
I'll Build A Stairway To Paradise (Gershwin—Da Sylva—Gershwin)
I'll Keep You Satisfied
I'm Gonna Sit Right Down and Cry Over You (Thomas—Biggs)
I'm In Love
India
Indian Rope Trick
In The Old Hillbilly Way
Isolation
It's For You
It's Only Make Believe (Twitty)
It's So Easy (Allison—Petty—Holly)

Johnny B. Goode (Berry)
Jubilee
Junk
Just Dancing Around
Just Fun

Keep Looking That Way
Keep Your Hands Off My Baby (Goffin — King)

Lawdy Miss Clawdy (Price)
Leave My Kitten Alone (McDougal — Turner)
Lend Me Your Comb (Twomey — Wise — Wiseman)
Like Dreamers Do
Little Eddie
Little Queenie (Berry)
Lonesome Tears In My Eyes (Burnette — Burnette — Burlison — Mortimer)
Look At Me
Looking Glass
Love Of The Loved
Lucille (Penniman — Collins)

Maisy Jones
Maybelline (Berry — Fratto — Fread)
Mean Mr. Mustard (Full Version)
Memphis (Berry)
Michael Row The Boat Ashore (Trad.)
Midnight Special (Trad.)
Miss Ann (Penniman)
Mamma, You've Been On My Mind (Dylan)
Moonglow
Move It (Samwell)
My Kind Of Girl

Nobody I Know
Not Guilty
Not Unknown

Oh Carol (Sedaka)
Oh My Love
Ooh! My Soul (Penniman)
On Moonlight Bay (With Morecambe and Wise) (Madden — Wenrich)
One And One Is Two

Peace Of Mind
Penina
Piano Boogie
Piano Theme
Picture Of You (Beveridge — Oakman)
Piece Of My Heart (Berns — Ragavoy)
Pink Litmus Paper Shirt
Polythene Pam (Full Version)
Pop Go The Beatles (Trad. Arr. Patrick)
Portrait Of My Love (Ornadel — West)
Proud As You Are

To Know Her Is To Love Her (Spector)
Tom Dooley (Trad.)
Too Bad About Sorrows
Too Much Monkey Business (Berry)
Turn Around (Holly)
Twenty Flight Rock (Cochran)

Watching Rainbows
What A Shame, Mary Jane Had A Pain At The Party
What'd I Say (Charles)
What's The New Mary Jane
When I Come To Town
When Irish Eyes Are Smiling (Davis — Mitchell)
Where Have You Been All My Life (Weill — Mann)
Whole Lotta Loving (Domino — Bartholomew)
Whole Lotta Shakin' Goin' On (Lewis)
Wild Honey Pie (Full Version)
Winston's Walk
Woman
World Without Love

Yakety Yak (Leiber — Stoller)
You Are My Sunshine (Davis — Mitchell)
You Win Again (Williams)
You'll Know What To Do
Youngblood (Leiber — Stoller — Pomus)
Your Feets Too Big (Benson — Fisher)
Your True Love (Allison — Petty — Holly)

Zero Is Just Another Even Number

Discography

Anytime At All; I'll Cry Instead; Things We Said Today; When I Get Home. [6 November 1964]

GEP 8931 Beatles For Sale
No Reply; I'm A Loser; Rock And Roll Music; Eight Days A Week. [6 April 1965]

GEP 8938 Beatles For Sale No. 2
I'll Follow The Sun; Baby's In Black; Words Of Love; I Don't Want To Spoil The Party. [4 June 1965]

GEP 8946 The Beatles Million Sellers
She Loves You; I Want To Hold Your Hand; Can't Buy Me Love; I Feel Fine. [6 December 1965]

GEP 8948 Yesterday
Yesterday; Act Naturally; You Like Me Too Much; It's Only Love. [4 March 1966]

GEP 8952 Nowhere Man
Nowhere Man; Drive My Car; Michelle; You Won't See Me. [8 July 1966]

MMT/SMMT 1 Magical Mystery Tour
Magical Mystery Tour; Your Mother Should Know; I Am The Walrus; The Fool On The Hill; Flying; Blue Jay Way. [8 December 1967]

BEP 14 The Beatles E.P.s Collection
This 14 E.P. Set Contains all of the above listed 13 E.P.s plus a free bonus E.P. not on sale separately. That E.P. is: **SGE 1 The Beatles**
The Inner Light; Baby, You're A Rich Man; She's A Woman; This Boy [7 December 1981]

LONG PLAY

PMC 1202 Please Please Me
PCS 3042
Side One
I Saw Her Standing There; Misery; Anna (Go To Him); Chains; Boys; Ask Me Why; Please Please Me.
Side Two
Love Me Do; P.S. I Love You; Baby It's You; Do You Want To Know A Secret; A Taste Of Honey; There's A Place; Twist And Shout. [22 March 1963]

PMC 1206 With The Beatles
PCS 3045
Side One
It Won't Be Long; All I've Got To Do; All My Loving; Don't Bother Me; Little Child; Till There Was You; Please Mister Postman.
Side Two
Roll Over Beethoven; Hold Me Tight; You Really Got A Hold On Me; I Wanna Be Your Man; Devil In Her Heart; Not A Second Time; Money. [22 November 1963]

PMC 1230 A Hard Day's Night
PCS 3058
Side One
A Hard Day's Night; I Should Have Known Better; If I Fell; I'm Happy Just To Dance With You; And I Love Her; Tell Me Why; Can't Buy Me Love
Side Two
Any Time At All; I'll Cry Instead; Things We Said Today; When I Get Home; You Can't Do That; I'll Be Back. [10 July 1964]

PMC 1240 Beatles For Sale
PCS 3062
Side One
No Reply; I'm A Loser; Baby's In Black; Rock And Roll Music; I'll Follow The Sun; Mr. Moonlight; Kansas City/Hey Hey Hey Hey.
Side Two
Eight Days A Week; Words Of Love; Honey Don't; Every Little Thing; I Don't Want To Spoil The Party; What

You're Doing; Everybody's Trying To Be My Baby. [4 December 1964]

PMC 1255 Help!
PCS 3071
Side One
Help!; The Night Before; You've Got To Hide Your Love Away; I Need You; Another Girl; You're Going To Lose That Girl; Ticket To Ride.
Side Two
Act Naturally; It's Only Love; You Like Me Too Much; Tell Me What You See; I've Just Seen A Face; Yesterday; Dizzy Miss Lizzy. [6 August 1965]

PMC 1267 Rubber Soul
PCS 3075
Side One
Drive My Car; Norwegian Wood (This Bird Has Flown); You Won't See Me; Nowhere Man; Think For Yourself; The Word; Michelle.
Side Two
What Goes On; Girl; I'm Looking Through You; In My Life; Wait; If I Needed Someone; Run For Your Life. [3 December 1965]

PMC 7009 Revolver
PCS 7009
Side One
Taxman; Eleanor Rigby; I'm Only Sleeping; Love You To; Here, There And Everywhere; Yellow Submarine. She Said, She Said.
Side Two
Good Day Sunshine; And Your Bird Can Sing; For No One; Dr. Robert; I Want To Tell You; Got To Get You Into My Life; Tomorrow Never Knows. [5 August 1966]

PMC 7016 A Collection Of Beatles Oldies
PCS 7016
Side One
She Loves You; From Me To You; We Can Work It Out; Help!; Michelle; Yesterday; I Feel Fine. Yellow Submarine.
Side Two
Can't Buy Me Love; Bad Boy; Day Tripper; A Hard Day's Night; Ticket To Ride; Paperback Writer; Eleanor Rigby; I Want To Hold Your Hand. [10 December 1966]

PMC 7027 Sgt. Pepper's Lonely Hearts Club Band
PCS 7027
Side One
Sgt. Pepper's Lonely Hearts Club Band; With A Little Help From My Friends; Lucy In The Sky With Diamonds; Getting Better; Fixing A Hole; She's Leaving Home; Being For the Benefit Of Mr. Kite.
Side Two
Within You, Without You; When I'm Sixty-Four; Lovely Rita; Good Morning, Good Morning; Sgt. Pepper's Lonely Hearts Club Band (Reprise); A Day In The Life. [1 June 1967]

PMC 7067/8** The Beatles (2 L.P.s)
PCS 7067/8**
Side One
Back In The U.S.S.R.; Dear Prudence; Glass Onion; Ob-La-Di, Ob-La-Da; Wild Honey Pie; The Continuing Story Of Bungalow Bill; While My Guitar Gently Weeps; Happiness Is A Warm Gun.
Side Two
Martha My Dear; I'm So Tired; Blackbird; Piggies; Rocky Racoon; Don't Pass Me By; Why Don't We Do It In The Road?; I Will; Julia.
Side Three
Birthday; Yer Blues; Mother Nature's Son; Everybody's Got Something To Hide Except Me And My Monkey; Sexy Sadie; Helter Skelter; Long, Long, Long.
Side Four
Revolution 1; Honey Pie; Savoy Truffle; Cry Baby Cry; Can You Take Me Back; Revolution 9; Good Night. [22 November 1968]

PMC 7070** Yellow Submarine
PCS 7070**
Side One
Yellow Submarine; Only A Northern Song; All Together Now; Hey Bulldog;

It's All Too Much; All You Need Is Love.

Side Two

Contains incidental music by George Martin and Orchestra as played in the film. [17 January 1969]

PCS 7088** Abbey Road
Side One

Come Together; Something; Maxwell's Silver Hammer; Oh! Darling; Octopus's Garden; I Want You (She's So Heavy).

Side Two

Here Comes The Sun; Because; You Never Give Me Your Money; Sun King; Mean Mr Mustard; Polythene Pam; She Came In Through The Bathroom Window; Golden Slumbers; Carry That Weight; The End; Her Majesty. [26 September 1969]

PXS 1** Let It Be
Side One

Two Of Us; (I) Dig A Pony; Across The Universe; I Me Mine; Dig It; Let It Be; Maggie Mae;

Side Two

I've Got A Feeling; One After 909; The Long And Winding Road; For You Blue; Get Back. [8 May 1970]
(PXS1 was a package containing the album plus a book called 'Get Back'. On 6 November 1970 the album was issued separately as PCS 7096.)

PCSP 717** The Beatles 1962 – 1966 (2 L.P.s)
Side One

Love Me Do; Please Please Me; From Me To You; She Loves You; I Want To Hold Your Hand; All My Loving; Can't Buy Me Love.

Side Two

A Hard Day's Night; And I Love Her; Eight Days A Week; I Feel Fine; Ticket To Ride; Yesterday.

Side Three

Help!; You've Got To Hide Your Love Away; We Can Work It Out; Day Tripper; Drive My Car; Norwegian Wood (This Bird Has Flown).

Side Four

Nowhere Man; Michelle; In My Life; Girl; Paperback Writer; Eleanor Rigby; Yellow Submarine. [20 April 1973]

PCSP 718** The Beatles 1967 – 1970 (2 L.P.s)
Side One

Strawberry Fields Forever; Penny Lane; Sgt. Pepper's Lonely Hearts Club Band; With A Little Help From My Friends; Lucy In The Sky With Diamonds; A Day In The Life; All You Need Is Love.

Side Two

I Am The Walrus; Hello Goodbye; The Fool On The Hill; Magical Mystery Tour; Lady Madonna; Hey Jude; Revolution.

Side Three

Back In The U.S.S.R.; While My Guitar Gently Weeps; Ob-La-Di, Ob-La-Da; Get Back; Don't Let Me Down; The Ballad Of John And Yoko; Old Brown Shoe.

Side Four

Here Comes The Sun; Come Together; Something; Octopus's Garden; Let It Be; Across The Universe; The Long And Winding Road. [20 April 1973]

PCSP 719 Rock And Roll Music (2 L.P.s)
Side One

Twist And Shout; I Saw Her Standing There; You Can't Do That; I Wanna Be Your Man; I Call Your Name ; Boys; Long Tall Sally.

Side Two

Rock And Roll Music; Slow Down; Kansas City etc.; Money; Bad Boy; Matchbox; Roll Over Beethoven.

Side Three

Dizzy Miss Lizzy; Anytime At All; Drive My Car; Everybody's Trying To Be My Baby; The Night Before; I'm Down; Revolution.

Side Four

Back In The U.S.S.R.; Helter Skelter; Taxman; Got To Get You Into My Life; Hey Bulldog; Birthday; Get Back. [11 June 1976]

PCTC 255 Magical Mystery Tour
Side One
Magical Mystery Tour; The Fool On The Hill; Flying; Blue Jay Way; Your Mother Should Know; I Am The Walrus.
Side Two
Hello Goodbye; Strawberry Fields Forever; Penny Lane; Baby, You're A Rich Man; All You Need Is Love. [19 November 1976]

EMTV 4 The Beatles At The Hollywood Bowl
Side One
Twist And Shout; She's A Woman; Dizzy Miss Lizzy; Ticket To Ride; Can't Buy Me Love; Things We Said Today; Roll Over Beethoven.
Side Two
Boys; A Hard Day's Night; Help!; All My Loving; She Loves You; Long Tall Sally. [6 May 1977]

PCSP 721 Love Songs (2 L.P.s)
Side One
Yesterday; I'll Follow The Sun; I Need You; Girl; In My Life; Words Of Love; Here, There And Everywhere.
Side Two
Something; And I Love Her; If I Fell; I'll Be Back; Tell Me What You See; Yes It Is.
Side Three
Michelle; It's Only Love; You're Going To Lose That Girl; Every Little Thing; For No One; She's Leaving Home.
Side Four
The Long And Winding Road; This Boy: Norwegian Wood (This Bird Has Flown); You've Got To Hide Your Love Away; I Will; P.S. I Love You. [28 November 1977]

PHO 7027 Sgt. Pepper's Lonely Hearts Club Band
Picture Disc. [January 1978]

BC 13 The Beatles Collection
A Boxed Set Containing The Following Albums: Please Please Me; With The Beatles; A Hard Day's Night; Beatles For Sale; Help!; Rubber Soul;

Revolver; Sgt. Pepper's Lonely Hearts Club Band; The Beatles; Yellow Submarine; Abbey Road: Let It Be; Rarities. [December 1978]

PCS 7184 Hey Jude
Side One
Can't Buy Me Love; I Should Have Known Better; Paperback Writer; Rain; Lady Madonna; Revolution.
Side Two
Hey Jude; Old Brown Shoe; Don't Let Me Down; The Ballad Of John And Yoko. [May 1979]

PCM 1001 The Beatles "Rarities"
Side One
Across The Universe; Yes It Is; This Boy; The Inner Light; I'll Get You; Thank You Girl; Komm, Gib Mir Deine Hand; You Know My Name (Look Up The Number); Sie Liebt Dich.
Side Two
Rain; She's A Woman; Matchbox; I Call Your Name; Bad Boy; Slow Down; I'm Down: Long Tall Sally. [October 1979]

PCS 7214 The Beatles Ballads — 20 Original Tracks
Side One
Yesterday; Norwegian Wood (This Bird Has Flown); Do You Want To Know A Secret; For No One; Michelle; Nowhere Man; You've Got To Hide Your Love Away; Across The Universe; All My Loving; Hey Jude.
Side Two
Something; The Fool On The Hill; Till There Was You; The Long And Winding Road; Here Comes The Sun; Blackbird; And I Love Her; She's Leaving Home; Here, There And Everywhere; Let It Be. [October 1980]

MFP 50506 Rock And Roll Music Volume 1
George Martin's re-mixed tapes as issued on American version of the original album, Capitol SKBO 11537. [October 1980]

MFP 50507 Rock And Roll Music Volume 2
As Above. [October 1980]

SM 701-8 The Beatles Box

This boxed set is available only from EMI's Mail Order Division: World Records. The Eight Albums contained are as Follows: [October 1980]

SM 701 Record 1
Side One

Love Me Do; P.S. I Love You; I Saw Her Standing There; Please Please Me; Misery; Do You Want To Know A Secret; A Taste Of Honey; Twist And Shout.

Side Two

From Me To You; Thank You Girl; She Loves You; It Won't Be Long; Please Mister Postman; All My Loving; Roll Over Beethoven; Money.

SM 702 Record 2
Side One

I Wan't To Hold Your Hand; This Boy; Can't Buy Me Love; You Can't Do That; A Hard Day's Night; I Should Have Known Better; If I Fell; And I Love Her.

Side Two

Things We Said Today; I'll Be Back; Long Tall Sally; I Call Your Name; Matchbox; Slow Down; She's A Woman; I Feel Fine.

SM 703 Record 3
Side One

Eight Days A Week; No Reply; I'm A Loser; I'll Follow The Sun; Mr. Moonlight; Every Little Thing; I Don't Want To Spoil The Party; Kansas City/Hey Hey Hey Hey.

Side Two

Ticket To Ride; I'm Down; Help!; The Night Before; You've Got To Hide Your Love Away; I Need You: Another Girl; You're Gonna To Lose That Girl.

SM 704 Record 4
Side One

Yesterday; Act Naturally; Tell Me What You See; It's Only Love; You Like Me Too Much; I've Just Seen A Face; Day Tripper; We Can Work It Out.

Side Two

Michelle; Drive My Car; Norwegian Wood (This Bird Has Flown); You Won't See Me; Nowhere Man; Girl; I'm Looking Through You; In My Life.

SM 705 Record 5
Side One

Paperback Writer; Rain; Here, There And Everywhere; Taxman; I'm Only Sleeping; Good Day Sunshine; Yellow Submarine.

Side Two

Eleanor Rigby; And Your Bird Can Sing; For No One; Dr. Robert; Got To Get You Into My Life; Penny Lane; Strawberry Fields Forever.

SM 706 Record 6
Side One

Sgt. Pepper's Lonely Hearts Club Band; With A Little Help From My Friends; Lucy In The Sky With Diamonds; Fixing A Hole; She's Leaving Home; Being For The Benefit Of Mr. Kite; A Day In The Life.

Side Two

When I'm Sixty-Four; Lovely Rita; All You Need Is Love; Baby You're A Rich Man; Magical Mystery Tour; Your Mother Should Know; The Fool On The Hill; I Am The Walrus.

SM 707 Record 7
Side One

Hello Goodbye; Lady Madonna; Hey Jude; Revolution; Back In The U.S.S.R.; Ob-La-Di, Ob-La-Da; While My Guitar Gently Weeps.

Side Two

The Continuing Story Of Bungalow Bill; Happiness Is A Warm Gun; Martha My Dear; I'm So Tired; Piggies; Don't Pass Me By; Julia; All Together Now.

SM 708 Record 8
Side One

Get Back; Don't Let Me Down; The Ballad Of John And Yoko; Across The Universe; For You Blue; Two Of Us; The Long And Winding Road; Let It Be.

Side Two

Come Together; Something; Maxwell's Silver Hammer; Octopus's Garden; Here Comes The Sun;

Because; Golden Slumbers; Carry That Weight/The End/Her Majesty. [October 1980]

PCS 7218 Reel Music
Side One
A Hard Day's Night; I Should Have Known Better; Can't Buy Me Love; And I Love Her; Help!; You've Got To Hide Your Love Away; Ticket To Ride; Magical Mystery Tour.
Side Two
I Am The Walrus; Yellow Submarine; All You Need Is Love; Let It Be; Get Back; The Long And Winding Road. [12 March 1982]

The following album is included because it incorporates Lennon—McCartney songs, recorded by The Beatles but yet to be issued by them.

NUT 18 The Songs Lennon and McCartney Gave Away
Side One
I'm The Greatest (Ringo Starr); One And One Is Two (The Strangers with Mike Shannon); From A Window (Billy J. Kramer and The Dakotas); Nobody I Know (Peter and Gordon); Like Dreamers Do (The Applejacks); I'll Keep You Satisfied (Billy J. Kramer and the Dakotas); Love Of The Loved (Cilla Black); Woman (Peter and Gordon); Tip Of My Tongue (Tommy Quickly); I'm In Love (The Fourmost).
Side Two
Hello Little Girl (The Fourmost); That Means A Lot (P.J. Proby); It's For You (Cilla Black); Penina (Carlos Mendes); Step Inside Love (Cilla Black); World Without Love (Peter and Gordon); Bad To Me (Billy J. Kramer and The Dakotas); I Don't Want To See You Again (Peter and Gordon); I'll Be On My Way (Billy J. Kramer and The Dakotas); Catcall (The Chris Barber Band).

PARLOPHONE EXPORT RECORDS
SINGLES
DP562 If I Fell/Ask Me Why
DP563 Dizzy Miss Lizzy/Yesterday
DP564 Michelle/Drive My Car
DP570 Hey Jude/Revolution

LONG PLAY
CPCS 101 Something New
Side One
I'll Cry Instead; Things We Said Today; Any Time At All; When I Get Home; Slow Down; Matchbox.
Side Two
Tell Me Why; And I Love Her; I'm Happy Just To Dance With You; If I Fell; Komm, Gib Mir Deine Hand.

CPCS 103 The Beatles' Second Album
Side One
Roll Over Beethoven; Thank You Girl; You Really Got A Hold On Me; Devil In Her Heart; Money; You Can't Do That.
Side Two
Long Tall Sally; I Call Your Name; Please Mr. Postman; I'll Get You; She Loves You.

CPCS 104 The Beatles VI
Side One
Kansas City/Hey Hey Hey Hey; Eight Days A Week; You Like Me Too Much; Bad Boy; I Don't Want To Spoil The Party; Words Of Love.
Side Two
What You're Doing; Yes It Is; Dizzy Miss Lizzy; Tell Me What You See; Every Little Thing.

CPCS 106 Hey Jude
Same track listing as PCS 7184.

PCS 7067-8 The Beatles (White Album)
Same track listing as normal PCS 7067-8 Release. But with Parlophone label instead of Apple.

With the exception of the Hey Jude album, which was released with an Apple label, all singles and albums were issued with a Parlophone label, including the Hey Jude/Revolution single and the double album The Beatles. This was because the Apple label design was not cleared for use in all countries to which the records were being exported, so to avoid legal problems these were pressed with a Parlophone label.

POLYDOR RECORDS
SINGLES
NH 66-833 My Bonnie/
The Saints [5 January 1962]
NH 52-906 Sweet Georgia Brown/
Nobody's Child [31 January 1964]
NH 52-275 Why/
Cry For A Shadow [28 February 1964]
NH 52-317 Ain't She Sweet/
Take Out Some Insurance On Me, Baby
[29 May 1964]

EXTENDED PLAY
H 21-610 My Bonnie
My Bonnie; Why; Cry For A Shadow;
The Saints. [12 July 1961]

LONG PLAY
236-201 The Beatles First
Side One
Ain't She Sweet; Cry For A Shadow;
(Let's Dance); My Bonnie; Take Out
Some Insurance On Me Baby; (What'd
I Say).
Side Two
Sweet Georgia Brown; The Saints;
(Ruby Baby); Why; Nobody's Child;
(Ya Ya).

Titles in parentheses performed by
Tony Sheridan and the Beat Brothers. All
other songs performed by either The
Beatles or Tony Sheridan and The
Beatles.
Re-Issued on 4 August 1967 under the
same title, second re-issue 18 June 1971
as The Early Years (Contour 287001),
third re-issue 4 June 1976 as the Beatles
featuring Tony Sheridan (Contour CN
2007). [19 June 1964]

2683-0068 The Beatles Tapes (2 L.P.s)
Interviews with each member of The
Beatles as given to David Wigg.
[30 July 1976]

LINGASONG RECORDS
SINGLES
**NB1 Falling In Love Again/Twist and
Shout** [25 May 1977]

Long Play
LNL1 The Beatles Live! At The Star Club

In Hamburg, Germany; 1962 (2 L.P.s)
Side One
I Saw Her Standing There; Roll Over
Beethoven; Hippy Hippy Shake;
Sweet Little Sixteen; Lend Me Your
Comb; Your Feets Too Big.
Side Two
Twist and Shout; Mr. Moonlight; A
Taste Of Honey; Besame Mucho;
Reminiscing; Kansas City/Hey Hey
Hey Hey.
Side Three
Ain't Nothin' Shakin'; To Know Her Is
To Love Her; Little Queenie; Falling In
Love Again; Ask Me Why; Be Bop A
Lula; Hallelujah, I Love Her So.
Side Four
Red Sails In The Sunset; Everybody's
Trying To Be My Baby; Matchbox;
Talkin' 'Bout You; Shimmy Shimmy;
Long Tall Sally; I Remember You.
[25 May 1977]

CHARLEY RECORDS
LONG PLAY
CRV 202 Hear The Beatles Tell All
Side One
Jim Steck Interviews John Lennon
Side Two
Dave Hull Interviews John, Paul,
George, Ringo. [20 February 1981]

PHOENIX RECORDS
LONG PLAY
PHX 1004 Early Years (1)
Side One
I Saw Her Standing There: Roll Over
Beethoven; Hippy Hippy Shake;
Sweet Little Sixteen; Lend Me Your
Comb.
Side Two
Twist and Shout; Mr. Moonlight; A
Taste Of Honey; Besame Mucho;
Reminiscing. [17 July 1981]

PHX 1005 Early Years (2)
Side One
Ain't Nothin' Shakin'; To Know Her Is
To Love Her; Little Queenie; Falling In
Love Again; Ask Me Why.
Side Two
Red Sails In The Sunset; Everybody's
Trying To Be My Baby; Matchbox;
Talkin'Bout You; Shimmy Shimmy.
[17 July 1981]

PHX 1011 Rare Beatles
Side One
Be Bop A Lula; Long Tall Sally; Your Feets Too Big; I'm Gonna Sit Right Down And Cry Over You; Where Have You Been All My Life.
Side Two
Sheila; Hallelujah, I Love Her So; Till There Was You; Kansas City/Hey Hey Hey Hey; I Remember You. [22 January 1982]

AFE RECORDS
LONG PLAY
AFELD 1018 Historic Sessions (2 L.P.s)
Side One
I'm Gonna Sit Right Down And Cry Over You; I Saw Her Standing There; Roll Over Beethoven; Hippy Hippy Shake; Sweet Little Sixteen; Lend Me Your Comb; Your Feets Too Big.
Side Two
Twist and Shout; Mr. Moonlight; A Taste Of Honey; Besame Mucho; Reminiscing; Kansas City/Hey Hey Hey Hey; Where Have You Been All My Life.
Side Three
Till There Was You; Ain't Nothin' Shakin'; To Know Her Is To Love Her; Little Queenie; Falling In Love Again; Ask Me Why; Be Bop A Lula; Hallelujah, I Love Her So.
Side Four
Sheila; Red Sails In The Sunset; Everybody's Trying To Be Baby; Matchbox; Talkin' 'Bout You; Shimmy Shimmy; Long Tall Sally; I Remember You. [25 September 1981]

AMERICAN RELEASES
CAPITOL/CAPITOL STARLINE*/APPLE**
SINGLES
5112 I Want To hold Your Hand/
I Saw Her Standing There [13 January 1964]
5150 Can't Buy Me Love/
You Can't Do That [16 March 1964]
5222 A Hard Day's Night/
I Should Have Known Better [13 July 1964]

5234 I'll Cry Instead/
I'm Happy Just To Dance With You [20 July 1964]
5235 And I Love Her/
If I Fell [20 July 1964]
5255 Matchbox/
Slow Down [24 August 1964]
5327 I Feel Fine/
She's A Woman [23 November 1964]
5371 Eight Days A Week/
I Don't Want To Spoil The Party [15 February 1965]
5407 Ticket To Ride/
Yest It is [19 April 1965]
5476 Help!/
I'm Down [19 July 1965]
5498 Yesterday/
Act Naturally [13 September 1965]
6061* Twist and Shout/
There's A Place [11 October 1965]
6062* Love Me Do/
P.S. I Love You [11 October 1965]
6063* Please Please Me/
From Me To You [11 October 1965]
6064* Do You Want To Know A Secret/
Thank You Girl [11 October 1965]
6065* Roll Over Beethoven/
Misery [11 October 1965]
6066* Boys/
Kansas City etc. [11 October 1965]
5555 We Can Work It Out/
Day Tripper [6 December 1965]
5587 Nowhere Man/
What Goes On [21 February 1966]
5651 Paperback Writer/
Rain [30 May 1966]
5715 Yellow Submarine/
Eleanor Rigby [8 August 1966]
5810 Penny Lane/
Strawberry Fields Forever [13 February 1967]
5964 All You Need Is Love/
Baby You're A Rich Man [17 July 1967]
2056 Hello Goodbye/
I Am The Walrus [27 November 1967]
2138 Lady Madonna/
The Inner Light [18 March 1968]
2276** Hey Jude/
Revolution [26 August 1968]

2490** Get Back/
Don't Let Me Down [5 May 1969]

2531** The Ballad Of John and Yoko/
Old Brown Shoe [4 June 1969]

2654** Something/
Come Together [6 October 1969]

2764** Let It Be/
You Know My Name (Look Up The
Number) [11 March 1970]

2837** The Long And Winding Road/
For You Blue [11 May 1970]

4274 Got To Get You Into My Life/
Helter Skelter [May 1976]

4347 Ob-La-Di; Ob-La-Da/
Julia [November 1976]

4612 Sgt. Pepper's Lonely Hearts Club
Band/With A Little Help From My
Friends/A Day In The Life [August
1978]

B5107 The Beatles' Movie Medley/
I'm Happy Just To Dance With You [30
March 1982] (7 and 12-inch versions)

EXTENDED PLAY
EAP 2121 Four By The Beatles
Roll Over Beethoven; All My Loving.
This Boy; Please Mister Postman. [11
May 1964]

R5365 4 By The Beatles
Honey Don't; I'm A Loser.
Mr Moonlight; Everybody's Trying To
Be My Baby. [1 February 1965]

LONG PLAY
CAPITOL/UNITED ARTISTS*/APPLE*
ST 2047 Meet The Beatles
Side One
I Want To Hold Your Hand; I Saw Her
Standing There; This Boy; It Won't Be
Long; All I've Got To Do: All My
Loving.
Side Two
Don't Bother Me; Little Child; Till
There Was You; Hold Me Tight; I
Wanna Be Your Man; Not A Second
Time. [20 January 1964]

ST 2080 The Beatles' Second Album
Side One
Roll Over Beethoven; Thank You Girl;

You Really Got A Hold On Me; Devil In
Her Heart; Money; You Can't Do That.
Side Two
Long Tall Sally; I Call Your Name;
Please Mister Postman; I'll Get You;
She Loves You. [10 April 1964]

UAS 6366* A Hard Day's Night
Side One
A Hard Day's Night; Tell Me Why; I'll
Cry Instead; (I Should Have Known
Better); I'm Happy Just To Dance With
You; (And I Love Her).
Side Two
I Should Have Known Better; If I Fell;
And I Love Her; (Ringo's Theme —
This Boy); Can't Buy Me Love; (A Hard
Day's Night). [26 June 1964]

*Titles In Paretheses Performed By The George
Martin Orchestra.*

ST 2018 Something New
Side One
I'll Cry Instead; Things We Said
Today; Anytime At All; When I Get
Home; Slow Down; Matchbox.
Side Two
Tell Me Why; And I Love Her; I'm
Happy Just To Dance With You; If I
Feel; Komm, Gib Mir Deine Hand.
[20 July 1964]

STBO 2222 The Beatles' Story (two L.P.s)
Record One
On Stage With The Beatles; How
Beatlemania Began; Beatlemania In
Action; Man Behind The Beatles -
Brian Epstein; John Lennon; Who's A
Millionaire? Beatles Will Be Beatles;
Man Behind The Music - George
Martin; George Harrison.
Record Two
A Hard Day's Night - Their First
Movie; Paul McCartney; Sneaky
Haircuts And More About Paul. The
Beatles Look At Life; 'Victims' Of
Beatlemania; Beatle Medley; Ringo
Starr; Liverpool And All The World!
[23 November 1964]

ST 2228 Beatles 65
Side One
No Reply; I'm A Loser; Baby's In Black;

Rock And Roll Music; I'll Follow The Sun; Mr. Moonlight.

Side Two

Honey Don't; I'll Be Back; She's A Woman; I Feel Fine; Everybody's Trying To Be My Baby. [15 December 1964]

ST 2309 The Early Beatles
Side One

Love Me Do; Twist And Shout; Anna (Go To Him); Chains; Boys; Ask Me Why.

Side Two

Please Please Me; P.S. I Love You; Baby, It's You; A Taste Of Honey; Do You Want To Know A Secret. [22 March 1965]

ST 2358 Beatles VI
Side One

Kansas City/Hey Hey Hey Hey; Eight Days A Week; You Like Me Too Much; Bad Boy; I Don't Want To Spoil The Party; Words Of Love.

Side Two

What You're Doing; Yes It Is; Dizzy Miss Lizzy; Tell Me What You See; Every Little Thing. [14 June 1965]

SMAS 2386 Help!
Side One

(The James Bond Theme); Help!; The Night Before; (From Me To You Fantasy); You've Got To Hide Your Love Away; I Need You; (In The Tyrol).

Side Two

Another Girl; (Another Hard Day's Night); Ticket To Ride; (The Bitter End/You Can't Do That); You're Gonna Lose That Girl; (The Chase). [13 August 1965]

Titles in parentheses performed by the George Martin Orchestra.

ST 2442 Rubber Soul
Side One

I've Just Seen A Face; Norwegian Wood (This Bird Has Flown); You Won't See Me; Think For Yourself; The Word; Michelle.

Side Two

It's Only Love; Girl; I'm Looking Through You; In My Life; Wait; Run For Your Life. [6 December 1965]

ST 2553 Yesterday ... And Today
Side One

Drive My Car; I'm Only Sleeping; Nowhere Man; Dr. Robert; Yesterday; Act Naturally.

Side Two

And Your Bird Can Sing; If I Needed Someone; We Can Work It Out; What Goes On?; Day Tripper. [20 June 1965]

ST 2576 Revolver
Side One

Taxman; Eleanor Rigby; Love You To; Here, There And Everywhere; Yellow Submarine; She Said, She Said.

Side Two

Good Day Sunshine; For No One; I Want To Tell You; Got To Get You Into My Life; Tomorrow Never Knows. [5 August 1966]

SMAS 2653 Sgt. Pepper's Lonely Hearts Club Band

As British album [2 June 1967]

SMAL 2835 Magical Mystery Tour

As British album [27 November 1967]

SWBO 101** The Beatles (two L.P.s)

As British album [25 November 1968]

SW 153** Yellow Submarine

As British album [13 January 1969]

SO 383** Abbey Road

As British album [26 September 1969]

SW 385** Hey Jude

As British album [26 February 1970]

AR 34001** Let It Be

As British album [18 May 1970]

SKBO 3403** The Beatles 1962 - 1966 (two L.P.s)

As British album [2 April 1973]

SKBO 3404** The Beatles 1967 − 1970 (two L.P.s)

As British Album [2 April 1973]

SKBO 11537 Rock And Roll Music (two L.P.s)

As British album [7 June 1976]

SMAS 11638 The Beatles At The Hollywood Bowl

As British album [2 May 1977]

SKBL 11711 Love Songs (two L.P.s)

As British album [24 November 1977]

SEAX 11840 Sgt. Pepper's Lonely Hearts Club Band
(Picture disc) [January 1978]
SEAX 11900 Abbey Road
(Picture disc) [February 1978]

SHAL 12060 Rarities
Side One
Love Me Do; Misery; There's A Place; Sie Liebt Dich; And I Love Her; Help!; I'm Only Sleeping; I Am The Walrus.
Side Two
Penny Lane; Helter Skelter; Don't Pass Me By; The Inner Light; Across The Universe; You Know My Name (Look Up The Number); Sgt. Pepper Inner Groove. [March 1980]

The Beatles Ballads
As British album [October 1978]

SV 12199 Reel Music
As British Album [12 March 1982]

Beatles' records also appear on the following record labels.
For convenience, the labels have been listed alphabetically.

ATCO RECORDS
SINGLES
6302 Sweet Georgia Brown/
Take Out Some Insurance On Me Baby. [1 June 1964]
6308 Aint She Sweet/
Nobody's Child [6 July 1964]
LONG PLAY
SD 33-169 Aint She Sweet
Aint She Sweet; Sweet Georgia Brown; Take Some Insurance On Me Baby; Nobody's Child.
Remainder of this album features The Swallows. [5 October 1964]

DECCA RECORDS
SINGLES
31382 My Bonnie/
The Saints [23 April 1962]

LINGASONG RECORDS
LONG PLAY
LS-2-7001 The Beatles Live At The Star Club In Hamburg, Germany; 1962 (2 L.P.s)

Side One
I'm Gonna Sit Right Down And Cry Over You; Roll Over Beethoven; Hippy Hippy Shake; Sweet Little Sixteen; Lend Me Your Comb; Your Feets Too Big.
Side Two
Where Have You Been All My Life; Mr. Moonlight; A Taste Of Honey; Besame Mucho; Till There Was You; Kansas City/Hey Hey Hey Hey.
Side Three
Hallelujah I Love Her So; Aint Nothing Shakin'; To Know Her Is To Love Her; Little Queenie; Falling In Love Again; Sheila; Be Bop A Lula.
Side Four
Red Sails In The Sunset; Everybody's Trying To Be My Baby; Matchbox; Talkin' 'bout You; Shimmy Shimmy; Long Tall Sally; I Remember You. [28 June 1977]

MGM RECORDS
SINGLES
K13213 My Bonnie/
The Saints [27 January 1964]
K13227 Why/
Cry For A Shadow [27 March 1964]

OLDIES RECORDS
OL 149 Do You Want To Know A Secret/
Thank You Girl [10 August 1964]
OL 150 Please Please Me/
From Me To You [10 August 1964]
OL 151 Love Me Do/
P.S. I Love You [10 August 1964]
OL 152 Twist And Shout/
There's A Place [10 August 1964]

PICKWICK RECORDS
LONG PLAY
PTP 2098 The Historic First Live Recordings (2 L.P's)
Side One
Where Have You Been All My Life; A Taste of Honey; Your Feets Too Big; Mr. Moonlight; Besame Mucho; I'm Gonna Sit Right Down And Cry Over You; Be Bop A Lula.
Side Two
Ain't Nothin' Shakin'; Everybody's Trying To Be My Baby; Matchbox; Talkin' Bout You; Long Tall Sally; Roll Over Beethoven; Hippy Hippy Shake.

Talkin' 'Bout You; Long Tall Sally; Roll Over Beethoven; Hippy Hippy Shake.

Side Three

Hallelujah; I Love Her So; Till There Was You; Sweet Little Sixteen; Little Queenie; Kansas City/Hey Hey Hey Hey; Hully Gully.

Side Four

Falling In Love Again; Lend Me Your Comb; Sheila; Red Sails In The Sunset; To Know Her Is To Love Her; Shimmy Shimmy; I Remember You. [June 1980]

SPC 3661 The Historic First Live Recordings—Volume 1

Album 1 of the above two-album set [September 1980]

SPC 3662 The Historic First Live Recordings—Volume 2

Album 2 of the above two-album set [September 1980]

POLYDOR RECORDS
LONG PLAY
24-4504 The Beatles - Circa 1960 - In The Beginning

Same track listing as the British The Beatles First Album (Polydor 236-201) [4 May 1970]

SWAN RECORDS
SINGLES
4152 She Loves You/
I'll Get You [16 September 1963]
4182 Sie Liebt Dich/
I'll Get You [21 May 1964]

TOLLIE RECORDS
SINGLES
9001 Twist And Shout/
There's A Place [2 March 1964]
9008 Love Me Do/
P.S. I Love You [27 April 1964]

VEE JAY RECORDS
SINGLES
VJ 498 Please Please Me/
Ask Me Why [25 February 1963]
VJ 522 From Me To You/
Thank You Girl [27 May 1963]
VJ 581 Please Please Me/
From Me To You [30 January 1964]
VJ 587 Do You Want To Know A Secret/
Thank You Girl [23 March 1964]

EXTENDED PLAY
VJ EP 1-903 The Beatles

Misery; A Taste Of Honey.
Ask Me Why; Anna (Go To Him).
[23 March 1964]

LONG PLAY
VJ LP 1062 Introducing The Beatles
Side One

I Saw Her Standing There; Misery; Anna (Go To Him); Chains; Boys; Love Me Do.

Side Two

P.S. I Love You; Baby, It's You; Do You Want To Know A Secret; A Taste Of Honey; There's a place; Twist And Shout. [22 July 1963]

VJ LP 1062 Introducing The Beatles

Same basic track listing as previous album except that Love Me Do and P.S. I Love You were replaced by Ask Me Why and Please Please Me. [27 January 1964]

VJ LP 1085 Jolly What! The Beatles And Frank Ifield On Stage

Please Please Me; From Me To You; Ask Me Why; Thank You Girl. Remainder of album features Frank Ifield. [26 February 1964]

VJ DX 30 The Beatles VS The Four Seasons (two L.P.s)

Record One: same track listing as the second version of the Introducing The Beatles album (VJ LP 1062) as released on 27/1/64.

Record Two: 12 tracks by the four seasons. [1 October 1964]

VJ LP 1092 Songs, Pictures And Stories Of The Fabulous Beatles

Same track listing as the second version of the Introducing The Beatles album (VJ LP 1062) as released on 27 January 1964. [12 October 1964]

The Beatles were also included on American various artists' compilation albums on the Capitol, Clarion, Metro, MGM and Polydor record labels. Most of these albums are now deleted.

INDEX

This index of song and album titles indicates the main text listing and descriptions of songs and single records and/or as individual tracks on albums, with secondary references chiefly to descriptions of alternative recorded versions. Albums are identified by (LP) and are listed according to their main entries within the text *and* Discography.

All the known unreleased tracks are listed in alphabetical order on pages 201-205.

(Throughout, indexing of the definite and indefinite article as the first word of a title has been avoided.)

Raunchy (Justis)
Red Sails In The Sunset (Kennedy—Williams)
Reminiscing (Curtis)
Rock Island Line (Arr. Donegan)
Rubber Soul

Save The Last Dance For Me (Pomus—Shuman)
Searchin' (Leiber—Stoller)
Send Me Some Lovin' (Price—Marascalco)
September In The Rain (Warren)
Shake Rattle And Roll (Calhoun)
Shakin' In The Sixties
Shimmy Shimmy (Massey—Sheubert)
She Came In Through The Bathroom Window (Full Version)
Sheila (Roe)
Shirley's Wild Accordion
Short Fat Fanny (Williams)
Shot Of Rhythm And Blues (Thompson)
Shout (Isley—Isley—Isley)
Side By Side (with The Karl Denver Trio) (Wood)
Singing The Blues (Endsley)
So How Come (No One Loves Me) (Bryant—Bryant)
Soldier Of Love (Lay Down Your Arms) (Cason—Moon)
Some Other Guy (Leiber—Stoller—Barrett)
Somethin' Else (Cochran)
Stand By Me (King—Leiber—Stoller—Jones)
Step Inside Love
Suicide
Sunshine Life For Me
Sure To Fall (In Love With You) (Perkins—Claunch—Cantrell)
Suzy Parker
Sweet Little Sixteen (Berry)
Swinging Days

Take Good Care Of My Baby (Goffin—King)
Talkin' 'bout You (Charles)
Tea For Two (Youmans—Caesar)
Teddy Boy
That Means A Lot
That's Alright Mama (Crudup)
The Art Of Dying (Harrison)
The One And Only
The Right String But The Wrong Yo—Yo (Perryman)
The Sheik Of Araby (Snyder—Wheeler—Smith)
The Years Roll Along
The Walk
Think It Over (Holly—Petty)
Thinking Of Linking
Third Man Theme (Karas)
Thirty Days (Berry)
This Is Some Friendly
Those Were The Days (Raskin)
Three Cool Cats (Leiber—Stoller)
Tip Of My Tongue